SAIS PAPERS
IN INTERNATIONAL AFFAIRS

Peacekeeping on Arab-Israeli Fronts

WESTVIEW PRESS / FOREIGN POLICY INSTITUTE
SCHOOL OF ADVANCED INTERNATIONAL STUDIES
THE JOHNS HOPKINS UNIVERSITY

SAIS PAPERS
IN INTERNATIONAL AFFAIRS   NUMBER 3

Peacekeeping on Arab-Israeli Fronts

Lessons from the Sinai and Lebanon

Nathan A. Pelcovits

WESTVIEW PRESS / BOULDER AND LONDON
WITH THE FOREIGN POLICY INSTITUTE
SCHOOL OF ADVANCED INTERNATIONAL STUDIES
THE JOHNS HOPKINS UNIVERSITY

A Westview Press / Foreign Policy Institute Edition

All rights reserved. No part of this publication may be reproduced or transmitted in any form or by any means, electronic or mechanical, including photocopy, recording, or any information storage and retrieval system, without permission in writing from the publisher.

Copyright © 1984 by The Johns Hopkins Foreign Policy Institute, School of Advanced International Studies

Published in 1984 in the United States of America by
 Westview Press, Inc.
 5500 Central Avenue
 Boulder, Colorado 80301
 Frederick A. Praeger, Publisher

Library of Congress Catalog Card Number: 84-51609
ISBN 0-86531-899-9

Composition for this book by The William Byrd Press, Richmond, Virginia, for The Johns Hopkins Foreign Policy Institute, SAIS.

Printed and bound in the United States of America
10 9 8 7 6 5 4 3 2 1

THE JOHNS HOPKINS FOREIGN POLICY INSTITUTE

Lucius D. Battle
Chairman

Philip Geyelin
Editor-in-Residence

Archie Albright
Executive-in-Residence

Harold Brown
*Distinguished Visiting Professor
National Security Affairs*

Murray Gart
Research Associate

Kristen E. Carpenter
*Managing Editor
Publications Program*

Janet Smith
Assistant to the Chairman

Robert E. Osgood
*Director of Research
Codirector, Security Studies Program
(on leave)*

Michael Vlahos
*Codirector
Security Studies Program*

Wilfrid Kohl
*Director
International Energy Program*

Christian A. Herter, Jr.
Fellow

Celeste R. Wilson
Programs Coordinator

George R. Packard
Dean, School of Advanced International Studies, The Johns Hopkins University

The Johns Hopkins Foreign Policy Institute (FPI) was founded in 1980 and serves as the research center for the School of Advanced International Studies (SAIS) in Washington, D.C. The FPI is a meeting place for SAIS faculty members and students, as well as for government analysts, policymakers, diplomats, journalists, business leaders, and other specialists in international affairs. In addition to conducting research on various policy-related international issues, the FPI sponsors conferences, seminars, and roundtables.

The FPI's research activities are often carried on in conjunction with SAIS's regional and functional programs dealing with American foreign policy, Latin America and the Caribbean Basin, Africa, the Middle East, the Soviet Union, U.S.-Japan relations, Canada, security studies, international energy, the Far East, Europe, and international economics.

FPI publications include the *SAIS Review*, a biannual journal of foreign affairs, which is edited by SAIS students, and SAIS Papers in International Affairs, a monograph series which is copublished with Westview Press in Boulder, Colorado. For additional information regarding FPI publications, write to: Managing Editor, FPI Publications Program, School of Advanced International Studies, The Johns Hopkins University, 1740 Massachusetts Avenue, N.W. Washington, D.C. 20036.

To the memory of Leamon Ray Hunt

ABOUT THE BOOK AND AUTHOR

Since 1948, the United Nations has sponsored virtually every third-party peacekeeping mission on Arab-Israeli fronts. Three recent events, however, have been responsible for significantly altering the pattern of peacekeeping in the region: the Camp David accords, which, because they were opposed in the U.N. by the Soviet Union and most Arab nations, prevented U.N. sponsorship of a Sinai peacekeeping force; the June 1982 Israeli invasion of Lebanon, during which the U.N. Interim Force was made to look ineffectual; and the Sabra-Shatila massacres in South Beirut three months later, which prompted the deployment of a multinational peacekeeping force. Dr. Pelcovits analyzes these events to answer the questions they raise about peacekeeping in the Middle East: What advantages are afforded by U.N. peacekeepers compared with non-U.N. missions? What net benefits are derived from American participation in a non-U.N. multinational operation? And how do they compare to the classic U.N. peacekeeping rationale of insulating disputed areas from superpower confrontation? Finally, what determines the success of such operations—geopolitical circumstance or institutional affiliation?

Nathan A. Pelcovits is a professorial lecturer at the School of Advanced International Studies, The Johns Hopkins University. He is the author of *Security Guarantees in a Middle East Settlement* (1976).

CONTENTS

Abbreviations xii

Preface 1

**Chapter 1. 1982: Turning Point for
Middle East Peacekeeping** 5
   The American Commitment:
      The Creation of the MFO   7
   Peacekeeping and Geopolitics   11

**Chapter 2. The Travails of UNIFIL:
Mandate and Expectations**..17
   "An Impossible Operational Position"   20
   Facts and Expectations:
      Disputes over UNIFIL's Role   23

**Chapter 3. Impartiality and Effectiveness:
Measuring Peacekeeping Success** 25
   High-threat Fronts: A Peacekeeping Paradox   26
   An American Presence in South Lebanon?   28

Chapter 4. The MNF in Search of a Mandate.................31
   Gemayel Campaigns for an Expanded MNF 33
   Israel-Lebanon Agreement on Troop Withdrawal 39
   Two Stubborn Problems 43
      Rebuilding the Lebanese Army 43
      Syrian Resistance 44

Chapter 5. Peacekeeping in Lebanon: The Three Sectors 47
   The South: UNIFIL Redux 47
   Prospects for a Multinational Force
      in Greater Beirut: Four Options 51
      Option 1: An Activist MNF 52
      Option 2: Phasing Out the American Contingent 55
      Option 3: Replacing the MNF with U.N. Peacekeepers 58
      Option 4: A Corps of Neutral Observers 62
   Disengagement on the Eastern Front 62

Chapter 6. The Multinational Force & Observers:
** Unique or Paradigm? 69**
   Success and Vulnerabilities 72
      Freedom of Navigation 74
      Dealing with Charges of Treaty Violations 75
      The MFO: How Long Will It Stay? 78

Chapter 7. The MFO and the U.N. as Peacekeepers:
** Costs and Benefits 81**
   Political Consensus and Institutional
      Adaptation 82
   Directing the Peacekeepers 88
   Meeting the Costs 89

Chapter 8. Third-Party Peacekeepers for the Golan
** and the West Bank? 93**
   The Golan Front 94
   The West Bank 97

Notes 101

Appendixes
- A. Documents Relating to the Sinai Multinational Force & Observers (MFO) *109*
- B. Documents Relating to Peacekeeping in Lebanon *139*
- C. Document Relating to the United Nations Disengagement Observer Force (UNDOF) *169*
- D. Security Council Resolutions on the United Nations Interim Force in Lebanon (UNIFIL) *173*

Index 179

ABBREVIATIONS

IDF	Israeli Defense Forces
MFO	Sinai Multinational Force & Observers
MNF	Multinational Force in Beirut
OGL	Observer Group Lebanon
OPs	Observation Posts
PLO	Palestine Liberation Organization
RDF	Rapid Deployment Force
SSM	U.S. Sinai Support Mission
UNDOF	United Nations Disengagement Observer Force
UNEF	United Nations Emergency Force
UNFICYP	United Nations Force in Cyprus
UNIFIL	United Nations Interim Force in Lebanon
UNMOs	United Nations Military Observers
UNOC	United Nations Operation in the Congo
UNTAG	United Nations Transitional Assistance Group
UNTSO	United Nations Truce Supervisory Organization

PREFACE

THE VIRTUAL DISINTEGRATION OF THE Multinational Force (MNF) in Beirut early in 1984, and the move to replace it with a U.N. peacekeeping presence, occurred several weeks after the final draft of this paper was completed. This has not altered, however, the main lines of the analysis. That the MNF would have a short half-life as peacekeeper was predictable, as it had compromised the essentials for effective peacekeeping—impartiality among all warring factions, a political consensus embracing all nations with important interests in the outcome of the conflict, a clear goal, and a coherent structure able to sustain the cooperation of all troop-contributors.

As this study demonstrates, the MNF experience can be understood only in the broader context and complex history of a series of successful and not-so-successful efforts to enlist third-party peacekeepers in the protracted Arab-Israeli conflict. International peacekeeping—that is, the use of military observers or troops from third countries to monitor truce lines or disengagement arrangements—has experienced its most varied and challenging tests on Arab-Israeli fronts. Third-party involvement in stabilizing the region has been a constant feature there since the 1948 war. Following each of five or six wars, some form of U.N. presence has been installed either to supervise truce lines or to monitor and verify security arrangements (demilitarized and limited-forces zones) mandated in disengagement agreements.

But the pattern has changed in important ways in the last few years, and what has happened is instructive not only for peacekeeping possibilities in the Middle East but for an understanding of the utility of peacekeeping elsewhere. Up until two years ago, peacekeeping missions on Arab-Israeli fronts—and in other regions for that matter—were mandated and managed by the United Nations. There was no practical alternative. In 1982 the picture and the options changed. In that year three events transformed the terms in which scholars and policymakers must henceforth think about the utilities of and options for enlisting peacekeepers in the Arab-Israeli conflict. These three events induced me to undertake the study.

The first and most revolutionary event was the deployment in April 1982 of the Multinational Force & Observers (MFO) to monitor the Sinai security arrangements mandated in the Egypt-Israel peace treaty of March 1979. The creation of the MFO, once it became clear that Soviet and Arab opposition would prevent the United Nations from taking on this responsibility, had profound implications for the future of peacekeeping in the region. For henceforth the question must be raised: Is this a unique case or does the MFO offer a model for other fronts? The second event occurred two months later when invading Israeli forces swept aside troops of the U.N. Interim Force in Lebanon (UNIFIL). The U.N. peacekeeping presence in southern Lebanon was made to look irrelevant, and during that summer the question of its future was debated by planners in Washington and at the United Nations. The third significant event occurred at the end of September. In the wake of the massacres in the Palestinian refugee camps of Sabra and Shatila in South Beirut, the MNF, comprised of American, French, and Italian troops, was dispatched to Beirut to help restore internal security and extend Lebanese government authority to the surrounding area. Its ambiguous mandate, loose command-structure, and eroding political base, as Syrian-backed opposition elements came to perceive the MNF as hostile, did not bode well for the success of the mission.

These events posed novel questions about peacekeeping options on Arab-Israeli fronts. How does one assess the balance of costs and benefits involved in fielding a U.N. force as compared with non-U.N. alternatives? What are the net benefits of American participation as compared with the classical rationale for U.N. peacekeeping, that is, insulating disputed areas from superpower confrontation? Is it geographic and political circumstance or the institutional framework within which a peacekeeping operation is launched and managed that counts most in determining effectiveness and durability? Is the MFO experience idiosyncratic or is it transferrable to other fronts? Is there a future for UNIFIL in Lebanon, and what might its mission be? What misjudgments led to the mistakes and troubles encountered by the MNF? Can they be avoided by a U.N. force in the face of Lebanon's endemic communal strife?

In pursuit of answers I went to the area in the spring of 1983 (March–May) to study the experience of UNIFIL, the MFO, and the MNF. I visited Egypt, Israel, and Lebanon, as well as force headquarters and field units of UNIFIL in southern Lebanon and of the MFO in the Sinai. I also spent the better part of a week at MFO headquarters in Rome. Apart from documentary sources, my findings are based largely on numerous conversations with American, Egyptian, Israeli, and U.N. officials; diplomatic and military analysts; academics; and officers serving with UNTSO, UNIFIL, and the MFO.

Acknowledgments must be more than pro forma. Since events were evolving and sparsely documented, I had to rely inordinately on the willingness of dozens of officials and officers to speak in confidence and with the understanding in most instances that their views would not be attributed. None, of course, is responsible for my misjudgments or errant statements, though I have taken pains to recall and record views in as fair a manner as possible. But the need to respect anonymity means that I can never adequately thank many of them for their time and advice.

I benefited immeasurably from the perceptive comments of friends and former colleagues in the Department of State and in American diplomatic missions in Cairo, Jerusalem, Tel Aviv, Rome, and New York. I am indebted to them for their sage counsel and hospitality. Respecting their wishes, I cannot name them, but I must acknowledge the encouragement and assistance of my friend and former colleague, Daniel Fendrick of the Office of Long-Range Assessments and Research.

Among those I am pleased to thank for advice and hospitality are the following U.N. personnel: Under Secretary–General Brian E. Urquhart and Mr. George Sherry at U.N. headquarters; Lt. Gen. Emanuel Erskine, chief of staff, and his staff at UNTSO headquarters in Jerusalem; Lt. Gen. William Callaghan, force commander, and his staff at UNIFIL headquarters in Naquora, as well as the commanders of the Finnish and Irish battalions who shepherded me around their sectors in the UNIFIL area of operation in April 1983. For encouragement to pursue this study and for many kindnesses I can now never repay, I am beholden to Leamon Ray Hunt, director-general of the MFO, who was assassinated by terrorists in Rome on February 15, 1984. I must also thank Lt. Gen. Frederik Bull-Hansen, the MFO force commander, and the MFO staff for their cooperation and hospitality during my visits to the Sinai and Rome headquarters. Among the staff who extended themselves I must single out Maj. Barry S. Sprouse, senior visits officer at MFO force headquarters, and Mr. W. J. Dieterich, public affairs officer at MFO headquarters in Rome.

In Cairo, I found exceptionally illuminating and helpful my visits with Adm. Mohsen Hamdy, head of the Egyptian liaison office with international organizations, and Under Secretary Shafei Abdul Hamid of the Ministry of Foreign Affairs.

In Israel, where I spent the better part of two months working out of the Harry S Truman Research Institute at Hebrew University, numerous officials at the Ministry of Foreign Affairs and Ministry of Defense were helpful. I am pleased to acknowledge the help and perceptive comments of Brig. Gen. Dov Sion, chief of Israel's liaison office with the MFO; deputy director of the Ministry of Foreign Affairs, Hanan Bar-On; and the ministry's assistant director, Gen. Michel Elizur. Although they are, of course, not responsible for what I have written, many of the ideas in the study were generated by talks with Israeli political and military analysts, among whom I am particularly indebted to former prime minister Yitzhak Rabin; Aharon Yariv, Yair Evron, Aryeh Shalev, and Nimrod Novik of the Jaffee Center for Strategic Studies, Tel Aviv University; Itamar Rabinovich, director of the Shiloah Center for Middle Eastern and African Studies, Tel Aviv University; Ze'ev Schiff of *Haaretz*; and Gabriel Sheffer, deputy director of the Leonard Davis Institute for International Relations, the Hebrew University in Jerusalem. Michael Brecher of McGill University, in Jerusalem at the time, was most generous with his time and counsel. Special thanks are due to the Truman Research Institute, and its director Zvi Schiffrin, for providing me with office space, administrative services, and a stimulating research atmosphere during my stay in Jerusalem.

I am most indebted to Maj. Gen. (ret.) Indar Jit Rikhye, president, and Peter Harvey, executive director, of the International Peace Academy (IPA) for their sustained interest, encouragement, and assistance. A grant toward the cost of preparing and publishing this study was made by the Ira and Miriam D. Wallach Foundation, for which I am most grateful. I should also like to thank Kristen E. Carpenter, managing editor of this series, for her skillful editing of the manuscript, and W. Mark Habeeb, a Ph.D. student at SAIS, for his help with research, indexing, and collecting documents.

NATHAN A. PELCOVITS

1.
1982: TURNING POINT FOR MIDDLE EAST PEACEKEEPING

For more than thirty years the United Nations (U.N.) played a constructive and virtually exclusive role in third-party peacekeeping between Israel and its neighbors. Since 1948 military observers of the U.N. Truce Supervisory Organization (UNTSO), including U.S. officers, have monitored armistice lines, supervised ceasefire arrangements, and verified arms-limitation zones. The earliest authentic U.N. peacekeeping *force*—if intervention in Korea is regarded as a quasi-enforcement operation and as legitimating American "police action"—was the first U.N. Emergency Force (UNEF I), deployed in the aftermath of the Suez War of 1956 to supervise the ceasefire and withdrawal and then to patrol the Sinai and Gaza border areas. In fact, UNEF I became the prototype for U.N. peacekeeping and the paradigm by which Dag Hammarskjold codified the rulebook for U.N. peacekeeping. The prerequisites for successful peacekeeping were defined as consent and cooperation of the parties, troop contingents volunteered by participants other than permanent members, impartiality, and use of force by U.N. troops only in self-defense.

Many thought the inglorious departure of UNEF I in May 1967, when U Thant recalled the force at President Gamal Abdel Nasser's behest, might have signaled the requiem for U.N. peacekeeping efforts in the region. But an unexpected sequel to the Yom Kippur War brought the second U.N. Emergency Force (UNEF II) to the Sinai with uncommon assignments—not only to monitor the disengagement, but to control a buffer zone and verify limitations on armed forces and armaments in designated zones. A parallel arrangement was devised for the Golan

Heights. A hybrid disengagement observer force, UNDOF, continues to keep watch on that front to this day.

By and large, the United States took the lead in these ventures, as it had in the Congo (UNOC, 1960–64) and in the installation of the U.N. Force in Cyprus (UNFICYP, 1964–present). America mustered the political consensus, provided indispensable logistical support, paid a disproportionately large share of the costs, and became the foremost champion of a dominant managerial role for the U.N. secretary-general. The American dedication to U.N. peacekeeping stemmed from a perceived national interest in insulating disputed or disorderly Third World areas from Soviet encroachment without incurring the onus and costs of unilateralism. From the U.S. perspective, U.N. peacekeeping served as a device for sharing responsibilities and costs.

By the end of 1978—that is, around the time of Camp David—some 14,000 personnel were serving in U.N. forces and observer groups in the Middle East (UNTSO, UNEF II, and UNDOF), Cyprus and Kashmir (UNMOGIP). In addition, plans were under way for the creation of a 7,500-man U.N. Transitional Assistance Group (UNTAG) to supervise Namibian elections and transition to independence. The United States had taken the lead in urging U.N. peacekeeping involvement in all these cases, including Namibia. America also was committed to paying about a third of the cost of U.N. peacekeeping and, in effect, acted as "contributor of last resort."[1]

True, international peacekeeping (which in practice meant U.N. peacekeeping) was self-limiting. Its authority and effectiveness depended on sustaining the political consensus, attracting a cross-section of troop contributors, and persuading the warring parties to cooperate with the peacekeepers rather than renew the fighting. But it was useful in certain conflicts, notably in the Middle East, where the balance of national interest lay in stabilizing a crisis while diplomacy attempted to move the conflict toward peaceful settlement.

American leaders often felt frustrated by the cumbersome and wasteful U.N. operations, which were always vulnerable to Soviet troublemaking. Still, if the alternative was to go it alone, as President Kennedy instructed Assistant Secretary of State Harlan Cleveland, the United States would opt to support, for instance, the U.N. action in the Congo despite all the frustration and cost.[2] Also, when it became clear that NATO would not or could not take over the British security responsibilities in the Cyprus troubles of 1963–64, the United States pressed the United Nations to deploy UNFICYP with the mandate of preventing the recurrence of fighting and of helping restore law and order.

A departure from this pattern occurred in 1975 when Israel insisted on an American presence as the sine qua non for the interim Sinai agreement. Despite misgivings in Congress, a civilian U.S. Sinai Support Mission (SSM) was established to keep watch over entrances to the passes and to manage a tactical early-warning system that monitored Egyptian and Israeli surveillance stations lodged on the heights overlooking the Giddi Valley. (The United States also conducted aerial surveillance with the knowledge and consent of the parties.) But this peacekeeping watch did not supplant the United Nations; it served to complement the U.N. peacekeepers who patrolled a demilitarized buffer zone.[3]

The Camp David accords, too, assumed that the United Nations would monitor the withdrawal of Israel from the Sinai and stay on to police the permanent security arrangements. Arab rejection of Camp David meant the Soviets would not acquiesce to a continued U.N. role. So, it became clear early in 1981 that the U.N. peacekeeping option was unacceptable. In accordance with a presidential pledge at the time the treaty was negotiated, the United States undertook to "ensure the establishment and maintenance of an acceptable alternative multinational force."

The American Commitment: The Creation of the MFO

In a protocol of August 1981, signed by the parties and witnessed by the United States, the Multinational Force & Observers (MFO) was established as a non-U.N. international organization to recruit and install in the Sinai a multinational force and corps of civilian observers to monitor the security arrangements of the Egypt-Israel peace treaty of March 26, 1979. A ten-nation, 2,500-man force was deployed in April 1982 as the Israelis relinquished their last holding in the Sinai: Colombia, Fiji, and the United States provided infantry battalions; Australia, France, Italy, the Netherlands, New Zealand, the United Kingdom, and Uruguay contributed specialized units; and the United States also provided a logistical support unit and approximately forty personnel for the civilian observer unit. Expenses, which come to about

$100 million a year, were split three ways by the United States, Egypt, and Israel.[4]

The mission of the MFO was to monitor and verify the security arrangements in Annex I of the peace treaty, which established limitations on men and arms permitted within the four zones—three in the Sinai and one in Israel along the international border. These were the duties that the U.N. force and observers had originally been expected to perform. In Zone A, nearest the canal (see map), Egypt was permitted one mechanical infantry division of up to a total of 22,000 personnel; in Zone B, four border battalions comprising up to 4,000 soldiers; and in the demilitarized Zone C, the treaty as amended by the protocol allowed only MFO military components, although Egypt may maintain civilian police units armed with light weapons. In Zone D, Israel was allowed up to four infantry battalions totaling not more than 4,000 personnel. Limits were also placed on the number and types of military equipment and arms allowed in each zone. Operationally, the peacekeepers were assigned four essential tasks: (1) operating checkpoints, reconnaissance patrols, and observation posts within Zone C and along the international boundary and line B; (2) periodic verification, not less than twice a month, of limitations on men and arms in the other three zones; (3) additional verification within forty-eight hours after receiving a request from either party; and (4) ensuring freedom of navigation through the Strait of Tiran in accordance with Article V of the treaty.[5]

This venture into non-U.N. peacekeeping was a historic departure in more ways than one, with profound implications for U.S. policy. In the first place, America assumed a commitment to organize the force and to keep it operating. Apart from ensuring that the force was effective and met the expectations of the parties, the United States, in effect, assumed responsibility for sustaining the political consensus on the basis of which the nine other countries were persuaded to participate in the MFO.

Second, for the first time since the Korean War, American troops (not civilian technicians or air-reconnaisance crews) became the mainstay of a multinational presence in an area where trouble could break out. It was the first time such a commitment had been made under non-U.N. auspices.

The third novelty was the need to invent an institutional structure. While the director-general of the MFO drew on the peacekeeping experience of the United Nations, there existed neither a political

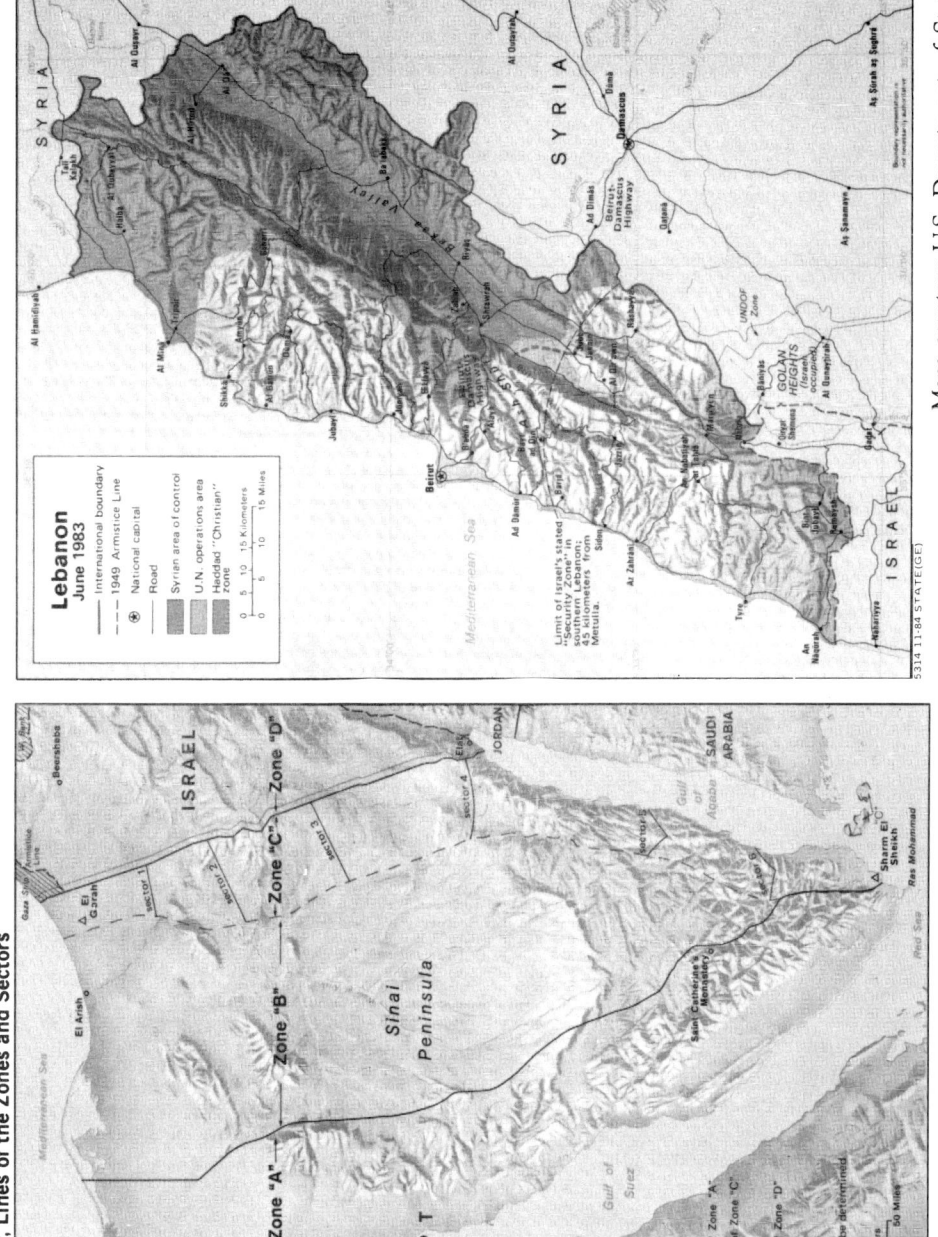

Maps courtesy U.S. Department of State

structure comparable to the Security Council nor an established institutional machinery. Moreover, operational procedures and a command structure had to be improvised.

The peacekeeping landscape was also altered by another event in 1982 when the U.N. Interim Force in Lebanon (UNIFIL) was swept aside and made to look ineffective during the Israeli invasion of Lebanon in June. In an unusually candid report, the new U.N. secretary-general, Javier Perez de Cuellar, lamented the spectacle of an almost unrelieved failure of the United Nations to carry out its major assignment to halt conflict and, specifically, to keep the peace in Lebanon.[6]

The third significant peacekeeping event of 1982 was the creation of the Multinational Force (MNF). Given Israeli opposition and distrust, U.N. observers could not be effectively deployed between the Israeli forces and the Palestine Liberation Organization (PLO), so a multinational force (comprised of a U.S. Marine contingent and French and Italian units) was rapidly organized to monitor the evacuation of the PLO fighters from Beirut. The multinational force was expected to withdraw a week or two after the evacuation was complete, turn the port over to the Lebanese army, and depart. This, indeed, is what happened. But the force soon returned.

At the urgent request of President Amin Gemayel following the assassination of President-elect Bashir Gemayel and the massacres in the refugee camps of Sabra and Shatila, the United States, again in partnership with France and Italy, formed a new multinational force to enable the Lebanese government to restore internal security in Beirut. The MNF's Italian unit was given the specific function of protecting the Palestinian refugee camps. In an exchange of letters with the Beirut government, dated September 25, 1982, the United States pledged to deploy "temporarily" a force of about 1,200 to help "establish an environment which will permit the Lebanese armed forces to carry out their responsibilities in the Beirut area." A marine amphibious unit was sent in because it was judged to have a less permanent cast than an army presence. The mission of the marines was described in somewhat less restrictive terms in President Reagan's letter to Congress four days later: They would be needed for only a limited period to meet the requirements of the current situation, but this step would support the broader objective of "helping restore the territorial integrity, sovereignty, and political independence of Lebanon."

Eventually it became clear that the United States had taken on a larger commitment: to keep American troops in Lebanon until the Beirut situation stabilized, the "full sovereignty" of the Lebanese government restored, the foreign forces withdrawn, and the Lebanese army rebuilt to the point where it could take over responsibility for maintaining order. By the end of 1982 the Gemayel government sought a U.S. commitment to increase the marine contingent, with parallel increases from France and Italy. The nature and duration of the peacekeeping mission were imperceptibly changing. But it remained undetermined where the expanded MNF would be deployed, and, as noted below, all planning on where and of what magnitude and in what manner any peacekeeping presence would operate was suspended while negotiations proceeded on effecting the withdrawal of all foreign forces—Israeli, Syrian, and PLO—from Lebanon.

The future of UNIFIL also remained uncertain; its term was renewed in October 1982 for three months and, the following January, for six months under the old mandate. (As noted below, further renewals extended the mandate to April 1984.) Questions were raised with regard to restructuring and perhaps expanding UNIFIL under a new mandate. A question was also posed as to whether a non-U.N. peacekeeping force should be considered or, for that matter, whether the peacekeeping task should be shared.

In the immediate aftermath of the invasion, planners in Washington projected an augmented UNIFIL, perhaps doubling the 7,000-man force, with an expanded mandate. This was thought to provide the best chance of an international force of sufficient size with international acceptability, although Israel's distrust of UNIFIL rendered the proposal problematic. Others stressed that direct U.S. participation (beyond sponsorship) was essential to strengthen the deterrent value of any international presence, to reassure the Israelis and persuade them to withdraw, and to provide the necessary psychological assurance to the government of Lebanon. While negotiations for withdrawal proceeded, proposals were advanced to divide the peacekeeping tasks among the parties, a multinational force, and UNIFIL II, although it was not clear where such a mixed force would be deployed and what its mandate would be.

Peacekeeping and Geopolitics

The events of 1982 posed novel policy considerations regarding third-party peacekeeping on Arab-Israeli fronts. How does one compare the cost-benefits of U.N. and non-U.N. options, of American participation as against the classical rationale for peacekeeping—that is, keeping disputed areas insulated from superpower confrontation? Is the experience of the MFO idiosyncratic, or can certain features be transferred to Lebanon, the Golan, or the West Bank? Is there a future for UNIFIL in Lebanon?

Most of the officials, diplomats, newsmen, and academics to whom I posed these questions during a visit to the area (March–May 1983) shared the presumption that the MFO experience was distinctive and would not be readily adaptable to other fronts. The propitious circumstances on the Sinai front could not soon be expected elsewhere—the stability prevailing in both Egypt and Israel, and their shared interest in observing the treaty; the fact that the peacekeepers were there to ensure a settlement already attained rather than to stabilize a crisis; and the commitment undertaken by the United States. Still, they could not exclude the possibility that certain aspects of the MFO experience might hold lessons for the multinational force in Lebanon and for a Syrian-Israeli settlement.

The initial focus of this study was to assess the balance sheet of costs and benefits (political, institutional, financial) that could reasonably be expected from recourse to a non-U.N. force as compared with a U.N. peacekeeping force. This mainly involved examining the MFO's origins and its first year of experience: How had the mandate, operating procedures, rules of engagement, logistical and financial challenges, command and control, etc., stood the test of time? What political and institutional problems had been encountered and overcome? What were the problems that might portend difficulties down the line?[7]

Clearly, the auspices under which a peacekeeping operation is undertaken—particularly whether it is launched and managed by the United Nations or by an autonomous organization—is far from irrelevant. Thus, in Lebanon the policy choice between extending the purview of UNIFIL (or UNTSO) to Beirut as against deploying the MNF in August and September 1982 was measurably affected by the auspices under which the peacekeepers would operate. The case is instructive. On August 1, 1982, the U.N. Security Council (S.C.) authorized the secretary-general (S.C. Resolution 516) to deploy U.N. observers to monitor the situation in Greater Beirut—then under siege by the Israeli Defense Forces (IDF)—in a campaign to force the PLO fighters to leave. Three days later the Security Council pressed Israel to comply with this decision (S.C. Resolution 517), and on August 12 passed S.C. Resolution 518, which "demanded" that Israel cooperate fully in the effort to secure the "effective deployment of the United Nations observers." It was not only Jerusalem's general disaffection with the United Nations nor even the harsh language of the resolution that led to Israel's refusal to cooperate with the UNTSO in Beirut. Rather, Israel doubted that General Erskine's group of twenty-eight observers (newly constituted as Observer Group Lebanon) could effectively ensure PLO withdrawal, especially as the Security Council had merely "taken note" of the PLO's "decision . . . to move the Palestinian armed forces from Beirut" in S.C. Resolution 517 of August 4. In Israel's eyes, only an American-led multinational force (the first MNF) had the credibility to ensure the departure of the PLO fighters.

Similarly, following the Sabra-Shatila massacres, the Security Council authorized the secretary-general (S.C. Resolution 521, September 19, 1982) both to increase the number of U.N. observers in and around Beirut from ten to twenty, and to consult with the Lebanese government on "possible deployment" of U.N. forces to assist the government in protecting the civilian population. The mandate was an appropriate one for U.N. peacekeepers, but the United Nations was not in a position to move rapidly and provide the kind of support required by Gemayel. The secretary-general was understandably reluctant to expand the observer corps or to dispatch troops from UNIFIL without further consultation and explicit approval from the Security Council. Gemayel preferred the American-French presence (the second MNF) not only because he thought it could deploy more rapidly to help him control Beirut's security situation, but, as noted later, because he viewed it as an instrument to bolster his political position.

On the other hand, the MNF participants and the Gemayel government preferred to have the United Nations monitor the (abortive) ceasefire of September 1983 between the Lebanese army and the opposition militias. However, the effort to enlist the fifty-man UNTSO team of observers in Beirut for this assignment had to be abandoned because the necessary consensus could not be mustered in the Security Council. By the same token, the MFO operation was facilitated by the fact that negotiators of the protocol could avoid the political hassle in the Security Council, and the MFO managers could finesse the question of "equitable geographic distribution" in recruiting the force. On the other side of the ledger, the need to improvise an institutional structure added to the costs and complications. On Arab-Israeli fronts, also, Israel's distrust of what it perceived as a hopelessly politicized United Nations might have proved an obstacle to enlisting U.N. peacekeepers—although not an insuperable one, as the history of UNEF II and UNDOF demonstrates.* (The costs and benefits of the U.N. option are delineated in chapter 7, along with a similar assessment of the MFO.)

Almost without exception, however, those interviewed tended to see the issue of the comparative advantages of U.N. and autonomous (non-U.N.) institutional auspices as secondary to that of the geographic and political circumstances under which a peacekeeping operation is installed. The success of the MFO (and the relative failure of UNIFIL) had less to do with the auspices under which these operations were launched and managed than with the political dynamic that animated them and the geopolitical circumstances in which they operate. Success seems to depend particularly on the prospect for reconciling the often differing expectations regarding the mandate and how to measure effectiveness.

Thus, the success of the MFO derived only partly from the fact that it escaped the constraints of peacekeeping under U.N. auspices. The MFO succeeded, in part, because of the skill with which the negotiators of the protocol reconciled the political demands of Egypt and Israel, and the manner in which the MFO leadership (particularly its director-general and force commander) managed the initial stages of the operation so as to enlist cooperation both of the parties and of the troop participants.

There were other advantages. The MFO's success as the world's first non-U.N. multinational peacekeeping force has hinged mostly on the fact that it buttresses a peace settlement already reached between the parties rather than stabilizing a crisis, as in Cyprus. In fact, some officers

---

* Some Israeli academics and diplomats contend that Israelis have been so traumatized by the drumbeat of invective and the double-standard applied to Israel in U.N. forums, that no U.N. operation is trusted to be either fair or effective. Others dispute this, pointing to periods of cooperation with U.N. peacekeepers on both Egyptian and Syrian fronts. Even more telling is the fact that the March 1979 treaty of peace between Egypt and Israel assigned the central role in monitoring the security arrangements to U.N. forces and observers. And it was Israel that was insistent on including a provision that U.N. personnel "will not be removed unless such removal is approved by the Security Council of the United Nations, with the affirmative vote of five Permanent Members, unless the Parties themselves otherwise agree." True, Israel would have preferred a non-U.N., American-led international force—for which Foreign Minister Moshe Dayan argued at Camp David—but in the circumstances, Israel's antipathy to the United Nations was overcome and Israel signed on to a permanent U.N. force for the Sinai.

at MFO headquarters contended that the Sinai force represented the only true *peacekeeping* operation in existence, the others being crisis or truce managers.

Beyond this, officials in Egypt and Israel basically agreed as to what to expect from the MFO and how it fit into the countries' security needs. Although Egyptian officials expressed less enthusiasm about its value, the MFO was seen on both sides as a confidence-builder in a still-fragile relationship in need of bolstering from the third "full partner" to the peace.

Both countries also perceived the MFO as theirs; as founders and financiers of the enterprise, they "owned" it and were thus inclined to be cooperative. Of course, all peacekeeping rests on the consent and cooperation of the parties, consent to launching the operation and cooperation with the force afterwards to ensure its effective functioning. Consent and cooperation, along with impartiality, are the cardinal principles whether peacekeepers are engaged in monitoring a buffer zone and damping down incidents, or contributing to internal stability.

But peacekeeping has the greatest prospect of succeeding when it rests on an agreement, whether a peace treaty or disengagement accord, rather than on a mandate perceived as externally imposed through the Security Council. Parties often "consent," as Israel did with UNIFIL, but cooperation may be reluctant because the peacekeeping force is seen as imposed by external pressure and as insufficiently responsive to security needs.

Another lesson from the MFO, which has proved particularly germane to Lebanon, is that peacekeeping works best when only two politically stable parties are involved. (This is true not only because it takes the consent of two to tango but because another pair or more of feet complicates the political choreography.) In turbulent Lebanon, security arrangements involving third-party peacekeepers must take into account myriad warring factions, irregulars, and, of course, the interests of a third state, Syria. The overriding question in Lebanon has been not the peacekeeping auspices but whether *any* third party—U.N. or MNF— could provide the necessary political and logistical muscle to ensure that the Lebanese security forces could stand on their own in reasonably short order. Without a stabilization of the crisis, no peacekeeping presence could be workable. The MFO was thus not so much a model for Lebanon and other Arab-Israeli fronts as a cautionary example of the limits of enlisting third-party peacekeepers in situations where the underlying political consensus was missing.

The key element in the creation of the MFO "alternative multinational force" (as in that of the MNF or any other such force on Arab-Israeli fronts) was the United States' commitment to provide a military presence and to take central responsibility for its durability and effectiveness. In effect, the U.S. military presence and overall political commitment was the key "circumstance" affecting the functioning of the force. This spelled the difference that made the force attractive to Israel and ensured its cooperation.* An American military presence has long been considered desirable by the Israeli political mainstream (particularly in the Labor alignment) not so much as guarantor but as a warrant that policies and outlook in Washington and Jerusalem will be aligned in a crisis. (Others in Israel, for example the school associated with former defense minister Ezer Weizman, have opposed any intermediary between Israel and its Arab adversary; and there are those, like Weizman's successor, Ariel Sharon, who feared the American presence would exact a price, putting a brake on Israeli military action should it be deemed necessary.)

For Israel, such an "alternative multinational force" possessed the dual advantages of an American presence and a U.N. absence. For the Arab partner, the American presence might be reassuring, but the exclusion of the United Nations entailed political costs. A dominant U.S. role in a multinational force also generates suspicion as to the extent of its international character. Although the U.S. commitment to the MFO virtually guarantees that the force will be materially supported and prove durable, the MFO leadership has been sensitive about any indications that Washington does not consider the MFO to be a fully autonomous, independent, *international* organization.

The MFO command has been successful so far in maintaining the international character and appearance of the force—a point on which Egypt is particularly sensitive. Experience appears to suggest, however, that in cases where the international acceptability of a peacekeeping operation is paramount (as for example, in Namibia), a U.N. framework would be preferred, assuming, of course, that other aspects—reliability, ability to respond, financing, etc.—could be managed.[8]

---

* At Camp David, the pledge to "ensure the establishment and maintenance of an acceptable alternative multinational force" was artfully phrased by the American delegation so as not necessarily to require American military involvement. Nevertheless, it is clear from the memoirs of the participants that Israel would not have found "acceptable" any multinational force lacking an American component.

2.
THE TRAVAILS OF UNIFIL: MANDATE AND EXPECTATIONS

AGREEMENT ON A FORMAL MANDATE does not necessarily mean agreement on perceptions and expectations vis-à-vis a peacekeeping force and how it fits the politico-security needs of adversaries. Nor does it ensure that the effectiveness of the force will be measured by the same yardstick. Therefore, the fate of any peacekeeping operation, whether under U.N. auspices or otherwise, depends on the ability of the parties as well as the peacekeepers to reconcile the often widely differing interpretations of the formal mandate and the disparate expectations regarding the peacekeepers' role.

Sometimes such differences are rhetorical and are subordinated to other considerations. Thus, Egyptian and Israeli officials still do not fully agree on the utility and mission of the MFO, carrying over the differences that first emerged during the protocol negotiations. For Egypt, the essence is that the MFO not be perceived as operating so as to impair Egyptian sovereignty in any way. Admiral Mohsen Hamdy, chief of Egypt's liaison system with international organizations, pictures Egypt as a gracious host and MFO personnel as guests for whom Egypt provides services and courtesies. Even in demilitarized Zone C, where the force is located, the provisions of the protocol relating to MFO functions have been construed by Egypt restrictively: The MFO "observes and reports" developments. Admiral Hamdy's opposite number, Brig. Gen. Dov Sion, stresses the autonomous, authoritative, activist character of the MFO in implementing the treaty's security provisions. So far, these controversial interpretations of the mandate have had only minor operational consequences—both nations have an overriding interest in ensuring the smooth functioning of the force. As noted below, these differences contain seeds of dissension that might later spell trouble should the political outlooks of the two sides diverge.

In the case of UNIFIL, on the other hand, the perceptual gulf between the United Nations and Israel and between the United States and Israel proved little short of disastrous. From the start, Israel perceived that UNIFIL had been imposed by President Jimmy Carter prematurely and without Israel's case being heard.* In discussions on a proposed U.N. force for southern Lebanon—even before the Litani Operation—Israel had in mind some form of disengagement arrangement whereby the U.N. force controlled up to the Litani River. Its primary goal was to keep the Palestinian guerrillas out and help Israel maintain its security belt. Now Israel found that its "chief friend and ally was pushing ahead with a policy which involved very little more than Israel's very early withdrawal, for Israel had no reason to think that a U.N. force would be able to keep the Palestinians under effective control."[9] At the United Nations as well there was reluctance to get entangled in a fractionated Lebanon. The Christians were eager to eliminate Palestinian influence in southern Lebanon, while the Muslim factions were more interested in the speedy departure of the Israelis. Indeed, Gen. Ensio Siilasvuo, then chief coordinator of U.N. peacekeeping operations in the Middle East, strongly opposed the idea of sending a U.N. force to the area.[10]

From the outset, Israel judged UNIFIL as a potential impediment to the existing security arrangements on its northern border and only marginally useful in deterring infiltration and shelling from PLO strongholds. In Israeli eyes, the UNIFIL mandate did not and, given the political dynamics in the United Nations, could not seriously take into account Israeli security concerns about its northern settlements. Some Israeli officials and academics conceded (if only in private) that the U.N. force might provide a third line of defense behind the Haddad enclave and the fence at the border. But the official Israeli assessment was that, on balance, the UNIFIL presence at times undermined Israel's security measures inasmuch as UNIFIL spent much of its efforts confronting Maj. Saad Haddad, Israel's protégé, rather than fighting the PLO terrorists. At

---

* Foreign Minister Dayan pressed the White House to delay Security Council action from Saturday to the following Monday so he could present Israel's case, and was turned down.

times, Israelis claimed certain UNIFIL units actually helped camouflage PLO operations by arrangements whereby the PLO agreed to leave the UNIFIL battalion alone if the latter turned a blind eye to PLO infiltration and military operations. (Reliable sources have claimed that documents captured during the June 1982 incursion substantiate such sweetheart deals between UNIFIL commanders and the PLO, although without implicating home governments. As of this writing, these documents have not been made public.)

UNIFIL's perspective was totally opposite. Israel was faulted by Lt. Gen. William Callaghan and his staff for forcing the U.N. force to "face both ways," that is, guarding UNIFIL's area of operation from Haddad and Israeli encroachment as well as from the PLO-controlled Tyre pocket and threats from north of the Litani. UNIFIL claimed that, except for very few incidents, the area of operation was not the source of infiltration or shelling. Artillery and rockets were shot "over the head" of UNIFIL battalions, actions beyond their ability or responsibility to stop. UNIFIL commanders and senior staff vehemently rejected allegations that the force remained passive (or even collaborative) in the face of attacks and confrontations from armed elements of the PLO and its leftist allies of the Lebanese National movement as well as from the Haddad side—known as "de facto forces" (DFF) in U.N. parlance.[11]

The prevailing assessment both at U.N. headquarters in New York and at UNIFIL headquarters in Naquora was that the readiness of U.N. peacekeepers to "take casualties" belied charges of passivity, let alone "collaboration." Indeed, as Under Secretary–General Brian E. Urquhart noted in a press briefing on January 13, 1983, this is precisely the sort of advantage afforded by a U.N. force: It is prepared to take the necessary risks and the "casualties incurred in taking those risks." Moreover, the readiness of any "alternative multinational force" to stay the course in the face of danger and attack was yet to be proved. (This judgment was made many months before the events of the autumn when the U.S. Marines and other units of the multinational force came under attack from Syrian-backed antigovernment militias and countered with artillery, naval, and air gunfire. Casualties mounted. The terrorist truck-bomb attacks in Beirut on October 23 on the marine compound and French paratroop barracks together claimed nearly 400 lives. The immediate reaction, both in Washington and in Paris, was to reinforce the determination to continue with the mission of the multinational force. But over time this tragic event helped erode the American resolve to stay.)

The case made both in New York and Naqoura, thus, has been that the UNIFIL area of operation did not become the route for infiltration and terrorist attacks on Israel's northern settlements. The sole exception was the attack by five Palestinians on Misgav Am (near Kiryat Shemona) in April 1980, when a group of children was held hostage in a kibbutz nursery. Three Israelis, including a child, died and ten soldiers were wounded before a special antiterrorist squad burst into the nursery and killed all five Palestinians. (Even this incident was not admitted as UNIFIL's fault since the infiltrators may have come through the gap between two battalion areas.) In any event, both in New York and Naqoura it was stressed that from the July 1981 ceasefire until June 1982, with the exception of one incident in May, not one rocket or artillery shell fell on northern Israel and that PLO infiltrators were always intercepted and disarmed by U.N. troops. So, the presumed ineffectiveness of UNIFIL could not have been the cause of Israel's invasion.

"An Impossible Operational Position"

Moreover, both UNIFIL officers and independent scholars like Alan James stress that the UNIFIL command was put into an impossible operational position because of the ambiguity of the mandate, the lack of specificity in the definition of objectives, and the territorial constraints. Following the civil war of 1975–76, the main PLO activity and threat to Israel's northern settlements were centered in southern Lebanon. On March 11, 1978, Palestinian guerrillas hijacked a tourist bus in northern Israel; thirty-five people were killed and twice that number wounded. Three days later Israel mounted the Litani Operation with the objective of clearing the PLO from southern Lebanon, but stopped short of Tyre partly to avoid further casualties and partly because of U.S. and world pressure for a ceasefire. On March 19, 1978, the U.N. Security Council adopted S.C. Resolution 425, which called for Israeli withdrawal "forthwith" and set up UNIFIL to confirm the withdrawal of Israeli forces, restore international peace and security, and assist the government of Lebanon in the restoration of its effective authority in the area. On the same day the Council adopted S.C. Resolution 426, which approved the secretary-general's terms of reference for UNIFIL, in effect adding a fourth element to the mandate: The force "will use its best efforts to . . . ensure that its area of operations is not used for hostile activities of any kind."

While the mandate assumed cooperation and compliance by the

parties, it prohibited any UNIFIL action that "could prejudice the rights, claims or positions of the parties concerned," thus setting up an inescapable conflict between its requirements and the security requirements of Israel (and of the PLO, for that matter). The parties' interpretation of their rights and needs served to frustrate the UNIFIL mission.

UNIFIL also was hampered by the territorial disposition of that part of southern Lebanon which did not fall into the perimeters of its "area of operation." As its forces withdrew from the southernmost strip of Lebanon, Israel turned over a 5–10 kilometer security enclave along the border to local militias under the command of Major Haddad.

As the Israelis withdrew, Palestinian and Lebanese armed elements attempted to move into the vacated areas, arguing that under the 1969 Cairo Agreement they were entitled to operate in southern Lebanon.[12] UNIFIL resisted these efforts, but in the end the PLO was permitted to hold onto certain "settlements" in the area of operations on the claim that they had never been evicted. Although the UNIFIL commander, Lt. Gen. Emanuel Erskine, argued that this area had been "clean" of Palestinians, the United Nations (and the United States) acquiesced in Yassir Arafat's claim. Some 300 (more than 700 by Israeli count) "armed elements" were permitted to move around in the UNIFIL area of operations. The PLO not only retained these sanctuaries but—using a similar argument that UNIFIL contingents should be deployed only in areas that had been occupied by the IDF—UNIFIL was excluded from operating in Tyre, which soon became the main base of guerrilla operations and artillery positions. The United Nations acquiesced to both the Israeli insistence on setting up the Haddad enclave and the PLO claim (strongly backed by the U.N.'s Arab group) that the Tyre pocket (including the port, the city, and the nearby Rashadiye camp) was operationally out of bounds to the United Nations.

The recriminations between UNIFIL and Israel, and the UNIFIL command's resentment of its undeserved reputation for ineffectiveness were almost inevitable. UNIFIL was given an impossible mission. It was left with an area of operation inadequate to the task of ensuring against infiltration and shelling. In addition, Israel insisted on looking after its own border security without regard to UNIFIL's mission. The United Nations' job was further complicated by the fact that the Haddad enclave was drawn in such a way that a salient from the south to Marjiyoun (Haddad's home base) effectively divided the UNIFIL area of operation. The assumption at UNIFIL headquarters that Israel wanted to retain this as the route for invasion was not borne out by events; in fact, the route through the gap was only one of four in the geography of the campaign.

The Israeli perspective was different. Although officials conceded that the UNIFIL command may have made a good-faith effort to carry out the mandate in the face of difficulties, reality fell far short of expectations. Infiltration of PLO guerrillas into the area controlled by UNIFIL took place gradually but steadily; PLO bases were tolerated. The UNIFIL version of the infiltration story was disputed. It was claimed that in the second half of 1980, sixty-nine successful infiltrations came through the UNIFIL zone in sectors held by the Dutch, Ghanian, Norwegian, Irish, Fiji, and Nigerian battalions. Also, it was charged, the UNIFIL zone became a PLO sanctuary from IDF pursuit and counteractions.[13]

More broadly, the prevailing doctrine among Israeli officials and strategists has been that any third-party peacekeeper with no direct stake in the security of the area naturally prefers not to confront PLO guerrillas and will therefore acquiesce in their presence and movements.[*] The U.N. practice of never fighting the PLO guerrillas and, at most, of taking away their arms which were then returned to PLO liaison officers in Tyre, made the U.N.'s claim of deterring infiltration unconvincing.

Although UNIFIL got consistently bad press in Israel, the private assessment of many military correspondents, academics, and even certain officials speaking off the record has been much more favorable. On balance, the UNIFIL presence was seen as helpful to Israel's security, albeit modestly. It had helped curb large-scale arms buildups and artillery concentrations in the area of operations and deterred, or at least complicated, infiltration.[14] In the Israeli Ministry of Foreign Affairs, the assessment was that as of the eve of the June invasion, the UNIFIL area of operation was "pretty quiet" and very few incidents originated there. Actually, Israelis thought the UNIFIL presence had become irrelevant because of PLO rockets and artillery that now reached Kiryat Shemona

---

[*] This lesson, it is said, was learned at the very beginning of UNIFIL's tour. On May 1, 1979, "armed elements" trying to infiltrate a UNIFIL position near Tyre were engaged by French troops and two infiltrators were killed. The next day a French truck was ambushed and its driver wounded. Reinforcements were engaged by armed elements deployed in the vicinity of Tyre and heavy fire-fighting ensued. On the same evening a French armored car was ambushed and set on fire and, in a separate incident that same night, the French battalion commander, Col. Jean-Germain Slavan was seriously wounded and one of his escort soldiers killed (as was the PLO escort). The French thereafter were instructed to show less zeal.

THE TRAVAILS OF UNIFIL   23

and Nahariya from positions outside its area of operation. Ironically, as some Israeli political leaders conceded in private, it was precisely because UNIFIL was largely effective in preventing PLO incursions that the PLO was forced to resort to long-range shelling. In effect, PLO actions evaded or "transcended" the UNIFIL presence, which now made little difference in controlling the PLO since it did nothing to hamper the few hundred "armed elements" in the PLO strongholds inside its area of operations and could not prevent the shelling of northern settlements.

Facts and Expectations: Disputes over UNIFIL's Role

In the aftermath of the Peace for Galilee Operation, disputes over facts and expectations regarding UNIFIL's role became less significant in U.N.-Israel relations than the perception that UNIFIL's main mission had become that of blocking IDF recruitment of local militias. Smarting from the humiliation of having been shown powerless to stop or even stem the Israeli drive, UNIFIL officers came to stress their mission as "custodians" of Lebanese integrity and sovereignty and as protectors of the "legitimate" local leadership against IDF and Israeli encroachment more generally. Although formal briefings continued to define the UNIFIL assignment in terms of the 1978 resolution, the interpretation of the mandate to restore Lebanese central authority had been stretched to the point where, in practice, the operational task became that of maintaining law and order in the sense, for example, of the UNFICYP mandate. Humanitarian responsibilities, now the main formal assignment of UNIFIL, were construed broadly as protecting the safety and welfare of the inhabitants.

Similarly—indeed, more vigorously—the military observers from UNTSO assigned to UNIFIL as the Observer Group Lebanon (OGL) have stressed that their primary mission is to reassure the local population and to help preserve Lebanese sovereignty and integrity for the future. Some sixty-five unarmed military observers (UNMOs) were assigned to OGL under UNIFIL's operational control. The UNMOs man five observation posts (OPs) along the armistice line, report and document any "violations" across the line, and patrol the roads in southern Lebanon. Their main purpose has been to show the international presence and the U.N. flag, to keep in contact with village leaders and notables, and to help pacify local disputes. Just as the OPs report and document only Israeli violations—overflights, vehicle traffic, and "permanent violations," that is, Israeli military facilities on the Lebanese side of the fence—so the protective function of the road patrols is intended mainly to show concern about the IDF presence and actions.

In effect, in the aftermath of the June invasion the United Nations quietly reinterpreted the mandate. The main task of the force and the UNTSO observers became that of "contributing to the maintenance of order and ensuring the security of the local population," as well as extending humanitarian and welfare help.[15] Because the PLO was no longer a factor (PLO power was always exaggerated in the eyes of many UNIFIL and UNTSO officers on the ground), UNIFIL's task became that of blocking what many perceived as an Israeli land-grab and of protecting the villagers' "freedom of choice." Thus, while agreeing that local security must rest on local militias and local authority (particularly the gendarmerie), UNIFIL doctrine and practice have distinguished between the villagers organized and equipped by Israeli security men and the "legitimate" local leaders who find shelter under the wings of UNIFIL. These leaders, it was claimed, looked to the U.N. force to preserve and restore their authentic authority until the central government could take over. And UNIFIL's mission was to monitor and contain the activities of Israeli-sponsored armed irregulars.

The controversy between Israel and UNIFIL over perceptions of events, the mandate, and effectiveness thus stemmed mainly from differing, indeed contradictory, notions of UNIFIL's role vis-à-vis Israel's security needs. According to the U.N. interpretation of the mandate, it was not UNIFIL's responsibility to take these needs into consideration. In fact, UNIFIL viewed Israel and its protégés under Haddad's command as destabilizing its mission and threatening Lebanese legitimacy and tranquility. From Israel's perspective, UNIFIL had become an impediment. For example, Israeli strategic planners were quite concerned about the human and political costs of UNIFIL resistance when planning the "Peace for Galilee" operation. In the end, Israel decided to accept the political costs and to attack through UNIFIL lines. On balance, UNIFIL had become a liability rather than an asset for those concerned with security on Israel's northern border.

3.
IMPARTIALITY AND EFFECTIVENESS: MEASURING PEACEKEEPING SUCCESS

CONTROVERSY OVER HOW TO MEASURE effectiveness, and contradictory expectations among the parties to a conflict, are apparent in many peacekeeping operations. An international force is under pressure from both sides to interpret the mandate in a manner that benefits one side or the other and is hard put to maintain impartiality. Thus, Archbishop Makarios pressed UNFICYP to "help maintain law and order," in the sense of U.N. support for local police authority, while the U.N. command considered that mandate required it to maintain peace impartially between the Greek and Turkish Cypriot communities.

The problem of expectations arises with particular force on Arab-Israeli fronts, where Israel's perception has been that the political climate in the United Nations infects its peacekeepers and impairs their impartiality to the detriment of Israel's security needs. Indeed, certain strategic experts are convinced that any multinational force linked to the United Nations carries so much negative baggage in Israel's domestic politics that U.N. peacekeepers cannot hope to get the necessary consent and cooperation, though these fears appear exaggerated, as UNEF II and UNDOF have demonstrated. Still, the negative Israeli feelings about the United Nations complicates the necessity for any U.N. force to prove impartiality and effectiveness.

More important than the U.N. label in explaining the protracted feud between Israel and the United Nations (often supported by the United States) over the effectiveness of UNIFIL was the Israeli perception that the peacekeeping force was not fully sensitive to Israeli concern about the safety of the northern settlements. Any multinational opera-

High-threat Fronts: A Peacekeeping Paradox

For Israel, any third-party force, U.N. or otherwise, can have only marginal value in its security calculations. This is particularly true with regard to a "high-threat" front such as southern Lebanon. With the end of the civil war in 1977, this border—for years the most tranquil—became the only actively threatening one. By raiding Lebanon to get at the PLO, Israel paid a doubly heavy price: Its raids contributed to the deterioration of Lebanon's unity and security, fueling instability on the border, and it roused hostility in the West, including the United States. Israel had to bow to American pressure and consented to the deployment of UNIFIL, although it was never convinced that UNIFIL could figure significantly in its security calculations. Haddad and the option of direct action by the IDF remained the pillars of security for the northern front.*

Paradoxically, on a front such as the Sinai, where the threat is less immediate because of a peace settlement and where distance assures more notice of attack on vital population centers, a third force can be accepted as adding to security. There, advantage was seen in an authoritative, activist peacekeeping force, especially as the multinational force in the Sinai was also a vehicle for an on-the-spot American presence to help guarantee the security provisions of the treaty. On the other hand, in a high-threat area like southern Lebanon—the security zone—Israel could never rely on a third force as part of its security system. At best, such a force has been accepted as symbolic or as a fig-leaf to help justify to the public the risks of withdrawing the IDF after the Litani Operation. To Israeli strategic planners it was clear that a battalion commander of an

---

* Before Israel's invasion of Lebanon in 1982, Major Haddad's militia played an important role in Israeli eyes in curbing Palestinian infiltration into northern Israel. Although Haddad commanded just 1,500 to 2,000 men—far too small a force to police the enclave effectively—its main value was to serve as the eyes and ears for the IDF in southern Lebanon. Its vulnerability lay in its inordinate dependence on one man who could not be replaced easily (Major Haddad died January 14, 1984) and who was perceived as the creature of the patron, Israel. Haddad's militia, in addition, lacked a solid political base among the majority Shiites. The IDF had tried to cultivate the local Shiite militias both before and after the 1982 invasion, but met with little success.

international peacekeeping force would never expose his men to the risks of determined guerrilla attacks; the peacekeeper has neither the national interest nor the mandate to take necessary and effective counteraction.

From their experience with UNIFIL, Israeli planners concluded that no third force could play a serious, reliable role in protecting the borders and that if an Israeli-sponsored, Haddad-led militia were not in the cards, at the very least the IDF must be assured of intelligence cooperation from the Lebanese army and of monitoring access to the security zone. (In the less sensitive area north of the Awali, as I note later, Israel was much less concerned, indeed almost indifferent, about the presence of a third force; it was prepared to withdraw with the assurance that no hostile forces would fill the vacuum and believed a U.S.-led multinational force could most effectively help buttress Lebanese authority there. In the end, Israel redeployed to the Awali line even though adequate arrangements to ensure order had not been completed.)

Here a paradox arises. Although it is argued that in an area such as southern Lebanon a peacekeeping force is symbolic at best, it is precisely here that Israel measured UNIFIL's effectiveness by its ability to control PLO infiltration and hit-and-run shelling of the northern settlements. As noted earlier, Israel saw UNIFIL as normally passive (or at times even collaborative) in the face of PLO threats and thus branded the U.N. force as ineffective whenever incidents occurred. The UNIFIL command contended that no peacekeeping force could be "100 percent effective" and, as General Erskine underscored during my conversations with him in the spring of 1983, the IDF itself had not succeeded in halting all terrorist action in the area.

Yet Israel tested UNIFIL's value by the strictest standard of 100 percent effectiveness. The reason Israel could not tolerate even sporadic PLO attacks and held UNIFIL accountable—if not for its failure to stop the attacks, then for inhibiting IDF counteraction—had to do with domestic political considerations. No government could afford to admit that the northern settlements could not be fully protected, nor could it accept without paying a high political price the fact of the hemorrhaging of the population from these settlements which followed terrorist attacks or shelling. Since UNIFIL could not prevent the shelling nor completely staunch infiltration through its area, it came to be viewed as more hindrance than help in the struggle against the PLO. This was especially true when UNIFIL, in exercising its responsibility to control unauthorized movement of armed persons in its area, often clashed with Haddad's people and other Israel-sponsored militiamen. The Begin government became especially frustrated with the situation after the stepped-up shelling in the spring of 1981.

Although the bad blood between the Israeli military and UNIFIL may be ascribed partly to Israel's distrust of any U.N. operation, in the main, controversy would have arisen if the peacekeeping operation had been under other than U.N. auspices. It is ironic that Israel's strategists discounted the peacekeepers as of marginal value in protecting the border, yet political logic required that UNIFIL be blamed for ineffectiveness in not stopping the attacks on Kiryat Shemona and Misgav Am.

In designing future peacekeeping mechanisms for Arab-Israeli fronts, the UNIFIL experience provides an important lesson. For Israel, any third-party force will play only a marginal role in security arrangements in any sector it views as high-threat, such as southern Lebanon. As the Israel-Lebanon negotiations that led to the agreement demonstrate, a third-party force may be acceptable in marginal roles—such as protector of refugee camps or as symbolic assurance to the local population that they have not been entirely forgotten—but not as buffer or guarantor of borders. A tentative conclusion is that any third-party peacekeeping force would not be acceptable as guarantor in areas designated as security zones. It is not just Israel's disaffection with the United Nations that is at play.

Moreover, a widely held premise has been that in security-sensitive areas such as southern Lebanon, Israel would prefer a multinational force with a U.S. core—such as the MFO or MNF—to a U.N. presence. Indeed, the conventional wisdom in certain Israeli academic circles is that a non-U.N. alternative (especially with a U.S. contingent) is always preferable. The logic appears to work the other way around.

An American Presence in South Lebanon?

It is true that in mid-June 1982, Prime Minister Begin urged the Reagan administration to field a multinational peacekeeping force in the south, similar to the Sinai presence, and indicated he would welcome a U.S. contingent within such a multinational force as guarantor and as the logical replacement for Israeli forces when they withdrew. Begin's purpose was not clear, although he may have been trying to involve the United States or to deflect plans (then prevalent in Washington) for a revived and expanded role for UNIFIL.

MEASURING PEACEKEEPING SUCCESS 29

At the time, Washington planners assumed that any multinational presence would be limited to two sectors, one incorporating the UNIFIL area of operation, but with its northern border moved up to the Zaharani River to correspond more or less to Israel's definition of its security zone. The second sector would include an area north of that, extending to Damur and stretching from the coast to the ridge line. (Oddly enough, the initial presumption was that Beirut would have to be excluded because likely troop-contributors would be reluctant to participate in a multinational force deployed there.) It was assumed that Israel wanted, above all, an American military presence corresponding to that in the Sinai. Such a presence would demonstrate a physical guarantee to police a buffer on Israel's northern border and would involve the United States more directly in the Lebanon problem. In Israel's view, a non-U.N. force had the additional advantage of involving the United States without a balancing Soviet role.

The United States, however, would have none of the Begin proposal, and within a very short time Israel cooled to the idea and soon expressed open hostility to *any* third-party force in the security zone. During his October 1982 visit to Washington, Foreign Minister Yitzhak Shamir told Secretary of State George P. Shultz that Israel opposed any third force in its security zone and that the assignments of any third party, whether U.N. or the MNF, outside the zone was of less immediate concern to Israel. Foreign Ministry officials interviewed in the spring of 1983 confirmed that this was still policy. The type of force, if any, to be deployed in the north and east was up to the Lebanese. Israel "wouldn't mind" having an international force there to monitor the Syrians in the Bekaa and to help the Lebanese oust the PLO from Tripoli.

Why did the Israeli government have second thoughts about an American presence, as part of the MNF, in the security zone nearest Israel's borders? One can only speculate, but it is clear that broader political-strategic considerations were at work than simply an assessment of the United States' utility as a guarantor. Apart from doubts as to whether such a force could be assembled or be more reliable than UNIFIL, an MNF presence on Israel's border could bring complications into U.S.-Israeli relations. Especially after the encounter between the IDF and the U.S. Marines in Beirut in the fall of 1982, Israeli strategists worried about confrontations of this kind. No matter how effective such a peacekeeping force might be, Israel could not exclude the possibility that the security mechanism would not be completely reliable and that the IDF might need to move into Lebanon again. Confrontation and even fire-fights with the peacekeepers could not be ruled out. So, ironically, some strategists argued that if circumstances and Arab politics required a third-party presence in the security zone, Israel should prefer the U.N. option precisely because the MNF is American! The reasoning was that, should it come to a confrontation with, for example, a Norwegian unit of UNIFIL, this would be less politically costly than confronting U.S. Marines. (This is not to say that Israel was unconcerned about the impact on its friendly relations with the Netherlands and Norway occasioned by clashes between Israel-sponsored militia and their contingents in UNIFIL; this is a major reason why Israel wanted UNIFIL removed.)

Another element that militated against an American security force in southern Lebanon or other high-threat areas on Israel's borders was that it would violate Israeli doctrine that American GIs must never be called on to shed their blood in defense of Israel. Former prime minister Yitzhak Rabin (who underscores this point in his memoirs, as he often did when he was ambassador to Washington during the Nixon administration) says Israelis are still sensitive on this point. Anathema to him and to many Israelis is the idea that any U.S. force, even as part of a multinational operation, would ever be put at risk of losing lives in a situation where the United States is perceived as defending Israel's security. For Israel, such a policy is seen as a losing game: If U.S. Marines take casualties fighting an IDF engaged in counterterrorist action, the political shock and cost to Israel's reputation would be tremendous. If casualties are taken fighting Israel's enemies, then Israel loses luster in American eyes as a country that no longer can boast that it fights its own battles if given the tools.

The upshot is that the acceptability of a U.N. force depends not only on its function and expectations—i.e., how effective it will be—but on the way it fits into the security considerations of the parties. On Arab-Israeli fronts, particularly where a third-party force operates in an Israeli security zone, two considerations apply. One is that any third force can realistically be assigned only minimal functions, mainly as a symbolic presence and to carry out ancillary tasks, such as protecting the refugee camps in southern Lebanon. The other—and more surprising—consideration is that in such a situation, an autonomous (non-U.N.) multinational force with an anchoring U.S. presence involves political costs that may make a U.N. force preferable.

4.
THE MNF IN SEARCH OF A MANDATE

A DIFFERENT POLITICAL LOGIC and other considerations came into play in assessing the suitability of third-party peacekeepers outside southern Lebanon. By mid-November 1982 a 4,300-man force comprising U.S. Marines (1,200), French troops (1,500), and Italian troops (1,400) was deployed in Greater Beirut to bolster the Lebanese army. Plans were soon under way to expand the force. When Lebanese Foreign Minister Elie Salem visited Washington in December he sought a commitment to increase the size of the marine contingent, as well as the French and Italian, to about 12–15,000, with the idea that the MNF could extend its area of operations, serve as logistical backup for the Lebanese army, and bring "the psychological security that cannot easily be defined." (Some even thought that, at its peak, a total of 25–30,000 troops would be required.)

During the fall, with the encouragement of the Gemayel government, the Reagan administration took the lead in courting other likely participants in an enlarged peacekeeping operation that would support the Lebanese army in taking over areas vacated by the withdrawing foreign forces (Israel, Syria, and PLO). Sweden, Austria, Belgium, Australia, and South Korea were sounded out; others, such as Greece, Turkey, and Spain, were considered likely candidates.

As explained to them, the scenario projected the expectation of a reasonably prompt withdrawal of all foreign forces and the need to extend, quickly and effectively, the control of the Lebanese army over all Lebanese territory. The idea then was that UNIFIL would be kept in place in the south while the MNF's area of operation would be expanded along the Beirut–Damascus highway at first as the forces of Syria and Israel disengaged. A parallel operation led by instructors from the U.S. and French armies could quickly train, reequip, and rebuild the Lebanese forces so that four brigades would be brought up to strength by February 1983 and three more be ready for action later that year. The French would also help improve air and naval capabilities. It was hoped that this effort would so rebuild the Lebanese force that peacekeepers could leave within a year or so after the departure of all foreign forces.

Apart from enlisting a small British unit that joined the MNF on line in Beirut, little headway was made. By the following summer the size of the force had increased modestly to about 5,400; by the end of 1983 it totaled almost 6,000. Some of the nations solicited declined to join on the plea of constitutional inhibitions barring participation in any non-U.N. multinational force. Others were concerned about the cost because each MNF participant paid its own way and no promises could be made about reimbursement; most were dissatisifed with the open-ended commitment and the ambiguous mandate. In general, nations were reluctant to participate because of the exposure to risk and to the possibility of entanglement in interfactional struggle. Nor did they accept the optimistic view that the Lebanese army could be ready to take over the security task within a year or two.

Strategists in the United States and elsewhere also expressed doubts about the organization and command structure. Unlike the MFO, each unit operated autonomously in the sector assigned to it. No overall commander was named, and operations were loosely coordinated through a liaison and coordination committee of national units. This committee, in turn, was supervised by a policy oversight committee comprised of the participating nations' ambassadors to Lebanon, chaired by President Gemayel or his designate. The structure served both as a channel of communication with the government of Lebanon and as a vehicle for coordinating field operations. When and if the role and requirements of an expanded MNF were clarified, planners assumed that a tighter command-and-control system would be devised.

When the multinational force came under attack from Syrian-backed antigovernment militias during the fight for the approaches to Beirut in September 1983, American and French units countered with artillery and naval and air gunfire, prompting senior American officers to urge the creation of a combined command and staff. Naval and air strikes against the antigovernment militias were less effective than they might

THE MNF IN SEARCH OF A MANDATE   33

have been because of desultory coordination. The basic flaw in the force structure became evident: It was not unified. Four loosely coordinated national contingents had separate commands, rules of engagement, and arrangements with the Lebanese government, and each made its own decisions on how best to defend itself and assist the Lebanese army. But some of the others opposed a unified structure. France, in particular, insisted on differentiating its Middle East presence from that of the United States. A combined command would complicate France's political desire to distance itself from certain U.S. policies. Still, the foreign ministers' consultation in Paris at the end of October 1983 concluded a working agreement that consultation and coordination at all levels had to be improved.[16]

Gemayel Campaigns for an Expanded MNF

By early 1983, as months passed with no apparent progress in the negotiations on withdrawal of foreign forces, the United States suspended diplomatic efforts to expand the multinational force and, more broadly, to engage third-party peacekeepers to help stabilize the Lebanon crisis. At the same time, the Gemayel government took another look at possibilities for sending UNIFIL troops to Beirut and other parts of Lebanon. One reason for the apparent cooling of American enthusiasm for an expanded MNF was the Pentagon's grave reservations about what appeared to be an open-ended and growing American commitment to sustain the Lebanese government and army. What had appeared to be provisional in September threatened to become permanent.

In fact, from the start, Defense Secretary Caspar Weinberger and the Joint Chiefs of Staff opposed American military involvement in Lebanon, fearing the marines would become caught in a Vietnam-like quagmire. Events in the fall of 1983 confirmed that their anxiety was not misplaced. Apart from concern about the diversion of military manpower and resources from what the Pentagon judged to be higher-priority missions around the globe, the military high command believed that however well-intentioned the U.S. presence might be, it could not carry out a neutral peacekeeping role for long in such a volatile area. The marines, they feared, would become much more hostage than deterrent.[17]

Apart from misgivings in the Pentagon, voices in official Washington began questioning the wisdom of the United States' growing involvement in supporting the Gemayel government. It was said that Gemayel wanted a massive Franco-American investment in his regime not only as guarantor of its survival and rich source of aid but as the foreign scapegoat for Lebanese shortcomings. In fact, from the outset certain American officials thought the MNF was a mistake and the entanglement in Lebanon "an accident waiting to happen."

At this time (January 1983), the UNIFIL mission in the south was renewed for six months as negotiations for withdrawal dragged on. The mandate was not changed and Lebanon's proposal for an expanded mandate was turned down by the Security Council. A three-month renewal in July and a six-month renewal in October extended the mandate on similar terms to April 19, 1984. No one wanted to rock the boat. Some of the troop-contributing countries, notably the Netherlands and France, urged the Security Council to devise a "more meaningful role" for UNIFIL than providing "protection and humanitarian assistance to the local population." The French representative noted that the force had demonstrated its usefulness by "restoring security to the countryside" and should be employed further in such tasks. On the other hand, Israel's representative declared that UNIFIL had outlived its usefulness.[18]

Meanwhile, seeing no hope for enlisting UNIFIL to stabilize the Beirut area, Gemayel early in the year revived his campaign for an expanded MNF. He gained the support of the defense minister of France, Charles Hernu, and of Italy, Lelio Lagorio. In a visit to Washington[19] they pressed the Reagan administration to move ahead with plans for expanding the size and role of the MNF. They joined in Gemayel's plea that the Lebanese president needed this kind of backing to establish a stable, unified nation sympathetic to the West. It is remarkable that the Europeans were now taking the lead in public, especially in view of the United States' virtuoso diplomatic effort in the fall. Lagorio underlined the "utmost importance to restore the sovereignty of Lebanon, [and] if this requires an increase in the size and scope of the [multinational] force, then we say 'yes' very quickly." Lagorio revealed that Gemayel told him the Lebanese army would need at least a year before it would be ready to police the country on its own, and that he planned to build up eight mechanized brigades for the task. Lebanese officials proposed an expansion of the force to more than 15,000.

President Reagan was reported at that time to share this concern for shoring up the Beirut government, and to be considering the need to keep the marines there to ensure stability after foreign forces left. It was reported that this diplomatic goal conflicted with the Pentagon's growing desire to get the 1,200 marines (later increased to 1,800) out of their exposed positions and then out of the country as quickly as possible; there were deep misgivings about sending even more troops. United States officials would make no commitment on the terms or duration of any such stay, but Defense Secretary Weinberger was quoted as saying the marines would withdraw as Lebanon became strong enough to take care of "these internal security matters" on its own. By June Ambassador Morris Draper was optimistic that, once the foreign troops had withdrawn, the MNF would not have to be in Lebanon very long. In a "few months," he said, the Lebanese army would have six completed brigades enabling the Lebanese to handle their own security.[20] (By the end of 1983 the forecast in Washington was that eight to ten trained and equipped brigades would be available by May 1984.)

Through the summer, as hopes waned for a speedy solution to the problem of Syrian troop withdrawal, the Gemayel government continued to press for an expanded multinational force with an enlarged area of operation. At a minimum he wanted a commitment for more active involvement in maintaining security around Beirut and in keeping the highways open to Damascus and the south. The need was urgent because in July Israel made clear its intention to withdraw from the Shuf (which it did early in September).* Gemayel pleaded for an expanded MNF to replace the IDF as a buffer force in the Shuf until a renovated Lebanese army could take on the job. In September, even as the marines were coming under fire, Gemayel urged that they leave the bunkers and be deployed as a symbolic presence alongside the Lebanese army as it moved outside the Beirut area.

As fighting broke out between the Lebanese security forces and Syrian-backed Druse and Shiite militias for control of strategic sites around Beirut, the peacekeeping rules were severely strained. Attacks on marine positions and other MNF units—culminating in the October 23

---

* Although it was problematic that the Lebanese army would be able to control the vacated areas, Israel clearly had signaled its intention to undertake a "partial, staged pullback," probably to the Awali River, at least two months before the IDF withdrew from the Shuf, as reported in Richard Bernstein, "Israelis Planning Partial Pullback," *New York Times*, July 6, 1983.

suicide truck-bombing of the marine compound and the French paratroop barracks—forced a reassessment of the MNF's passive role. Rules of engagement* were stretched to allow artillery, naval, and air strikes against attackers, and later against Syrian antiaircraft positions that had fired on American reconnaissance aircraft. The incremental escalation of force—much of it deployed to support the Lebanese army—resulted in an enlarged MNF commitment to the survival of the Gemayel government and its ability to extend its authority outside the Beirut area.

Though dispatched to Lebanon as an impartial buffer and stabilizing force, the MNF now found itself actively involved in fighting to support the embattled Lebanese army. In the eyes of many Lebanese and Europeans, the French reprisal raids against Shiite Moslem positions and American shelling and bombing of Syrian and Druse forces ended any neutral role for the multinational force and called the entire mandate into question. The MNF predicament was how to remain "peacekeepers" in a situation where the classic rule of impartiality among warring factions made less and less sense. United Nations Under Secretary—General Urquhart declared that the MNF had lost its ability to help bring peace to Lebanon by "drifting into the reprisal game," and that the force had departed from the essential requirement that peacekeepers must be rigidly impartial.[21]

The march of events had overtaken the mission—originally defined in September 1982 as providing peacekeepers for a limited period to meet the "urgent requirements" of the current situation, with the hope for "prompt withdrawal of all foreign forces." Almost a year later, on August 30, 1983 (after the marines had come under mortar fire), the president reminded Congress that their continued presence was "essential to the objective of helping restore the territorial integrity, sovereignty, and political independence of Lebanon." In practice, this came to mean that the peacekeepers would now furnish the military and political muscle to shore up the Lebanese government until the Lebanese army could be modernized and trained to take over the job. Indeed, in a radio broadcast on December 10, President Reagan said the marines would leave "once

---

* On the rules of engagement under which the marine contingent operated in Beirut, see the Long Commission Report on the October 23 truck-bombing of the marine compound, key sections of which are reproduced in Appendix B.

internal stability is established . . . and withdrawal of all foreign forces is achieved."*

In some quarters sentiment grew for an open policy of transforming the peacekeeping presence into an instrument for sustaining the Gemayel government both militarily and diplomatically. It was proposed that the MNF units be consolidated under a unified command and that the passive posture be abandoned for one of patrolling and more direct assistance to the Lebanese army.[22] The *Economist* (September 10, 1983) called for more precise aims of the multinational force: a limited operation but specifically in aid of Lebanon's own army.

The Reagan administration resisted any formal enlargement of the marines' role, however. The more activist posture and rules of engagement for the marines and other MNF units, in addition to the increased aid to the Lebanese army, were portrayed as consistent with the original objective.† No change was required. Clearly neither the Congress nor the country was in a mood for expanding the American commitment.

By the end of the year the tide was running against the administration's policy, and the search was on for an honorable disengagement. Public support for the marine's mission was fading rapidly. Congressional uneasiness grew about the exposed positions of the marines and doubts about the effectiveness of the mission. Dug in and providing only a minimal visible "presence," the marines had become a lightning rod for attack rather than reassurance for the population. The airport, which the marines were mandated to keep open, was frequently closed because of shelling. Some political leaders called for immediate withdrawal, others for a disengagement timetable. Some feared the operation was moving the United States closer to war, others that the Syrians would outstay the Americans anyway, especially with an election year coming up. There

---

* Even before the October 23 massacre President Reagan declared on October 19 that the United States would not allow Syria "aided and abetted by 7,000 Soviet advisors and technicians" to destroy chances for stability in Lebanon. The stakes had been raised five days earlier when the president told a press conference that the MNF was deployed to "provide . . . stability so that when the Lebanese forces moved out as other forces [i.e., Syrian, Israeli, PLO] left there could be the maintenance of order behind them."

† Secretary of State Shultz told the Senate Foreign Relations and House Foreign Affairs committees on September 21, 1983: "From the beginning, we have had essentially three policy objectives in Lebanon: the withdrawal of all external forces . . .; a sovereign, independent Lebanon dedicated to national unity and able to exercise its authority throughout its national territory; and security for Israel's northern border."

was a sense of foreboding that American diplomacy was headed for failure because of its reliance on tacit promises from such moderate nations as Egypt and Saudi Arabia—promises that guaranteed a Syrian withdrawal in return for an Israeli agreement to pull out. Pressures mounted in Congress to change the bargain worked out with the president that had authorized him to keep the marines in Lebanon until April 1985.[23] On December 22, 1983, seventy congressmen urged the House leadership to review the American military involvement in Lebanon because the marines role had changed from "neutral peacekeepers to active participants in a civil conflict."[24]

Misgivings about the marines mission were reinforced by the report of the Defense Department's commission, which investigated the October 23 truck-bombing on the marine compound. Made public on December 29, the report not only faulted the military for failures of intelligence and command, but called into question the entire mission. The commission found that although the "environment" of the mission had been transformed from one of "evenhanded and neutral" peacekeeping to that of partisan support for the Lebanese army, neither the military objective nor the rules of engagement had been adjusted. The report gave new impetus to congressional and public demands to cut short the marines' stay. Congressional "reassessment" of the entire Lebanon venture followed. The report impelled Walter Mondale, a leading Democratic aspirant for the presidency, to call for the immediate withdrawal of the marines to be carried out over a period of forty-five days.[25] Political analysts speculated that the administration would soon be driven to scale back its ambitious goals in Lebanon and that the marines would be pulled out after a short breathing spell to allow Gemayel to negotiate a compromise with the political dissidents.

The administration's declared policy was not altered, however. President Reagan told a press conference on December 14 that the marine presence remained absolutely necessary, the mission was sound, and progress was being made toward the original goal of withdrawal of foreign forces and the "reinstitution of the Government of Lebanon and helping them . . . to train and raise a force which can assume control over their own territory." (Earlier in the month, President Gemayel was pressed during his visit to Washington to broaden the base of his government as the key to internal stability and, consequently, to the early departure of the MNF). Still, it was clear that constraints on an activist role for the multinational force—not to speak of its expansion as contemplated early in 1983—was no longer considered a realistic option for stabilizing Lebanon.[26]

Israel-Lebanon Agreement on Troop Withdrawal

The peacekeeping situation was further complicated by Syria's vehement opposition to the May 17, 1983, Israel-Lebanon withdrawal agreement which had been negotiated under American sponsorship. The May 17 accord provided for an end to the state of war, future "normalization" of intergovernmental and trade ties, and total withdrawal of Israeli troops subject to security arrangements for southern Lebanon. The agreement was endorsed by both parliaments, but President Gemayel withheld formal ratification. At the time, most Arab nations—Syria, Libya, and South Yemen being the exceptions—agreed with the Beirut government that this was the best deal Lebanon could hope to negotiate under the circumstances. It was clear to Beirut that if the security arrangements in the May 17 accord were not implemented, Israel would remain in southern Lebanon and make unilateral arrangements to protect its northern border.

But Syria was adamant that the accord be annulled as a condition of its cooperation with any political settlement in Lebanon.* The accord came to symbolize for Syria and the Lebanese opposition the political advantages gained by the Phalangists as a result of the Israeli invasion. At the Geneva national reconciliation talks at the end of October, Syrian-backed opposition leaders called for renegotiation of the agreement. A decision was reached neither to ratify nor to abrogate the

---

* Damascus did not specify the unacceptable elements of the agreement, but Lebanese diplomats and analysts speculated that apart from the normalization features of official liaison and trade links, Syria was most offended by the equating of its military presence in Lebanon with that of Israel as a "foreign force." This point was underscored by the Syrian representative in the Security Council on October 18, 1983. In addition, Syria was offended by the provision in Article 4 of the agreement that "all agreements and arrangements enabling the presence and functioning on the territory of either party of elements hostile to the other party are null and void." Some scholars concluded that Syrian opposition flowed more generally from Syrian anxiety that "Israeli domination" of southern Lebanon would pave the way to a peace with Lebanon which diminished chances for Syria's recovery of the Golan. See, e.g., J. G. Jabbra and N. W. Jabbra, "Lebanon: Gateway to Peace?", *International Journal* 38 (Autumn 1983): 606 f.

agreement but to empower Gemayel to discuss with Western and Arab countries an acceptable alternative formula.²⁷

Despite reports that the May 17 agreement had been given a lower profile in Israel's policy calculations and that revisions were not ruled out,* realistically there was little room for compromise on the security features. Whatever concessions might be negotiable on "normalization," implementation of the military provisions in the security arrangements had to be regarded as the minimal condition for total Israeli withdrawal from the security zone. And, in accord with the side-letters and understandings defining the conditions for implementing the agreement, Israel's withdrawal was conditioned on the departure of all PLO "armed elements" and assurance of the "simultaneous" departure of the Syrian troops.†

Given domestic pressures in Israel to speed a pullout of the IDF from Lebanon, the government appeared ready to negotiate the timing of withdrawal and not insist on the simultaneous departure of the Syrians. But even should the May 17 accord be formally abrogated and new security arrangements negotiated to assure the protection of Israel's northern border, certain elements in the security arrangements were key and unlikely to be materially altered by subsequent negotiations.

One was the establishment of a forty-kilometer security zone (or

---

* Some Israeli political analysts later considered the May 17 accord unrealistic because there was little hope that the Lebanese army could effectively extend Beirut's authority to the south. The official position, as articulated by Ambassador Yehuda Blum in the U.N. Security Council on October 18, was that Israel remained "determined to proceed toward full and speedy implementation" of the accord.

† While the side letters and understandings are not accessible, their main points are known. Israel's withdrawal was conditioned on that of the PLO armed elements and "simultaneous" Syrian withdrawal as noted, and Israel reserved the right to suspend its withdrawal without reciprocal action by Syria. Israel did not get the right it sought to operate from bases within Lebanon on its own. Joint Lebanese-Israeli forces could operate on a 24-hour basis as necessary, but Israeli personnel in the supervision centers (which supervised and directed the joint teams) were to be "stationed in Israel when not engaged in activities in the centers." (This provision is contained in the published "agreed minutes.") Israel did retain the right to aerial reconnaissance. There was apparently a separate understanding on Haddad's future in addition to his being named deputy commander of the territorial brigade. According to some, Israel got an American "green light" to return to Lebanon if its security were again threatened. See Jabbra & Jabbra, pp. 606–8 and J. H. Sigler, "United States Policy in the Aftermath of Lebanon," ibid, 570–71.

security region, as it was termed in the accord). Second, no permanent IDF presence would be allowed within the zone. Police and security functions would be the sole responsibility of Lebanese authorities, but they were obligated to enforce special security measures aimed at detecting and preventing hostile activities. The Lebanese army, police, and internal security forces (Ansar) would be the only organized forces permitted in the security region, except for the protective functions assigned to UNIFIL. Moreover, of the two Lebanese brigades to be stationed in the zone, one would be a "territorial brigade" integrating local militias (including that led by Haddad, who would be named deputy brigade commander according to a separate understanding) that would operate in the southernmost sector closest to the Israeli border.

The third key feature was a joint Lebanese-Israel mechanism for supervising the security arrangements. A security-arrangements committee (with equal numbers of Lebanese and Israeli officers, plus U.S. representation) would oversee joint supervisory teams to verify on a regular basis implementation of security safeguards, check border security, and ascertain the rectification of complaints. Supervision centers, manned by Lebanese and Israeli officers, would operate around the clock to supervise and direct the joint teams and serve as centers of communication and information-processing.

Not only the Israeli press but the Shamir government visualized the security arrangements as enabling the IDF to withdraw completely from Lebanon. By November 1983 a national consensus embracing both the government and Labor party leaders favored a pragmatic and flexible approach whereby IDF withdrawal would not necessarily be contingent on a reciprocal, let alone "simultaneous," pullback of Syrian troops. Israeli planners both in the Defence Ministry and academia (such as Amiram Nir of Tel Aviv University's Center for Strategic Studies), advocated a unilateral, phased Israeli withdrawal not linked to a reciprocal Syrian pullback or formal ratification of the May 17 accord. A first step might be to move from the Awali line and from urban centers to a line on the Zaharani River south of Sidon, while holding on to IDF positions on the eastern front. All such plans were to be coordinated with the Lebanese government and with Washington so as to avoid creating the kind of political strains that emerged during the September redeployment from the Shuf. The plan hinged on Lebanese army units being capable of taking over the area vacated, and the southernmost strip being policed by the territorial brigade in which Haddad's militia would be integrated. (It was also clear that until a political arrangement could be worked out with Damascus, the IDF would keep some troops on the high ridges overlooking Syrian positions in the Bekaa Valley).[28]

Thus, until the May 17 arrangements—or something much like them—were implemented, Israel's pragmatic alternative was to establish itself in a narrower security zone which would tie down fewer troops. But for the longer term it was clear that any Israeli government would hold fast to the essential features of the military provisions of the May 17 pact: In the forty-kilometer security zone that Israel had defined on the northern border, Lebanese security forces would have the sole responsibility for internal security, subject to certain security measures verified by a joint Lebanese-Israel military mechanism. In effect, it was to be a bilateral system, with third-party peacekeepers assigned a circumscribed role.

Two provisions in the May 17 accord dealt with peacekeeping. For southern Lebanon, the central government "may request appropriate action in the U.N. Security Council for one unit of UNIFIL to be stationed in the Sidon area" (at the northern border of the Israeli-Lebanese security zone) to support the Lebanese armed forces in "asserting governmental authority and protection in the Palestinian refugee camp areas," including sending teams to these areas in the vicinity of Tyre. But police and security functions remained the sole responsibility of the government of Lebanon.

The other provision relating to peacekeeping (Article VII) declared that nothing in the agreement would preclude the deployment on Lebanese territory of international forces requested and accepted by the government of Lebanon to assist in maintaining its authority, although "new contributors" to such forces would be selected from states having diplomatic relations with both Lebanon and Israel.[29]

The meaning of the provision puzzled U.N. officials and troop-contributors. Did it portend an expanded multinational force and a diminished U.N. role in protecting the southern camps? Negotiators assured them there was no hidden meaning, simply a saving clause that reserved to the Lebanese government the right to determine the international peacekeeping assistance it might request for the area outside the southern security zone. How and where an expanded MNF or U.N. force would be deployed, as well as the terms of the mandate, were left in abeyance until a parallel agreement could be reached on Syrian withdrawal. Still, at the time the assumption in Washington was that (*a*) an expanded MNF would indeed materialize, and (b) initially it would be deployed along the Beirut–Damascus highway and, probably, along the roads north to Tripoli and south to Sidon. The mandate would provide for a passive presence to reassure the government and forces of Lebanon; the MNF would be involved in internal security only when requested by the Lebanese—just "being there" would be its main contribution. The stated assumption of both the MNF contributors and of the government of Lebanon was that, once all foreign forces had withdrawn, the troops would be needed for a year at most. By that time it was projected that the Lebanese security forces, composed of some eight retrained and re-equipped brigades, would be able to handle the problem of internal order. Left open for later consideration was whether U.N. peacekeepers would be enlisted to bolster Lebanese authority.

Two Stubborn Problems

All plans for moving ahead with security arrangements and for enlisting third-party peacekeepers hinged on surmounting two obstacles: (1) the slow pace at which the Lebanese army was being retrained, and (2) Syrian resistance.* The official view in both Washington and Beirut was that with six completed brigades already available and two more soon to be retrained and reequipped, the Lebanese would be able to handle the problem within a maximum of one year after the departure of all foreign forces—an assessment judged as overly optimistic by many observers.

Rebuilding the Lebanese Army. From the start, assessments in Washington on the duration of the marine's stay in Beirut were based on a best-case scenario. Syria, it was assumed, would withdraw its troops and cooperate in bringing stability to Lebanon once an arrangement guaranteeing Israeli withdrawal were negotiated. A rapidly trained and equipped Lebanese army would somehow be immune to the social and confessional fissures in the larger Lebanese society and would soon be in condition to back up central-government authority countrywide. Opti-

---

* High-ranking Lebanese officials were quoted to the effect that they would not have signed the troop withdrawal agreement had they known that Washington would be so ineffective in inducing Syria to withdraw from Lebanon. Thomas L. Friedman, "For Lebanon and U.S., Problem of Confidence," *New York Times*, October 15, 1983.

mistic reports on progress in the training of Lebanese armed forces kept flowing into Washington, and doubts voiced by some American instructors were discounted.

Sanguine American estimates of how long it would take to rebuild the Lebanese army were at first perceived by planners in the Israeli Defense Ministry as a notional position adopted to spur negotiations for withdrawal of foreign forces; they were astonished to discover that this judgment was held as a real possibility. The Israeli military believed that, at best, the Lebanese forces during the first year could be capable of a modest assignment, such as taking over a small area vacated by Israel and, then, only with backup of the multinational force. Israeli experts estimated that Lebanon needed about five years. In fact, one of them believed it would take "at least" five years, and then only if social and political divisions could be bridged.

In point of fact, although six brigades were supposed to have been available then, widespread doubts were raised in July about the readiness of the Lebanese army to take over the contested Shuf Mountains as Israel redeployed southwards. Secretary of State Shultz went out of his way during his Middle East trip early in July to discourage any idea that U.S. Marines of the multinational force might fill the vacuum left by the departing Israelis.[30]

Syrian Resistance. The other obstacle—Syrian opposition—proved even more intractable. Even before the mid-May Lebanese-Israel agreement, there was considerable skepticism about Syria's intention to withdraw from Lebanon given its historical claims, its strategic interests in the Bekaa, and the assessment in Damascus that Syrian interests could be best preserved by staying. The Israel-Lebanese agreement was portrayed as impairing Syrian security interests and unacceptable on political grounds. Moreover, it appeared doubtful that any parallel agreement would reassure Syrians that they would be better off by leaving than staying.* In any event, experts such as former U.S. ambassador Talcott W. Seelye were convinced that Damascus would seek to dissociate any eventual Syrian withdrawal from the Israel-Lebanon agreement and to link any arrangement to Syria's wider regional concerns.

---

* Secretary of State Shultz was reported to have realized after his visit to Damascus on July 5, 1983, that Syria was adamantly opposed to a Syrian troop pullout that was linked in any way to an Israeli withdrawal, by Bernard Gwertzman, "U.S. Failure with Syrians," *New York Times*, July 7, 1983.

THE MNF IN SEARCH OF A MANDATE

By the end of 1983, not only old Syria hands were arguing that Syria would persist in its policy and could afford to wait out the United States and its allies—even despite air strikes against Syrian batteries in Lebanon. Sol M. Linowitz, special Middle East envoy for the Carter administration, judged that President Hafez al-Assad was apt to respond to military pressure by standing his ground, anticipating that the United States would not unleash an all-out attack on him and thereby risk direct Soviet military involvement.[31] In the press and in Congress arguments were made with increasing regularity that neither political reconciliation in Beirut nor an expansion of the Lebanese army's security responsibilities nor a face-saving plan for the marines' departure could be worked out without an accommodation with Syria. At the same time, as the military balance in the Beirut area shifted in favor of its Druse and Shiite allies, Syria appeared less inclined to cooperate either in fostering reconciliation and a stable settlement in Lebanon or in achieving an accommodation on troop withdrawal.

In Israel, too, Syria was increasingly viewed as the key to any settlement or even to stabilizing the crisis. The security system in the May 17 accord could not be put into effect without a redistribution of political power in Beirut, which depended in large measure on Syrian acquiescence. Sentiment grew for an accommodation with Syria based on a tacit accord on issues of mutual security concerns. This was believed essential by many U.S. and Israeli analysts because of Syria's emergence as the predominant Arab military power.[32]

More to the point of the peacekeeping utility of the MNF, and particularly the American component, hostility to the American military presence by Syrian-backed Lebanese factions mounted throughout the second half of 1983. It became highly problematic that American troops (if not Western troops more generally) could long continue to function in the guise of peacekeepers. Whether Soviet-inspired or not, Syrian officials and media continually referred to the multinational force as "foreign," and it appeared that in any arrangement for withdrawal of all external troops Syria would insist that the U.S. contingent, if not the others, depart. Syria's Foreign Minister Abdel Halim Khaddam, addressing the U.N. General Assembly on September 28, 1983, declared that the Western multinational force must withdraw from Lebanon because it posed "a grave threat to security and peace in the region."

Syria's opposition to the U.S. presence in the multinational force was just part of its militant drive to achieve a predominant voice in Beirut's affairs. The Reagan administration viewed it as a calculated attempt, aided by the Soviets, to destroy chances for stability in Lebanon and to change the overall balance there to its advantage. Whatever the Syrian design, one result was to erode the marines' ability to serve as peacekeepers in the classic sense inasmuch as a key party to the internal conflict—the Syrian-backed opposition militias—regarded them as politically partisan and had therefore dramatically withheld consent and cooperation for the MNF venture. More broadly, Washington and Damascus were in direct political conflict, the purpose of the one being to protect and sustain the Gemayel regime, and of the other to eliminate it or subordinate it to Syrian dictates.

The MNF thus was subjected to opposing pressures. The Gemayel government wanted the MNF to stay as reinforcement and "psychological security";* Syria wanted it to leave along with other "foreign forces."

To complicate peacekeeping prospects even further, as the Syrian influence over opposition elements grew during the September fighting, there were signs that problems could arise even with non-U.S. peacekeeping troops operating under U.N. auspices or cover. Following the ceasefire of September 26, 1983, Syrian-affiliated Lebanese militias demurred to proposals that U.N. observers supervise the truce along the 60-kilometer line east and southeast of Beirut. Two points were at issue. One was whether the observers would be unarmed supervisors, as the Syrian-backed Druse and Shia factions preferred, or observers-cum-troops, which the Lebanese government and army wanted. More important was the other issue. The Syrian-backed factions not only ruled out MNF auspices for the observers but also objected to U.N. auspices on the ground that U.N. peacekeepers tend to stay for good and that the U.N. Secretariat is under inordinate American influence. They preferred a "neutral," non-U.N. multinational corps of observers serving under their own flags. The longer-range implications of this, however, were ambiguous since these factions agreed to accept not only Greek but Italian observers even though Italy was at that time integral to the multinational force.[33]

---

* Pleading for the marines and other MNF units to remain, Gemayel argued that the role of the marines had not changed as a result of the October 23 attack. They continued to play a "crucial and successful role" in facilitating the extension of Lebanese government authority, and their presence expressed the "West's commitment to peace and stability" in Lebanon and the region. Gemayel did not refer to the MNF as a peacekeeping operation, but did stress that the marines had come to Lebanon not to "fight our war but to help establish peace and restore democracy. Your young men are not in Lebanon to engage in combat." Amin Gemayel, "Yes, the Marines Have a Mission," *Washington Post*, Outlook, October 30, 1983.

5.
PEACEKEEPING IN LEBANON: THE THREE SECTORS

SUCH CONSIDERATIONS SUGGESTED THAT a mixed peacekeeping system would have to be devised for Lebanon. Peacekeeping functions and mandate would need to be adapted to the special requirements of three sectors. In the south, peacekeeping must take account of Israel's security concerns, particularly in providing assurance that the Palestinian armed elements will not be allowed to reinfiltrate the security zone. An acceptable third-party role, as projected in the Lebanon-Israel agreement, appears to be the extension of UNIFIL's presence as international reassurance for the Lebanese authorities and as protector of the refugee camps. Second, in the center (Beirut and the Shuf), the function needed would be that of peacekeeper among rival factions once a ceasefire or security arrangement among them held. Here a major need would be to help the government that would emerge from a political compromise extend the perimeter of its authority beyond Beirut, reaching out along the highways to Damascus, Tripoli, and Sidon. An ancillary peacekeeping task in this sector would be to continue to protect the refugee camps and vulnerable civilian population. A third and entirely different peacekeeping function would be needed in the east along the Bekaa front: to police a Syrian-Israeli disengagement, in effect an extension of UNDOF's role on the Golan.

The South: UNIFIL Redux

The security arrangements anticipated in the May 17 agreement between Israel and Lebanon on troop withdrawal were based on two principles: (*a*) the Lebanese security forces would be the "only organized armed forces and elements permitted within the security region," and (*b*) a security-arrangements committee of the two parties would oversee verification by joint supervisory teams. The residual UNIFIL presence was limited to one unit stationed in the Sidon area to help the Lebanese government assert its authority and to help protect the refugee campsites in both the Sidon and Tyre areas. It remained unclear if this assignment was subject to negotiation so as to permit, for example, the extension of the UNIFIL presence in the northern reaches of the security zone. Israel would in all likelihood accommodate the U.N. presence operating in the area far removed from its border. Indeed, by the end of 1983, as Israel was planning to redeploy its troops from the Awali line to the Zaharani River, circles close to the Shamir government signaled that Israel would be open to proposals that UNIFIL monitor the vacated area. Earlier, former prime minister Rabin of the Labor opposition had proposed that a U.N. force take over the area between the Awali and Zaharani rivers as part of a security arrangement that would involve handing over to local militias internal security tasks in part of the security zone immediately north of the border. (There was little prospect, however, that the U.N. Security Council would sanction an arrangement that would remove much of the UNIFIL presence from the southernmost sector, where it monitored Israel's incursions, to become a buffer force in the northern sector of the security zone, where it would essentially monitor anti-Israel attacks.)

The U.N. leadership and many of the troop-contributing countries were disappointed with the small role assigned to UNIFIL and had reservations about limiting the mandate to protecting the Palestinian camps at Tyre and Sidon. Although controversial, the assignment did reflect the growing prominence of UNIFIL's humanitarian and protective role since the invasion of June 1982.

Some of the troop-contributing countries, however, would be satisfied with the protective-humanitarian mission only if it were part of a broader, "more meaningful" mandate to help restore security and central authority in the south. A wider interpretation of the protective function would appear to be necessary for UNIFIL to attract or retain troops from countries like the Netherlands which have expressed sensitivity on this point.[34]

UNIFIL could also be assigned a broad, protective role outside the security zone, an option left open in the Israel-Lebanon agreement: That is, the government of Lebanon reserved the right in the accord to request the deployment of "international forces"—the U.N. was not specified—to assist in maintaining its authority. Whatever other peacekeeping tasks UNIFIL might assume elsewhere in Lebanon, it would appear to be prudent and sensible to expand its protective and humanitarian functions beyond the south. As noted earlier, UNIFIL in practice expanded its humanitarian activities in the south during the Israeli occupation (within limits permitted by the IDF) and came to view itself as the custodian of Lebanese legitimacy, as well as defender of the "free choice" of local leaders and protector of the Palestinian population. The renewed mandate on October 18, 1982 (S.C. Resolution 523), in fact, added a new and specific task that the force should "assist the Government of Lebanon in assuring the security of *all* the inhabitants of the area without any discrimination." As noted above, the secretary-general's report on UNIFIL for the first half of 1983 underscored the function of "ensuring the security of the local population" and of extending humanitarian assistance to them. The secretary-general also stressed that the local inhabitants "value the protection and stability" provided by UNIFIL.

Moreover, S.C. Resolution 521, which authorized additional U.N. observers in Beirut in the wake of the Sabra-Shatila massacres, also requested that the secretary-general consult on additional steps the council might take—including the deployment of U.N. forces—to assist the government in ensuring full protection for the civilian population in and around Beirut. At the time, the government of Lebanon preferred the MNF option (having concluded that its interests were best served by relying on the Franco-American partnership at the core of the MNF effort), but the notion of an international force with a specifically humanitarian role was thus accepted in principle by the Security Council. The issue came to the fore vis-à-vis the protection of the refugee camps in southern Lebanon.

As a stopgap measure, the Security Council on July 18, 1983, approved a Lebanese request to extend UNIFIL for a further interim period of three months. UNIFIL's mandate was left unaltered and was renewed for six months on the same terms in October. During the debate certain troop-contributors expressed concern because of the continuing uncertainties regarding UNIFIL's future role. The Dutch declared they would withdraw their battalion in October unless "entirely new circumstances" prevailed and a viable role were devised for U.N. peacekeepers. In the end they were persuaded to stay on for another six-month term.

The apparent narrowing of UNIFIL's role accounted for part of the increased disquiet in the United Nations. During my visit in April 1983, officers of certain battalions expressed reticence about assuming the unorthodox assignment of protecting refugee camps. (The Finnish battalion was an exception, declaring its readiness to do anything asked by the United Nations.) Their reluctance was understandable. If the arrangement envisioned in the Lebanon-Israel agreement materialized, the United Nations would protect the refugee camps only at the request of the government of Lebanon—and, presumably, the same rule would apply elsewhere in the country should UNIFIL's sway be extended. United Nations troops would, in effect, be employed to assert the authority of the government; yet, ironically, the protection thus afforded the refugees would most likely be enlisted against depredations by Lebanese allied with the government.

UNIFIL's role outside the camp areas was left ambiguous in the May 17 agreement. If its role as protector were limited to the camps, what about the unassimilated Palestinians (say 250,000) living outside the camp areas who might need protection following the departure of the IDF? Protecting them could involve "internal policing," an unpalatable task for most of the troop contributors.

A third concern was this: Would protection of the camps mean just keeping out marauders, or would it mean that U.N. forces must also prevent the camps from being taken over by PLO militants and converted into terrorist bases? It is likely that the U.N. force would at least be expected to assist Lebanese authorities in this latter task. Apart from UNIFIL's being perceived as helping to "ghettoize" the Palestinians, U.N. personnel might be required to exercise police functions (security checks, identity cards, searches, informers, etc.)—functions with which troop-contributing countries might not wish to be associated.

Given these concerns, it becomes important to reassess UNIFIL's role as protector and dispenser of humanitarian services and to cast it in a broader context than that of simply protecting refugees. This would mean focusing the UNIFIL role on protecting Lebanon's civilian population as a whole without discrimination as suggested in S.C. Resolution 521, and as reflected in UNFICYP's mandate during the first ten years of deployment (1964–74). As noted above, this overall protective function was the central theme of the secretary-general's report on UNIFIL for the first half of 1983.

In Lebanon, as in Cyprus, the primary concern about the anticipat-

PEACEKEEPING IN LEBANON: THE THREE SECTORS 51

ed role of protecting the civilian population was that it might involve the U.N. force in the morass of internal security. The same concern applies to any international peacekeeping effort. Yet, in practice, the essence of most successful peacekeeping has been to serve as intermediary and policeman between feuding communities (Greek and Turkish Cypriots, tribal provincial groups in the Congo), even though international peacekeepers deny that such duties are part of the authorized mandate. If the broader purpose of the peacekeepers in Lebanon would be to help the government assert its sovereignty, then, functionally, this may well require a more relaxed interpretation of their operational role in helping to maintain civil order. A revised mandate for UNIFIL must focus on ensuring internal stability and protecting civilians.

Prospects for a Multinational Force in Greater Beirut: Four Options

By the same logic, any international peacekeeping role in Beirut and central Lebanon, whether by the MNF or an international force that might replace it, would entail some involvement with internal security. Earlier in the year (1983) planners made certain assumptions about such a role: that following an agreement on withdrawal of the Syrian forces, the MNF would be enlarged and move out beyond Beirut. It was anticipated that the MNF's main role would continue to be that of bolstering the authority of the central government as it increased the area under its control, but the MNF's operational function would remain the same. (Its projected assignment was to include protecting the refugee camps and nearby local population, a task performed by the Italian contingent from the start.)

Initially, planners in Washington did not envisage the U.S. contingent as providing anything more than a presence that bolstered the confidence of the Lebanese army. As one authoritative source noted, the marines were not out patrolling, guarding villages, arresting people, making sweeps in the countryside, or otherwise actively involved in internal policing. Congress, it was assumed, would never approve a mandate that actively involved U.S. forces in this manner. And, under the arrangement authorizing the deployment of the marines in Beirut, congressional approval was required for any change in the mission or deployment.

Yet, despite such opposition to involvement in Lebanon's internal security, any multinational force operating in this sector could not escape "helping" the Lebanese authorities perform such policing tasks as patrolling and manning checkpoints, just as UNIFIL has done in the south. Indeed, the Italian contingent all along patrolled the refugee camps in southern Beirut, and British troops policed certain Beirut neighborhoods and protected government buildings. An either/or assumption was made by planners: If there were no political agreement with the Syrians, no one could keep order in the contested areas, while, if an accommodation were reached, Lebanese security forces would soon be able to cope with only a helping, passive, and short-term presence by a multinational force.

Events proved that the choice was not likely to be that clear cut. Starting with the troubles in September 1983, the multinational force became more actively involved in helping Lebanese authorities manage internal strife. And, in discussions of the MNF participants with the Lebanese government on extending the purview of Lebanese security forces and police along the coastal highway to Sidon, Gemayel urged that the peacekeeping troops accompany Lebanese units as they moved into the new areas. In theory, there were four possible options for peacekeeping in the Beirut area and the adjoining parts of central Lebanon.

Option 1: An Activist MNF. The option advocated by the Lebanese government throughout 1983 was this: to restore central government authority beyond Beirut the MNF would need to be expanded and become an activist force. But this was not acceptable to the MNF participants; in particular, in the United States a course of this kind had become less and less politically defensible. By late fall 1983 and expanded MNF committed to sustaining Lebanese authority and rebuilding the Lebanese army—which had looked so promising at the beginning of the year—was no longer a realistic prospect. The notion of the MNF accompanying the Lebanese army as it moved into sensitive areas—favored by Lebanese officials—was now almost universally judged imprudent and politically unacceptable. Indeed, as noted earlier, pressures kept mounting for a reassessment of U.S. policy toward the Gemayel government and the creation of a face-saving formula that would permit the speedy disengagement of the marines from the strife-ridden Beirut area.

What was the alternative? At the end of 1983 some officials and commentators advocated the redeployment of the marines to less-exposed positions. Pentagon planners talked of shifting them south and west of the airport, along the coastal highway to Sidon, to shelter them from sniper and mortar fire. Secretary of Defense Weinberger was reported eager to move the marines to the safety of ships offshore. Still others suggested that part of the force be moved to the Damur airstrip, a position that would afford a better platform for returning artillery fire. Lebanese plans to deploy units along the coastal highway south of Beirut were coupled with a proposal that some 500 marines move in behind them as symbol of support for the Gemayel regime.

Officers on the ground, as well as on the Joint Staff, were reported to be skeptical about the value of shifting the marines. Moving them out of the airport to higher ground might make them vulnerable to urban terrorism and still leave them exposed to mortar and artillery fire. In any event, because of the U.S. commitment to secure the airport for other MNF units should emergency evacuation be necessary, some marines would have to remain. Weinberger's desire to keep marines offshore also involved certain risks; ferrying them ashore by helicopter would still make them vulnerable to hostile fire. There had to be every expectation that no great tactical advantage would be gained by this course of action; the marines would still be sought out as targets by antigovernment and Syrian-backed forces. Besides, the resolution authorizing the executive to keep the marines in the MNF for eighteen months (until April 1985) was based on the understanding they would remain in Beirut; consultation with Congress was required for changes in the deployment or mission. And the Reagan administration was loath to take action with regard to redeployment, fearing that any move to redefine their mission would spark a renewed, divisive debate in an election year.

Nor was it realistic to assume that the United States' MNF partners would accept the activist role and be prepared to move into the exposed positions vacated by U.S. troops. During the fall of 1983 the Italian and British parliaments viewed with growing alarm the American and French air and naval strikes against Syrian-backed militias. American air strikes against Syrian antiaircraft batteries early in December were cause for particular anxiety. Such action was seen as transforming the MNF role from peacekeeper to partisan in an internal conflict.

In Italy, concern for the safety of its troops in Beirut spurred talk about a "delicate search for a way out." Public demands for a pullout were endorsed by President Sandro Pertini, who warned against Italy's "getting entangled in a war which is none of her concern." The government which earlier that year had backed Gemayel's plea for an expanded force now moved ahead with plans to reduce the Italian contingent of 2,100 (the largest in the multinational force) by half. As of the end of 1983, the Italian government had made no move to pull out any part of its contingent. Observers attributed the delay to official reluctance to give up the international prestige attached to Italy's growing prominence as peacekeeper. Besides, the Italians were concerned that the safety of the refugee camps in their charge be assured before they left. It was clear, however, that if internal security in Beirut deteriorated, domestic pressures to withdraw would intensify. In Britain, news that its small, 115-man contingent had also come under fire angered members of parliament, some of whom blamed the government for subservience to the United States and demanded the withdrawal of the British unit. There was particular concern about the vulnerability of troops guarding government buildings. Any indication that the U.S. Marines were pulling back would bring pressures on the government to move the British unit to a safer position.

In France there was little public pressure to bring the 1,750-man contingent home: historical and cultural ties were widely accepted as justifying France's involvement in Lebanon. Nevertheless, questions were raised about France's neutrality, and there was growing concern that French troops were becoming prime targets for terrorist groups. Whether for political or tactical reasons, the government felt compelled at the end of 1983 to pull French units out of exposed positions in the southern suburbs of Beirut; these were taken over by the Lebanese army, which promptly came under fire from Shiite Moslem militiamen. (France's move was unilateral, no advance notice having been given to the other contingents.)* Of all the units, however, the French were most likely to stay so as to avoid the appearance of abandoning Lebanon until an alternative peacekeeping presence could be brought in.

For the time being, allied restiveness about the MNF mission was contained, and all three countries joined the United States at a NATO meeting in Brussels late in the year in a pledge to keep their units in

---

* There were also reports at year's end that France planned to return to their positions in southern Lebanon some 480 troops that had been detached in September 1982 from its UNIFIL battalion for service with the MNF in Beirut.

Lebanon.[35] It was clear, however, that sentiment favoring an expanded and activist multinational force to bolster the Gemayel government, evident earlier in the year, had vanished. Nor were America's partners in a mind to take over on behalf of Gemayel's army those strategic positions vacated by the United States as the marines moved to safer positions. The MNF in its present form had failed in its objectives as peacekeeper and had drifted into becoming a backstop for the Lebanese army. It became increasingly clear in Western capitals that this arrangement could not work without some progress toward national reconciliation and a broader-based government in Beirut.

Moreover, the transformation of the MNF's role came to be seen in the United States and Europe as operating at cross-purposes to broader Western objectives of reaching an accommodation with Syria by providing some recognition of its role and "legitimate interests" in the region. Without an accommodation, it was argued, the Lebanese crisis could not be solved nor Syria persuaded to withdraw its troops. And, although President Assad did not respond positively to diplomatic overtures to cooperate in stabilizing the Lebanese crisis, officials in moderate Arab countries and in Western capitals believed Damascus was interested in a negotiated solution.

The prime inducement for Syria to negotiate seriously on troop withdrawal and to refrain from interfering with efforts at political compromise in Beirut was the prospect of hastening the departure of the American force. From the beginning, Syria's (and the Soviet Union's) primary aim had been to keep any U.S. military presence out of Lebanon. At the same time, the U.S. interest was in paving the way to a pullout of the marines without opening the door to a Syrian takeover of Lebanon and without being perceived as betraying the commitment to Gemayel. In a sense, the United States and Syria shared an interest in getting the marines out in a manner that did not hand the other side strategic or political advantage.

Option 2: Phasing Out the American Contingent. At the end of 1983 the limited convergence of American and Syrian interests suggested a peacekeeping alternative which was gaining favor among Washington planners who were seeking a formula for an honorable withdrawal of the marines: convert the MNF into a more neutral multinational peacekeeping presence from which American ground forces were phased out. Restructuring the multinational force in this way would allow it to resume the original peacekeeping mission with the "consent" of all parties concerned and serve to foster conciliation. (Recall that the original deployment of the MNF had the consent of the Moslem opposition factions because it had gone in to protect the refugee camps in the wake of the Sabra-Shatila massacres.)

This formula held promise only if there were no dramatic shift in the balance of military power around Beirut so as to favor the Syrian-backed Moslem militias. A bargain might then be struck whereby Syria and its friends would not impede the peacekeeping mission of the multinational force for a transitional period during which the U.S. land contingent would be phased out and the force reconstructed. (In principle, there was no reason to exclude participation of American officers at the headquarters of a reconstituted force nor to discontinue American logistical help. The United States would also continue and perhaps accelerate the program of military aid to help train and modernize the Lebanese armed forces.) Under this plan, the U.S. naval presence would continue to be stationed offshore and the marine contingent be put on board the vessels. Their continued presence offshore would symbolize America's resolve to maintain a stabilizing presence, provide a visible show of support and psychological assurance to the Lebanese government, and pose a credible deterrent to Syria and Syrian-backed factions against any temptation to renege on the bargain.*

In addition to the naval presence and a strengthened program to train and reequip the Lebanese armed forces, the potentially erosive effect on Lebanese morale of phasing out the marines could be tempered by significantly increasing economic aid. No concrete plans for an economic reconstruction program were known to be under way in Washington at year's end. But, even as congressional pressure grew for a speedy withdrawal of the marines, so did misgivings about the effect of a hasty pullout on American credibility and influence in the region. To offset what some officials and congressional leaders perceived as the

---

* Some analysts questioned the wisdom of moving offshore, arguing that naval vessels would be particularly vulnerable to surface-to-surface missiles. Many naval experts, however, contended that the risk was appreciably less than that faced by land forces. In any event, removing the marines from shore to ships would have no military impact on the ground since they had performed virtually no military functions. It was not the marine presence that supported the ability of the Lebanese Army to hold such key points as the Suk al Gharb ridge line around Beirut; it was the navy's aircraft and guns that had from time to time provided fire support. See Drew Middleton, "U.S. Ships Off Lebanon: No Sitting Ducks," *New York Times*, December 22, 1983.

PEACEKEEPING IN LEBANON: THE THREE SECTORS

destabilizing effect of the marines' departure, Senator John Tower (R.-Tex.), chairman of the Senate Armed Services Committee, on returning from a trip to Lebanon early in January 1984, urged the United States to "expand her program of economic and military assistance to Lebanon."[36] In effect, this would entail changing the nature of the American presence so as to deemphasize the military program and highlight the reconstruction and economic stabilization program.

By early December 1983 plans for a phased withdrawal of American troops were under consideration, although not in the context of the kind of reconstructed force suggested here. The plans, as reported in the press, had the marines first being moved to a safer site south of Beirut and along the coastal road, and then, sometime early in 1984, moving them to ships offshore. The marines would return to the beach from time to time as reassurance to Gemayel. According to this plan, as the Lebanese army became better trained and as national reconciliation progressed, the marines would board ship and sail away.[37]

A multinational force reconstituted along these lines (that is, with the U.S. ground forces phased out) would be workable only if the European contingents—particularly the Italian and French—stayed on as its core and were reinforced by troops from nations considered by all parties as genuinely neutral and politically unthreatening. Symbolic troop contributions would render the force even more viable.

Among likely contributors of armed units mentioned at the end of 1983 were Australia, New Zealand, Greece, Pakistan, and Sweden. The Italians would need to remain for reasons cited earlier: their perceived impartiality and acceptability to all sides, and their role as protectors of the Palestinian refugees. The French would be key, given their historical and emotional ties to Lebanon and their readiness to play an activist peacekeeping role in Lebanon. (The French contingent of the MNF was the first to arrive and the last to leave when the force first came to Beirut—Frenchmen are proud of this.) Some believed that France would not be averse to playing a leading role in a multinational force (from which the U.S. contingent had withdrawn) as the "indispensable Western power in the Middle East." President François Mitterrand had expressed the hope that a significant French presence could provide Arab countries with an alternative to alliances with Moscow and Washington, and that Paris wanted to assist in bringing "political peace" to all countries in the region.[38]

Option 3: Replacing the MNF with U.N. Peacekeepers. Even if it proved feasible as a stabilizing mechanism for the immediate crisis, such a reconstructed multinational force (outside the U.N. framework) could not be expected to last for long given its fragile political and institutional base. Domestic pressures were mounting in Britain and Italy to disengage from their peacekeeping commitments in Lebanon. It was a sensible option only so long as the Soviet Union and Syria persisted in opposing a U.N. alternative. By the end of 1983 a consensus emerged both in the West and at the United Nations that stabilizing the central and northern sectors of Lebanon over the longer range would require replacing the MNF with a U.N.-affiliated peacekeeping presence.

France took the lead in the diplomatic effort,* and the proposal picked up wide support, particularly from the British, Italian, Egyptian, and Netherlands delegations at the United Nations. The United States viewed the substitution of a U.N. for an MNF force as a most dignified screen for disengagement, and in line with historic U.S. policy of enlisting the United Nations in crises where the American interest lay in denying a disputed area to adversaries rather than asserting direct control. The Reagan administration's position, while not unfavorable, was cautious. It supported the proposal in principle but with the caveat that the wishes of the government of Lebanon were the critical element and, in any event, that the U.N. option was workable only if factional fighting were brought under control and the political situation in Beirut stabilized.

United Nations Secretary-General Perez de Cuellar and the U.N. Secretariat endorsed the proposal so that—subject to Security Council authorization—the United Nations was available and ready to assemble a peacekeeping force. Perez de Cuellar told a year-end conference that a U.N. peacekeeping force could preserve order in the Beirut area more effectively than the multinational force. Such a force, he observed, would have a broader base of support within the international community and a greater likelihood of acceptance by the local population. Urquhart had stressed all along that only a U.N. presence could provide the necessary broad political base and coherent command structure that would assure durability. He also noted that Lebanon's fragile political

---

* As early as September 1983 the idea of a U.N. replacement for the MNF was broached by French Foreign Minister Claude Cheysson to Soviet Foreign Minister Andrei Gromyko during the latter's visit to Paris.

situation demanded that certain prerequisites be satisfied: (1) not only would the Lebanese government have to issue a formal request, but a political arrangement would have to be devised to assure the cooperation of all warring factions; (2) a durable political consensus would need to be mustered for the Security Council's authorization and mandate, including, of course, securing Soviet assent to withhold the veto; and (3) obtaining troops from nations that were acceptable to all parties.

The problem was to surmount Soviet and Syrian objections. Earlier in the fall Moscow objected to exploring even the idea of a U.N. force in Beirut on the ostensible grounds that the Lebanese crisis was purely internal. It had little desire to help the United States extricate itself from a difficult situation. On the other hand, a U.N. force assured the Soviets a voice in the peacekeeping venture through its weight in the Security Council. Moreover, removal of the American military presence—which posed the risk of armed encounters between the superpowers—could best be assured by replacing the MNF with U.N. peacekeepers. Political analysts argued that a diplomatic effort to change the Soviet Union's mind could be productive: Moscow had sufficient interest in stabilizing the Lebanese situation because it had to harbor some anxiety about being dragged into a confrontation with the United States or Israel by Syria's militancy. (At the same time, it was clear that the Soviets would accept U.N. peacekeepers in Beirut only if the West made credible its resolve to keep some variant of the MNF in place should the U.N. option fall through.)

The Soviets would, of course, insist on certain conditions, but these were consonant with those acceptable to the West and the United Nations; that is, that the troops be drawn from countries other than permanent members of the Security Council, that the force be authorized by and answerable to the Security Council, and that it be acceptable to the Syrian-backed opposition elements as well as to the Gemayel government.

Should the Soviets go along with the U.N. option, it was unlikely that Syria would resist for long. As noted earlier, Syria had opposed U.N. involvement in the supervision of the September 26 ceasefire as "internationalizing" the Lebanon crisis and tending to become a permanent fixture. Among Syria's allies in Lebanon, Druse leader Walid Jumblatt, while preferring the U.N. to the MNF as less biased, had misgivings about any international force; such a presence tended to permanently divide a country on the pattern of Cyprus. But even Jumblatt was reported to be not totally opposed to the U.N. option, provided the force was composed of "totally neutral" countries. Still, it was reasonable to assume that Syria and the Syrian-backed elements in Lebanon—as well as the rest of the Arab world—would prefer the U.N. option to the prospect of a continuing Western-dominated military presence in Lebanon. Over the years, Syria has found the United Nations, and more particularly the Security Council, a politically comfortable vehicle for dealing with Israel at arm's length. By year's end, there was reason to believe that once an internal political accommodation was reached in Lebanon, all key parties would find a U.N. peace-monitoring presence compatible with their interests.

Several approaches to enlisting the United Nations were conceivable. One would be to restructure the MNF as an autonomous force institutionally separate but operating under U.N. sanction. (Italy had for some time been pressing for a U.N. imprimatur for the MNF or any autonomous peacekeeping force operating in the Beirut area.) This loose affiliation with the United Nations might be preferred by certain opposition elements in Lebanon which suspect that a U.N. operation would be harder to oust than an autonomous force.

Considerations both of world politics and of peacekeeping effectiveness suggested a more direct, operational U.N. involvement. Two possibilities would be (*a*) increasing the 50-man corps of U.N. observers in the Beirut area to some 500–600 military observers; and (*b*) extending the reach of UNIFIL northward with a mandate adapted to the conditions of central Lebanon. An alternative would be to form an entirely new U.N. force, but it might be politically easier to adapt the UNIFIL mandate. In any event, replacing the MNF with U.N. peacekeepers would enable the United Nations to recruit observers and troops from neutral and nonaligned countries as well as from Western nations (such as the Federal Republic of Germany) with a stake in the Middle East's stability and oil supplies.

During deliberations on devising a mechanism to supervise the September 26, 1983, ceasefire, the UNTSO option was favored by the MNF participants as well as by the Lebanese government; some argued that a U.N. observer corps would be a sensible and workable option for the longer term. Under the circumstances, the Gemayel government would almost certainly find it acceptable. Experts on U.N. peacekeeping, both within and outside of the Secretariat, urged the United Nations to assume the task, stressing that the United Nations alone possessed the requisite trained, impartial, and experienced field and staff people to effectively monitor the ceasefire. Urquhart urged in mid-December 1983 that the fifty-man U.N. observer group be reinforced as the most efficient solution and that it be given the necessary authority and resources to carry out the mission. United Nations observers in the Beirut area, he observed, were regarded as impartial by all factions, were acquainted with the local commanders, and had the credibility to mediate when fighting flared up.

To function effectively, an expanded corps of U.N. observers stationed in central Lebanon would need a new Security Council mandate and, consequently, Soviet acquiescence. Such a mandate would authorize the group to supervise any ceasefire negotiated among Lebanese factions, help damp down fighting, and provide reassurance to the local population by patrolling and showing the flag. Their presence would help promote stability as negotiations progressed on national reconciliation and on a security plan for the Beirut area.

An observer group, however, could not undertake the necessary function of interposing warring factions in the manner of the U.N. force in Cyprus during the troubles in the 1960s. More effective—and probably indispensable if the crisis in the Beirut area is to be stabilized—would be the deployment of a peacekeeping force in central Lebanon either by extending the UNIFIL area of operation north of the Litani or by installing a new one. Either way, a new Security Council authorization would be needed. The mandate could be patterned on that of UNIFIL: to help keep the peace locally by interposing as necessary among feuding factions, and to support Lebanese authorities in providing public safety, civilian protection (including that of refugees), and humanitarian services. More broadly, the peacekeepers could help the Lebanese government restore central authority to areas from which external forces had withdrawn. Clearly, the mission would be workable only if a political accommodation were reached among warring factions.

The makeup of the force could be patterned after UNIFIL, with perhaps some additional "neutrals" acceptable to opposition elements. The French battalion in UNIFIL—part of which was detached for MNF service—could serve as the anchoring presence, and the Italian logistical unit could move up from the south. Other battalions and supporting services could be shifted, in agreement with the Lebanese government and troop-contributors, as certain UNIFIL responsibilities in the south are phased out. UNIFIL's protective and humanitarian activities, including those for Palestinians, could be extended up north.[39]

Option 4: A Corps of Neutral Observers. A corps of observers made up of countries perceived by all the Lebanese feuding parties as neutral and organized outside the U.N. framework—envisaged as part of the ceasefire arrangement of September 1983—could conceivably be a fourth option for policing the central sector on a long-range basis. At the time, the various political factions and militia leaders agreed to establish a security committee (composed of representatives of the Lebanese army and opposition militias) to supervise the observer group and receive its reports on ceasefire violations. At the Geneva national reconciliation talks early in November, it was agreed to ask Italy and Greece to provide 600–800 unarmed military observers serving under their own national flags to monitor the ceasefire. As of the end of 1983 the precise role and mandate of the observer corps were still under discussion; sources in Beirut speculated that the observers would not try to enforce compliance but would depend mainly on "moral persuasion."[40]

Difficulties were encountered from the start. Italy insisted on some kind of U.N. connection for the observers, a proposal rejected by Syrian-backed militia leaders. And, as noted earlier, by the end of year Italy was having second thoughts about participating at all. At one point, sources in Athens indicated that Greece was prepared to send only 100 military personnel. These complications discouraged any further plans for creating a non-U.N. observer peacekeeping mechanism in the Beirut area to replace the MNF.

It was thus doubtful that an autonomous, non-U.N. observer force would prove to be a realistic option. Whatever value an observer force with a tenuous U.N. affiliation might have in policing a ceasefire, its institutional base would be too weak and its political authority too insubstantial to make it an effective peacekeeping presence for central Lebanon even for the short term.

Disengagement on the Eastern Front

A third and completely different task for international peacekeepers in Lebanon would be to police disengagement on the Bekaa front between Syrian and Israeli forces. What appeared to be needed was an arrangement not unlike the one for the Golan. That is, a peacekeeping mechanism to buttress an explicit or tacit understanding between Israel and Syria, and to establish a demilitarized buffer to be policed by an

PEACEKEEPING IN LEBANON: THE THREE SECTORS 63

international force on the pattern of UNDOF. A companion arrangement would define the "red line" below which Syria would move only at the risk of a strong Israeli response;[41] a parallel "red line" would be established for Israel.

By the fall of 1983 it was clear that simultaneous and full withdrawal of Syrian and Israeli forces from all of Lebanon would not soon be achieved, so that any peacekeeping function on the Bekaa front had to flow from an arrangement, formal or tacit, between Israel and Syria putting some distance between the two armies. Although no grand, comprehensive solution was feasible, the disengagement of forces on that front would appear to satisfy the current interests of both countries in avoiding war, as well as Lebanon's national interest in regaining sovereignty over as much of its territory as possible.

Would Syria be receptive to the idea? Despite the escalation in Syrian rearmament and tough talk in Damascus,* the assessment in Washington was that Syria did not seek large-scale hostilities with Israel. In a November 1983 interview with columnists Rowland Evans and Robert Novak in Damascus, President Assad recalled with nostalgia the 1974 disengagement agreement on the Golan sponsored by Henry Kissinger, hinting he would be open to U.S. proposals for a parallel arrangement on the Bekaa line where Israeli and Syrian troops were face to face. (Syria's continued faith in the tranquility of the Golan was evidenced by its building of new civilian housing near Kuneitra). Nor would this be inconsistent with Assad's long-range plans for improving the strategic balance in his favor. Syria had reason to be anxious about Israel's military presence on that front: Israeli artillery was emplaced just 30 kilometers from Damascus, and the IDF held positions at the mountain passes on approaches to the Syrian capital and on Jebel Baruk, a 6,000-foot mountaintop overlooking the Bekaa where Israeli radar reaches to Damascus and beyond, and where electronic devices can intercept Syrian communications and monitor Syrian military activity.

The calculus on the Israeli side also pointed toward interest in a disengagement arrangement. True, an influential constituency argued

---

* Syrian defense minister, Maj. Gen. Mustafa Tlas, in an interview with a pro-Libyan Beirut magazine, *Al Kifah Al Arabi*, threatened suicide attacks on American warships and highlighted Syria's ability to hit any place in Israel with missiles; but he underscored that Syria still sought a strategic balance with Israel. *New York Times*, November 20, 1983.

that Syria would not abandon the ultimate intention of incorporating Lebanon into Greater Syria, which would thus imperil Israel, and that it would be foolhardy to contemplate abandoning a strategic stronghold like Jebel Baruk short of agreement on total and simultaneous withdrawal. But sentiment on the other side was growing. Prime Minister Yitzhak Shamir, interviewed on Israel television on November 9, 1983, indicated that Israel was approaching the time when "Operation Peace for Galilee" could be ended.[42] Because the main objectives of destroying the PLO infrastructure and keeping terrorists at a distance from its northern border had been achieved, Israel could now consider removing its military presence from Lebanon—so long as security arrangements in the south would ensure that "we won't be attacked by terrorists after we leave Lebanon." In reacting to the announcement that Syria had mobilized its forces, Shamir declared the previous day: "We have no interest in waging war on anybody, including Syria. And I hope Syria does not desire at this moment to have a confrontation with us." Even before the Syrian-backed assault on Arafat's positions in Tripoli, observers noted that Damascus held the key to containing PLO terrorist attacks on the northern settlements, since Syria alone had the power to unleash or rein in the guerrillas, they pointed to the fact that no terrorist attacks had originated in Syrian territory on the Golan front. The safety of the northern settlements, it was argued, hinged on involving Syria in an arrangement that made it responsible for curbing the Palestinians. Israeli strategists also noted that the Syrian army did not cross the line previously held on the Beirut–Damascus road when the IDF pulled back from the Shuf to new positions on the Awali River early in September 1983.[43]

Influential academics and politicians associated with the Labor alignment saw disengagement as part of any broader agreement to stabilize Lebanon and reduce Israel's costly involvement there. Aharon Yariv, director of the Tel Aviv University Center for Strategic Studies and former chief of military intelligence, observed early in November 1983 that Syria was aware it was not strong enough to wage war and could not count on its allies. The time was thus ripe, he argued, for a tacit arrangement with Syria to disengage forces: The Israelis would withdraw on the condition that the Syrians would not advance and would cooperate in deterring terrorist attacks on Israel's northern settlements. The IDF would pull back from positions that put Damascus in artillery range, and Syria would pull back the three divisions it had introduced into Lebanon to protect its flank. Yariv even counseled Israel to hold in abeyance the May 17 accord and to tacitly recognize Syria's "special position" in Lebanon. Later that month, former prime minister Rabin advocated a unilateral Israeli pullback from the Awali line to a narrower buffer zone about 48 kilometers deep. An expanded U.N. force would police the zone in tandem with Israeli units and local militia. In Rabin's view, the Israeli withdrawal need not be contingent on a reciprocal Syrian move.[44]

Other military analysts urged that any plans for redeploying from the Awali to the Zaharani River (designed to reduce the area and inhabitants under IDF control) be coupled with a broader arrangement for disengagement from the "confrontation border" with Syria. Israeli officers on the Bekaa front suggested to visitors the value of each side making local withdrawals in order to reduce the danger of escalation from isolated incidents. (Hirsh Goodman, military analyst for the *Jerusalem Post*, argued that even abandoning Jebel Baruk as part of the deal should not involve a high security cost because its contribution to intelligence-gathering had been overrated.) It was reported at year's-end that Israel had asked the United States to explore with Syria the possibility of a disengagement to reduce the risk of war through miscalculation, and that Israel would consider favorably any proposals for a U.N. force or the Lebanese army to take over the vacated area.[45]

Reflecting this growing sentiment for disengagement, former foreign minister Abba Eban argued that the same rationale which convinced both sides to sign the 1974 disengagement agreement now argued for a similar arrangement on the Bekaa front. Given Syria's radical ideology and goals, he stressed, conditions did not exist for a normal peace or an "affirmative relationship"; history had shown, however, that Syria under Assad is capable of pragmatic arrangements to reinforce conditions for avoiding war. The 1974 arrangement demonstrated that, once an agreement was reached, it could benefit both sides—in the past nine years not a single shot had been fired nor had any terrorist infiltrations taken place across the Golan disengagement line.[46]

The 1974 precedent would also apply to the diplomacy necessary to conclude a disengagement agreement for the Bekaa front. Since the condition of an "affirmative relationship" (Eban's term) was lacking, no arrangement could be devised without a diplomatic broker, and only the United States was in a position to serve as intermediary. Although Syria opposed a U.S. military presence in Lebanon, in its view, only America possessed the standing and credibility to bridge the differences and to pressure Israel to make the necessary concessions such as abandoning its position on Jebel Baruk. As noted earlier, Assad recalled the success of the Kissinger diplomatic shuttle of 1974 that resulted in the Golan disengagement. For Israel, only the United States could be trusted to be sensitive to its security concerns in negotiations for disengagement. It was reasonable to conclude that without an American diplomatic initiative no arrangement could be achieved.

What third-party force could realistically carry out the functions now performed on the Golan by UNDOF.* It is almost inconceivable that the Syrians would accept a multinational force patterned on the MNF—particularly if it included a U.S. contingent. The Bekaa front would require a peacekeeping presence operating in a sanitized area exempt from superpower involvement; this would exclude at least the United States, if not France—a permanent member of the Security Council. The experiences of UNDOF and UNEF II demonstrate that peacekeeping forces can enlist the cooperation of the states involved provided they can be relied upon to discipline any irregular forces, such as Palestinian guerrillas, in the area under their control. One has to conclude that part of the peacekeeping arrangements on the eastern Lebanon front would require a force under U.N. auspices similar to UNDOF.

In sum, recognizing that a final settlement for Lebanon could be a long-term affair, an interim plan for phased withdrawal and separation of forces on the Bekaa front would appear essential. Reports early in the fall of 1983 indicated that Israel might be amenable in principle to a separation-of-forces agreement with Syria to reduce the risks of accidental encounters. Syria was likely to find such an agreement desirable because it would protect its security interests in a most vital sector. If the

---

* UNDOF's mandate from the Security Council was to supervise the ceasefire and monitor the demilitarization between Israeli and Syrian forces of May 31, 1974. Operationally, this has entailed the deployment of peacekeepers (some 1,300, including logistical personnel, as of the fall of 1983), within and close to the area of separation, to ensure that there were no military forces within it. UNDOF operates static positions and observation posts that are manned 24 hours a day and sends out mobile patrols at irregular intervals but on predetermined routes. UNDOF also conducts fortnightly inspections to ensure that limits on arms and forces in the designated area of limitation are observed. Liaison officers from the parties accompany the UNDOF inspection teams. For years the situation has remained quiet, and few serious incidents have been reported. See *Report of the Secretary-General of the United Nations Disengagement Observer Force* (for the period May 21, 1983–November 21, 1983), U.N. Document S/16169, November 21, 1983.

agreement involved transferring control of the Jebel Baruk lookout from the IDF to international peacekeepers, Syrian participation could almost certainly be assured. Indeed, an arrangement to separate forces should be easier for Syria to accept than the 1974 disengagement in the Golan, which imposed restrictions on its freedom of military action on its own sovereign territory.

In any case, the model would be that of UNDOF or UNEF II: a disengagement agreement or understanding between Israel and Syria, with which Lebanon would be associated, providing for a demilitarized "area of separation." This buffer zone would be under the civilian control of the government of Lebanon but be policed by an international peacekeeping force. It must be presumed that this force would operate under the auspices of and be managed by the United Nations. No other third-party peacekeeping force could conceivably take on the assignment.

6.
THE MULTINATIONAL FORCE & OBSERVERS: UNIQUE OR PARADIGM?

DEPLOYMENT OF THE MFO IN THE Sinai introduced a novel pattern of peacekeeping into the area.[47] It is unique as the first sizable peacekeeping operation not under U.N. auspices and, as noted earlier, the first since the Korean War in which American troops (as distinguished from civilian observers) were stationed in a troubled area as the mainstay of an international presence.

The MFO's major advantage is that it was established by the parties themselves to buttress the Egypt-Israel peace treaty. It is not constrained by the requirement that the force composition reflect "equitable geographic distribution," nor does it come under the constant scrutiny of the Security Council, requiring Soviet acquiescence and Third World blessing. It was founded and has been largely financed by the parties, which thus have a stake in cost-effectiveness and financial accountability.

Furthermore, the MFO was designed to be durable, and its mandate was not made subject to periodic review and renewal. Above all, it is based on an unprecedented American commitment—made by the president when the treaty was negotiated—to establish and maintain an "alternative multinational force" if the U.N. force (provided in the treaty) did not materialize. Although some U.S. officials present at its creation claim that this pledge was artfully drafted so as "not necessarily" to require American military involvement, it is hardly conceivable that any "alternative multinational force" would have proved satisfactory for Israel without an American component. The United States provides the anchoring presence (a battalion from the 82nd and 101st airborne divisions in rotation), largely manages the logistics, paid the lion's share of the start-up costs, and shoulders a third of the operating cost of a budget that amounts to about $100 million a year. In addition, the U.S. presence has not blocked direct relations between the parties but has served to bridge them.

The MFO has been a successful operation mostly because it fit into the political and security needs of the key parties concerned. The MFO works for Israel because it has effectively supplemented Israel's strategic interests by bolstering and verifying the security provisions of the treaty and, above all, by providing a dominant role for the United States in policing those provisions. It also locks the United States into a security rationale linking U.S. security concerns in the eastern Mediterranean with long-range Israeli concerns. Israel did not need an American guarantee as much as a quasi alliance in which both countries would define security requirements in a compatible way. During the negotiations and to this day Israel has evinced an interest in a maximalist interpretation of the MFO's mandate—autonomous, activist, and with its authority flowing from the treaty and protocol, not deriving from Egypt's sovereignty over the Sinai.

Egypt, not happy about the MFO's open-ended term, acquiesced in its establishment as a "confidence-builder" because the MFO was the price of Israel's relinquishment of the Sinai and because Egypt sees some value in an international presence as guarantor. Egypt, however, has been very sensitive about any hint that the presence and activities of the MFO could impair its sovereignty; the troops are welcome "guests," but their responsibilities and authority are to be interpreted in the most minimal way. Egypt accepted the MFO not only as the price for recovering the eastern Sinai but as a way to involve the United States as a "full partner" in the peace. Nevertheless, it is very sensitive, as is the MFO leadership, that MFO be perceived not as a U.S. presence but as an "international" one.

Operationally, these differences have not been significant, and minor disputes over presumed violations have been readily reconciled. Perceptual differences, however, abound. Egypt would like to see the MFO's size and budget reduced, while Israel has been more concerned about the force's ability to carry out its task in an activist, maximalist manner. Egypt looks forward to an early departure of the force, while Israel cautions that any talk of a near-term dismantling of the force (through withdrawal of the Europeans, for example) would destabilize the peace. Israel stresses the American "look" of the force, Egypt the international aspect. For example, Israel is not displeased when the U.S. battalion is seen as a nucleus of the rapid deployment joint task force, but Egypt is very unhappy. Nevertheless, both sides ascribe value to the MFO as a confidence-builder while the peace is still in its infancy and as a token of the United States' commitment to the peace. Some Israelis see the key value in the MFO's responsibility to ensure freedom of navigation through the Strait of Tiran, an aspect the Egyptians would just as soon were not flaunted since they regard Egypt itself as guarantor of the terms of the treaty, which include freedom of navigation.

The U.S. connection with the MFO has given rise to a certain ambivalence in Washington. Those who championed a U.S. presence in the "alternative multinational force"—particularly those advocating close strategic relations with Israel—see the MFO as fitting into the broader U.S. strategic interests in the area. That is, a U.S. presence is a visible token of American power on the ground and of America's commitment to the stability of the region. The advantage of the peacekeeping assignment is that the United States can demonstrate this commitment in a politically sanitized, multinational context.

During the hearings in Congress,[48] however, concern was expressed that such an open-ended involvement could draw the United States into conflicts in the region against its will and national interests. Similar misgivings surfaced when the marines were sent to Lebanon as part of the MNF. In both cases, congressional misgivings stemmed partly from the open-endedness of the commitment, partly from the risk of being drawn into hostilities, and partly from the cost. The MNF was cause for particular concern because of the perception in Congress that the executive may have circumvented the War Powers Resolution. During hearings on the MFO protocol, the U.S. negotiators underscored administration assurances that the letter and spirit of the War Powers Resolution would be respected, and that Congress would be kept fully informed about changes on the ground that could affect the American commitment. In addition, any change in U.S. participation in the Sinai force would be subject to congressional approval. (Similar assurances were given when the marine unit was assigned to the multinational force in Beirut.)

Many U.S. strategists and military leaders were not reconciled to the obligation imposed on the military establishment to supply a battalion of the 82nd or 101st airborne divisions for peacekeeping duties for an indefinite period. As one knowledgeable senior military officer put it, the Sinai commitment, in effect, costs the Eighty-second Airborne Division one of its active brigades, taking it out of the front line, so to speak. The assignment also diverts resources and sends elite combat troops on what they regard as a marginal mission, taking each battalion, as it is rotated, out of its normal training and readiness cycle for close to a year—six months on location, three to get ready, and two to three to unwind and convert from peacekeeping to combat soldiers.[49]

Others, including commanders on the spot, assessed the assignment more favorably, citing the value of desert training for line and support units and for training in squad leadership. In general, the benefits of the assignment were seen to outweigh the costs. Some viewed this experience as compatible with training requirements for troops likely to be attached to the rapid deployment task force.

Another aspect of the dominant U.S. presence in the Sinai operation has been of concern to the MFO leadership: Some in Washington have tended to treat U.S. participation in the Sinai force as solely an American exercise and thus occasionally fail to respect the MFO's autonomous, international character. Some congressmen and generals, it is charged, acted as though the MFO installation were no different from a U.S. base in the Sinai, and were unwilling to accept the restraints on what a U.S. battalion could be expected to do (e.g., in regard to training) while participating in an international force. Nor did they sufficiently respect Egyptian sensitivities about what transpired on its sovereign territory. Still, on balance, U.S. policy has been perceived by the MFO leadership as fully supportive of its mission.

Success and Vulnerabilities

On April 25, 1983, the organization and troop-contributing countries celebrated the first anniversary of the MFO with a dress parade at headquarters in El Gorah, entertainment by Fiji and Colombian troops, and motorcycle races in the sand dunes. It has indeed been a success story whose pivotal figures are the negotiators of the protocol, led by Michael Sterner of the State Department, and his associates who persuaded nine other countries to join in the endeavor; Director-General Hunt of the United States and the Force Commander Bull-Hansen of Norway, whose diplomatic and managerial skills helped put the MFO on its feet; and the cooperation of the two chiefs of the Liaison System, Admiral Hamdy of Egypt and Brigadier General Sion of Israel.

Things that go right are easily taken for granted. Success is never unalloyed, however, and, over time, the effectiveness of any peacekeeping operation can be eroded. Speculation is that the MFO will endure for at least five years (the shortest assessment) but, more likely, for decades. It is unlikely that Israel would agree to the removal of MFO until tranquility prevails on all its borders. Vulnerabilities could cause problems for the force over the long run and are worth analyzing if the MFO is to be considered a model for other fronts.

What are these vulnerabilities? Financing is usually a critical problem in international peacekeeping endeavors, but the MFO has enjoyed more financial stability and better accountability than is generally the case for U.N. peacekeeping. One hears some grumbling about rising costs (much higher than expected), and the parties have been known to demand inspections of the detailed accounts, although this has been resisted by the MFO management. The parties are now persuaded that rigorous, joint budget-planning suffices. Still, as long as the parties (and the United States) continue to see political-security value in the perpetuation of the MFO, neither Congress nor the finance ministers of Egypt and Israel are likely to balk at the cost.

Nor are the differences over the optimum size of the force likely to become a major source of controversy. The force became larger than originally conceived because of Israel's insistence on three battalions. Although limited to an overall complement of 2,500–2,600 men, the MFO command was required to field three infantry battaltions. This produced some operational strains in assuring adequate support services, and the managers were forced to rely inordinately on expensive civilian-contract personnel. On the other hand, the Egyptians would like to see the force reduced. In their view, a much smaller force could easily back up the thirty to fifty civilian observers who carry out the key provisions of the treaty and protocol—to observe and verify the limitations on arms and men in Sinai zones A, B, and C, and in the adjoining Zone D on the Israeli side. In fact, authoritative Egyptian sources claim that the task could well be performed by a corps of observers patterned on the Sinai Field Mission.

These minor differences are likely to be smoothed over, although the issues of size and cost could be troublesome if ever Egypt or Israel were to seek some pretext for evading the obligations of the treaty. More ominous are three vulnerabilities, three fault lines in the structure, which over time could cause problems.

Freedom of Navigation. Under Article V of the treaty,[50] included in the protocol by reference, the MFO is charged with "ensuring the freedom of navigation through the Strait of Tiran." The blockade of the strait and the Gulf of Aqaba has triggered war more than once, so Israel emphasizes the MFO's responsibility to ensure freedom of navigation as integral to the security arrangements. Egypt is concerned that the provision to "ensure" not be interpreted in a manner that infringes on its sovereignty. These are territorial waters, it is claimed, and Egypt can be relied on to "ensure" free navigation to all as a matter of "trust and sovereignty." According to Egypt, the MFO's task at the strait is to "observe and report," just as it is elsewhere in the demilitarized Zone C where the force is deployed.

Does it matter? It would appear so in political and operational terms. Politically, Israel's confidence in the integrity of the MFO is based on the expectation that it will take the steps necessary to ensure, in the sense of "enforce," free navigation if it is ever threatened. Operationally, too, there could be a difference as to what the force would do in certain circumstances.

The MFO avoids taking a stand on legalities. The technical procedures for observing and reporting are the same as those applied elsewhere in Zone C, and "ensure" does "not include the use of force by the MFO to counter or control a deliberate or substantial military action undertaken by a state. [The MFO's] action would be to inform all parties involved in the situation, and to request immediate cooperation in settling matters which arise."[51] In effect, the function has been viewed as no different from observing and reporting elsewhere in the demilitarized Zone C. Indeed, the "operational concept" for the MFO is designed to deal with activities throughout Zone C, as well as the Strait of Tiran, and no formal distinction is maintained as to its responsibilities in the strait.

In practice procedures proved more complicated. The MFO has relied on observation posts (OPs) installed on either side of the narrow strait—manned by American troops—and on Italian coastal-patrol boats operating out of Sharm el-Sheikh to observe and report on all traffic and any incidents. The U.S. battalion also has employed helicopters to observe.

Observation and patrolling have certainly been more regular and energetic, and responses to any suspicious incidents are more rapid. In operational terms, "ensure" has come to mean procedures for "containing" the situation by calling on violators to cease and desist, relying on the Egyptians to remove the interference, but to do so themselves if this should be necessary.

The scenario presumably would unfold as follows: Should something unorthodox be observed, any suspicious activity or acts of interference with free navigation (mine-laying, for example, or overt interference with shipping), the MFO would notify the Egyptian police and assist them as necessary. If the Egyptians were delayed or for any reason failed to take effective action against such acts of interference, the MFO would "contain the situation." Various techniques would be employed. Although not disclosed, such techniques presumably would not exclude direct action to halt the interference. Once the situation is contained, the MFO would await the arrival of Egyptian authorities to take control of the situation.

The MFO leadership believes this procedure is a workable reconciliation of the differences in Egyptian and Israeli interpretations of what it is obliged to do to ensure freedom of navigation, that the technique of containment will work, and that the MFO will not be required to take more aggressive action.

Is this sufficient? What if the Egyptians drag their feet or dispute the facts? At bottom, a problem might arise if Israel and Egypt disagree about the facts and Israel demands that the MFO take action which Egypt might oppose. Suppose, for example, Iran were to interfere with Iraqi arms shipments through the Jordanian port of Aqaba and the Egyptians turned a blind eye. Does this mean that the MFO is responsible for halting the interference? Would it be able to do so? How should the United States respond if the MFO calls for assistance?

Dealing with Charges of Treaty Violations. How to handle charges of violations—an issue raised mainly by Israel—is the second point of potential discord. If it is not managed well, this issue could undermine good relations and thus the stability of the system. The problem arises mainly over two disputed points of interpretation of treaty provisions and the MFO's obligations regarding them.

One has to do with infiltration through the demilitarized Zone C and across the border, involving hostile acts (mine-laying) and the smuggling of arms and infiltration of terrorists. Article III, section 2 of the treaty states that "each party undertakes to ensure that acts or threats . . . will not originate from or not be committed from within its territory

... by any force subject to its control or by any other force stationed on its territory" against the population, citizens, or property of the other.[52] This provision is included by reference in the protocol governing MFO responsibilities, but the obligation this imposes on the MFO remains ambiguous.

Most unauthorized movement through Zone C and across the border consists of Bedouins, who have ignored frontiers since time immemorial and who sometimes smuggle wristwatches, tape-recorders, and similar goods. The MFO's position has been that routine border-control is a matter between Egypt and Israel. What remains uncertain is the amount of such traffic, how much of it is habitual Bedouin visiting and "commerce" across the border, and how much has hostile intent. If border-crossers are carrying hand-grenades or rifles with intent to take hostile action, the question of the MFO's responsibility arises.

The Egyptians deny that such traffic takes place on a serious scale. They claim they are doing the best they can with the limited police force allowed them in the zone, and that it is not their responsibility to help Israeli immigration and customs officers control their side of the border. Israel contends that this stand is disingenuous and ignores Egypt's obligation under the treaty to ensure that acts or threats against Israel do not originate in Egyptian territory. In Israel's eyes, this provision is integral to the security arrangements. Some Israelis have charged that the source of much of the hostile traffic, guerrilla infiltration, and smuggled arms was to be found in Cairo, and that Egyptian authorities must have been cognizant of it. Without a cooperative and effective procedure to control this movement, they say, confidence in the integrity and workability of the system is undermined. Moreover, Israeli security forces must shoulder a costly burden for a task that should be shared by Egypt and the MFO. Aside from the MFO's legal obligation to take counteraction, the Israeli position is that the MFO is an active participant in the security system and thus should be responsible for policing and halting hostile infiltration.

The MFO has walked with care. Within the zone the MFO is naturally in control of its own movements and installations, commanding "freedom of movement" and brooking no restrictions on its operations (while respecting Egyptian sovereignty). It has taken no responsibility, however, for the "internal function" of law and order. As one authoritative source at MFO headquarters put it: The MFO may have the authority under the protocol to "lean on" the parties to fulfill their responsibilities under the treaty, but it must be careful not to go beyond its authority. The MFO must not in any way get involved in "controlling" the border, for such activity not only goes beyond what the MFO is authorized to do but, perhaps more important, exceeds its mandate and would thus invite criticism.

Nonetheless, MFO patrols and observations posts have been positioned and moved about to ensure that the force is alert to potentially hostile traffic; patrols have been particularly active on the border. If a patrol observes what appears to be peaceful movement or activities, both sides are notified. (This includes, for example, reporting flares shot from the Israeli side in the course of military exercises.) If suspicious movements or activities are noticed, the MFO tracks the putative infiltrators and assists the parties in "carrying out their responsibilities." If there is reason to believe that the traffic is surreptitious and hostile, the MFO does not rule out counteraction. At that point, the procedure might be to arrest the suspect and turn him over to the authorities.

So far, this cautious procedure has not been a serious impediment to the functioning of the system. The fact that occasions for MFO action have been few and far between underscores the advantage of managing such a peacekeeping operation in a thinly populated desert terrain. Still, responsible and authoritative Israeli sources, official and otherwise, have expressed anxiety that such differences over the extent of MFO responsibility for controlling infiltration could become a source of tension and trouble down the road.[53]

The other source of contention between Egypt and Israel has arisen from certain ambiguities in the military annex regarding restrictions on arms and men in Zone A. Recriminations over this matter have flared up in the meetings of the Joint Liaison Committee and in exchanges between the parties. The formal provision in the security annex is that in Zone A, Egypt is allowed a mechanized infantry division consisting of three infantry brigades and one armored brigade, with supporting artillery and antiaircraft battalions and a specified number of artillery pieces, tanks, antiaircraft guns, and armored personnel carriers. Total personnel is not to exceed 22,000. The number of battalions in the infantry and armored brigades is not specified. Israel has contended that while the number of battalions stationed in Zone A is technically not violative, it so exceeds the normal count of battalions for a mechanized division that it violates the spirit of the accord. Egyptian authorities rejoined that totals have not been exceeded—if the military annex stipulates four brigades, then that is what Egypt has, and if each brigade consists of four to five battalions or more, this should not be anyone's concern, but rather be left to the discretion of Egyptian military commanders. The commander of a brigade has latitude to organize and deploy his force as needed for military exercises.

The United States and the MFO have supported the Egyptian interpretation, which is based on rules and procedures that prevailed during the Sinai Field Mission era. Israel, usually legalistic in interpreting such provisions, maintained that the spirit of the accord and the impact on Israeli security sensitivities should be taken into account. That is, the MFO should be concerned about "excessive" battalions even though the numerical count of total personnel stipulated in the annex has not been exceeded. Israel argued that an abnormal count of battalions for a mechanized division raises suspicions that these battalions could be deployed as nuclei and rapidly reinforced to full size.

The Israeli position has been that the concern of the United States and MFO should not be with the legalities but with taking measures that foster confidence. If one party, as in this case, believes it has reason to suspect that restrictions in military annex are being circumvented, the MFO should take a more assertive approach in reconciling the differences. More broadly, Israel has charged that certain violations based on national-source intelligence had not been "certified" by the MFO and thus was not followed up. Israel reasons that because the whole idea of the peacekeeping presence is to enhance confidence, the MFO and Egypt should not turn a blind eye to Israeli concerns. Again, although this did not emerge as a major concern during the first year, it could become a source of instability down the line.

The MFO: How Long Will It Stay? Any peacekeeping venture is subject to a multitude of problems that affect the willingness of troop-contributors to stay—weariness, the need to bring troops home, dissatisfaction with reimbursement. Regional political circumstances can change. Participating countries may then drop out and replacements will have to be found. In the end, if the United States is left alone in the Sinai (with perhaps one or two others, but otherwise without international cover) there may be rumblings in Congress about the U.S. shouldering of this endless task alone.

The problem of dropouts has always been a vulnerability of peacekeeping. In this case, because the mandate is open-ended, the MFO

THE MFO: UNIQUE OR PARADIGM? 79

faces uncertainty about the duration of its stay. Israel postulates that the MFO will be needed for a very long time, counted in decades. Egypt wants the MFO to think in a more limited time frame. Should equipment be purchased for the long or short term? Construction was designed on the assumption that the MFO would last for ten years. But reasonable projections on the MFO's life span are based on mutable conditions and events in the region, so that no one knows how long the MFO will remain. The MFO cannot ignore what happens in other parts of the Middle East. If confidence grows and both sides feel reasonably comfortable with border and security arrangements, they may look around and ask: Why are we spending $100 million a year on this? MFO managers and budget planners must live with this uncertainty and now plan on an annual basis.

Troop-contributors from Europe, Australia, and New Zealand signed up for two-year terms, and all sides would like to see them stay; conversations started the fall of 1983 about renewals. Other contributors such as Colombia and Fiji (which provide the other two battalions) had signed up for five years. The MFO's main concern would be replacing the specialized contingents—communications, transport, medical—if for any reason the present array is not renewed. So far, the MFO leadership sees no reason for concern.

The problems faced during the first round of recruitment could presage trouble in finding replacements. Certain European countries were uneasy from the start about participating in a non-U.N. international force. In addition, acceptability of the troops to both Egypt and Israel had to be taken into account. For instance, neither side wanted contingents from the Soviet sphere, and Israel would not accept troops from countries with which it had no diplomatic relations. Egypt opposed African participants so as not to stir up divisiveness in the Organization of African Unity (OAU) about the Camp David accords. For the United States, the problem was and remains not so much balancing the force geographically, but to ensure that the MFO be seen as supported by its allies—from Europe mainly, but also from Latin America, Australia, and New Zealand. Troop-contributors pledged to give adequate notice of intent to depart before the end of the contract term so that there would be time to recruit replacements; an escape clause was provided for extreme situations. But, essentially, MFO managers must rely on an American guarantee that the necessary troops will be available.

In the longer range, the MFO is vulnerable to political developments in the area. If the outlook appears stable, Europe may well feel that its contribution is no longer needed; parliamentary pressure to disengage would most probably ensue. Congress may then be reluctant to continue the American commitment without the support of key Europeans.

More disturbing would be the opposite situation. Strains in political relations between Egypt and Israel that followed the invasion of Lebanon did not impair the stability of the Sinai arrangements. But a threat of hostilities on other Arab-Israeli fronts might be seen by some of the Europeans as menacing the Egypt-Israeli peace. Certain troop-contributors might then pull out to avoid getting involved in hostilities or in response to political pressures from Arab countries. (It will be recalled that the Europeans initially agreed to share the peacekeeping burden in the Sinai with great reluctance and only in the expectation that stability on that front would help move along the peace process toward the goal of a "just, comprehensive, and durable settlement of the Middle East conflict.")[54]

In the United States, the concerns first expressed during congressional hearings on the MFO's establishment would again surface: concern about its utility as a peacekeeper, the cost, and the exposure of U.S. troops to entangling hostilities. Paradoxically, the durability of the MFO may well depend on its marginality, on its being perceived as useful and supportive in maintaining stability and buttressing a settlement, but not crucial in sustaining the peace. If it becomes a protector and guarantor, interposing the warring parties, many troop-contributors would have second thoughts.

In spite of the potential for trouble down the road, the near-term prospect is for continued acceptability and durability of the force.

7.
THE MFO AND THE U.N. AS PEACEKEEPERS: COSTS AND BENEFITS

WHAT DOES THE EXPERIENCE OF THE MFO suggest about the balance of advantage and disadvantage, of cost-benefit calculations, in enlisting a non-U.N. force when the U.N. option is not available?

Only tentative conclusions can be drawn at this point, partly owing to the short time the MFO has been in operation but mainly because of the unique circumstances in which it has operated. In numerous, separate conversations with MFO and U.N. officers, as well as with American, Egyptian, and Israeli officials and academics, I found a near-consensus that the MFO's success can be largely attributed to the propitious circumstances in which it was launched and the "clinical" environment in which it operated. That is, the peacekeepers were installed to back a settlement already attained between two (and only two) stable nations with a mutual interest in observing the treaty arrangements. Moreover, the favorable terrain—sparsely populated desert—has eased the task of monitoring and verification.

These advantages would have been enjoyed in equal measure by a U.N. force, which was originally contemplated. In fact, as the MFO's annual report emphasizes, the origins of the MFO and its mandate lie in Annex I of the peace treaty under which the parties "request the United Nations to provide forces and observers to supervise the implementation" of the security arrangements. It was only Israeli importunings and the expectation that Security Council approval would be difficult to obtain that led to President Carter's promise to "take those steps necessary to ensure the establishment and maintenance of an acceptable alternative multinational force." So that the principle that created the MFO, as well as the functions and mandate, derived directly from the treaty.

81

It is usually claimed, with justice, that given the negotiating compromises in the Security Council, a U.N. mandate is likely to be nonspecific, ill-defined, ambiguous, and often unrealistic, thereby complicating the peacekeeping operation. A case in point, of course, is the unrealistic mandate and conflicting expectations that severely constrained the effectiveness of UNIFIL. But this need not be the case. As the origins and experience of UNEF II and UNDOF demonstrate,[55] a mandate and terms of reference derived from a disengagement agreement between adversaries—which both are therefore motivated to observe—can produce a realistic basis for U.N. peacekeeping. Indeed, as noted earlier, the mandate and terms of reference embodied in the MFO protocol were those contemplated for a U.N. force and observers under terms of the Egypt-Israel treaty of 1979. Had the Security Council authorized such a U.N. peacekeeping operation, its task—policing demilitarization and verifying limited-forces zones—would have been almost identical with those undertaken by the MFO. By the same token, a non-U.N. multinational force such as the MNF in Lebanon can be plagued by a vague and ill-defined mandate and loose operating procedures. So, one must conclude that favorable political circumstance and the existence of a precedent agreement between the parties largely determine the specificity and realism of the mandate.

Political Consensus and Institutional Adaptation

The crucial differences in the characteristics of the U.N. and the alternative model resulted from the centrality of the U.S. commitment to organize and sustain the MFO, and the need for the architects of the Sinai force to build a new political-institutional structure. While the director-general of the MFO drew liberally on the U.N.'s peacekeeping experience and institutional memory, he had to invent a new international institution. There existed neither a political infrastructure comparable to the Security Council, nor a permanent secretary-general who could draw on the authority and prestige of his office, nor a seasoned Secretariat. The director-general had to improvise operating procedures and a command structure, and do so under severe constraints.*

---

*From August 3, 1981, when the MFO protocol was signed, to the arrival of the first units at El Gorah in March 1982, only seven months were available for construction, recruiting, equipping, transporting, writing operation procedures, and negotiation of the status-of-forces agreements.

THE MFO AND THE U.N.: COSTS AND BENEFITS

Nevertheless, certain advantages were derived from reliance on the United States and the need to operate outside an established international framework. Advantage lay in greater flexibility and freedom from politicized constraints so characteristic of Security Council decision-making, where extraneous concerns are often grafted onto peacekeeping decisions and thus impair their efficacy. Because the key requirements for launching the MFO were (1) consent of the parties and (2) the U.S. commitment, the MFO was easier to create. There was no need for long consultations in the Security Council to bring on board all those who can help or who can cause trouble. (Though, once the decision is made, recruitment of participants may be easier for the United Nations, as noted below.)

In addition—other things being equal—Israel's trust and cooperation are more readily obtained for a non-U.N. force, particularly if a U.S. presence is its central feature. Israel's long-standing distrust of the United Nations, and its perception of lack of impartiality among certain U.N. contingents and observers means that a non-U.N. presence such as the MFO stands a better chance of gaining Israeli cooperation.

Yet another advantage is that the MFO's existence does not depend on the weakest link in the world political consensus, nor does it need to run the gauntlet in the Security Council to assure its survival. Moreover, should the initial political underpinnings of the enterprise (authorization and renewal of the mandate in U.N. cases) be eroded, the United States becomes the guarantor of last resort. An autonomous force is also more responsive to changing U.S. needs—an advantage for the United States.

In the case of the MFO, the United States' commitment was underscored from the start by its decision to provide civilian observers to verify the security arrangements and to continue the aerial surveillance of the Sinai in support of the MFO's operation. Another advantage deriving from the U.S. commitment was that the MFO could draw on the existing logistical system and expertise of the Sinai Field Mission.

By the same token, both U.S. dominance and the lack of a broad political base that would have been derived from Security Council authorization raised misgiving about the genuine international character and legitimacy of the force. It complicated the task of attracting a broadly based group of participants. The United Nations attracts widespread political support for its peacekeeping ventures partly because, as Dag Hammarskjold taught, peacekeepers in Third World disputes insulate the conflict from superpower confrontation. (One of Dag Hammarskjold's rules was that the permanent members of the Security

Council, particularly the superpowers, were not acceptable as peacekeepers because they inevitably infected the peacekeeping venture with their ideological biases.) An additional attraction of a U.N. force, at least in the eyes of the U.S. Congress and public, has been that it provides a more equitable sharing of the burden of world stability. In U.N. peacekeeping, the U.S. commitment is limited by the extent of its political-financial contributions and, above all, by the fact that U.S. troops are not exposed to hostilities. Supporting U.N. peacekeeping ventures is, in effect, a policy of limited liability. The United States cannot extricate itself as easily and with as minimal political cost from the MFO or the MNF as it did, for example, twenty years ago in the Congo.

In the case of the MFO, any large falloff of participants would not only erode the international character of the force but put a greater burden on the United States. Should this happen, the limit of congressional tolerance is not clear, particularly should the situation expose U.S. troops to a greater risk of involvement in hostilities.

Still, as the debate about the MFO showed, where the United Nations is unwilling to take on the task or is unacceptable for one reason or another, Congress has been prepared to commit U.S. troops if they are deemed essential to stability and if the balance of costs and benefits is acceptable. Should the situation change and the peacekeeping operation no longer be perceived as effective in stabilizing a strategic area like the Sinai, or itself become a source of friction between the parties, support will likely be withdrawn.

Of course, the United Nations is not immune to the erosion of a political consensus. In fact, as the Congo and UNEF II demonstrated, when the world consensus on the value of a peacekeeping venture disintegrates, both the political underpinnings in the Security Council and offers by troop-contributors vanish, and the operation must be terminated.

These political considerations—a broader base of political support for U.N. operations as against the political-financial commitment—have their most pronounced impact on the recruitment efforts, the viability of the institutional structure, and the stability of financing.

The United Nations has a wider range of countries from which to choose, whose acceptability to the parties is the only limiting factor. Constitutional-political constraints inhibit some—the Nordics, Dutch, Irish, and Japanese, among others—from serving in a multinational force not under U.N. authority. Thus, Sweden declined to participate in the MNF in Lebanon because of political misgivings and constitutional impediments. Finland would not consider serving in a non-U.N. force. Even France was at first reluctant to go into Lebanon as part of a multinational force without U.N. blessing and U.N. cover, though in the end it bowed to Gemayel's plea. The U.N. cover is politically necessary for some countries to certify international legitimacy and "acceptability." In the case of Namibia, for example, this element is so important that it is inconceivable that key countries engaged in the Namibia issue would entertain even the notion of a non-U.N. force should the proposed UNTAG fall through.

Any venture undertaken outside the U.N. framework thus narrows the spectrum of potential participants. In fact, the main difficulty encountered by the founders of the MFO was in recruiting the right mix of participants, partly because of constitutional-political inhibitions, and partly because of continuing Arab opposition to the Camp David accords. In fact, Arab opposition, reinforced by the Soviets, is what prevented the Security Council from authorizing a U.N. force to monitor the Sinai security arrangements in the first place.

At the same time, as the MFO experience demonstrates, an autonomous, non-U.N. force can be more selective and flexible in its recruiting efforts because it is not bound by the U.N. rule of "equitable geographic distribution." The problem for managers of peacekeeping operations is to achieve a delicate balance between geography (to satisfy political sensitivities) and military competence (to satisfy operational requirements). Within the admittedly narrow range of countries willing or persuaded to serve, the MFO was free to concentrate on acquiring the battalions and specialized units to meet the operation's requirements.

The problem of recruitment has another aspect which appears to give the advantage to the United Nations. The U.N. Secretariat has more experience and flexibility in seeking troop-contributors; it also knows where to look. In effect, recruitment has been institutionalized. The United Nations also can draw on existing peacekeeping operations to man the first phase of a new venture. UNEF II got under way expeditiously by drawing on the U.N. force in Cyprus. Within forty-eight hours nearly 600 Finnish, Austrian, Swedish, and, soon thereafter, Irish troops were flown from Nicosia to interpose Egyptian and Israeli forces and to arrange a disengagement. UNEF units and UNTSO observers were subsequently recruited for UNDOF to carry out monitoring and verification duties under the terms of the May 1974 Israeli-Syrian disengagement agreement. The nucleus of UNIFIL was formed within days of Security Council authorization by detaching troops from Swedish, Iranian, and Canadian units serving with UNEF and UNDOF.

On the other hand, in both the MFO and MNF, the United States had to improvise procedures to help recruit a suitable force and assure political and logistical support. In the case of the MFO, this was not too onerous a constraint. The director-general was technically limited to recruit only from those nations agreeable to the parties. He was able at the outset to negotiate agreements for two of the three infantry battalions needed from Colombia and Fiji, both of which had experience with Middle East peacekeeping with the United Nations. The United States already had assured the parties of an infantry battalion and logistics and observer units. Thus, at a fairly early stage the MFO could count on the three infantry battalions needed for Zone C, in addition to observers for verification duties. Both as a token of international acceptability and to demonstrate that the U.S.-sponsored treaty had allied support, it was necessary to recruit contingents from NATO and other allies. From January to March 1982, talks with European Community and British Commonwealth nations resulted in agreements with Italy to provide and man the coastal-patrol unit, with Australia and New Zealand for a combined helicopter squadron, with France for an air-transport unit, with the Netherlands for communications and military police units, and with the United Kingdom for a headquarters unit. These, then, supplied visible political support as well as specialized services. Overtures to the Nordics were not productive, except for Norway, which consented to the appointment of Lieutenant-General Bull-Hansen (who had had a U.N. peacekeeping command in the Sinai) as force commander and three officers for his staff.

On balance, then, U.S. and MFO diplomacy overcame the obstacles inherent in non-U.N. ventures. Although political qualms were not entirely stilled, the MFO constituted a breakthrough and established a precedent for an alternative peacekeeping force for times when the United Nations was either unwilling to act or unacceptable to the parties, and when circumstances permitted.

The lack of an existing administrative and political structure created initial difficulties for the MFO. Without one, MFO managers could not hope to match the experience or facilities of the United Nations, particularly in moving expeditiously to launch and establish the operation. In fact, to a large extent the MFO drew on U.N. experience and procedures for logistics to get off to a promising start. More than half the Fijian soldiers in the MFO battalion had served in UNIFIL, and Colombia called its battalion "Colombia Tres" to denote that it was Colombia's third contribution to international peacekeeping.

Structural impediments aside, the MFO benefited from its ability to create new institutional procedures free of the United Nations' bureaucratic encrustation and the cumbersomeness typical of long-established institutional procedures. Unlike U.N. operations, which are characterized by a sprawling variety of equipment and maintenance standards among the various contingents, the MFO quickly established a unified supply, transport, and maintenance system—standardization of equipment facilitated maintenance. A unified and cost-effective logistical system was in place from the start. Here the value of the U.S. presence and commitment was made manifest.

The supply system is managed by the U.S. Army's logistics support unit, which is responsible for medical dispensaries, weapons and equipment maintenance, and explosive-ordnance disposal. The Uruguayan contingent operates the MFO's truck fleet and maintains the road network. On balance, the MFO has demonstrated that a fledgling institution is capable of introducing novel and creative ideas into international peacekeeping, particularly in logistics.

A new and more supple institution such as the MFO can also more easily accommodate a liaison system to facilitate communication between the parties, reconcile disputes, and consult on implementation of the security arrangements. Although the mechanism for bilateral liaison and coordination is provided in the security annex of the treaty (originally to have been implemented by a U.N. force), the procedures developed by the MFO stress the diplomacy of reconciling differences at the force commander's level, with the director-general intervening only as needed. Contested matters rarely are brought to the foreign offices, let alone to the ministers.

MFO doctrine stresses that the force can function smoothly if it supports, not substitutes for, the bilateral relationship defined in the treaty and protocol. As one of the negotiators of the protocol subsequently put it, the force is there not to guarantee or arbitrate but to help the parties work out their problems. The liaison system is designed to help the parties communicate and reconcile claims and disputes before they become political. MFO officers meet almost daily with Egyptian and

Israeli counterparts. Meetings at the level of the liaison chiefs are supposed to be held once a month; the force commander is invited when MFO matters are discussed or at the request of either party. Egypt normally has so requested. Israel's main complaint has been that periodic meetings are skipped too often. But it is not only (and, according to Egyptian officials, not mainly) the formal meetings that count, but rather the continuous telephone link which serves both as hotline and for day-to-day communication.

Although the same mechanism theoretically could have operated as well under U.N. auspices, in times of political tension (such as the Lebanon invasion) there might have been greater temptation to escalate and politicize disputes, exposing them to the vagaries of Security Council discussion. In the final analysis, though, the stability of the system depends not on the efficiency of the liaison mechanism but on the health of the bilateral relationship. Israel's unhappiness at the cooling of relations after the Lebanon invasion (when the Egyptian ambassador to Israel was brought home), in addition the deceleration of commercial and cultural normalization, have fueled suspicions and put a greater burden on the joint liaison system than it was intended to bear. Conceivably, this could adversely affect the attitude of troop participants.

Directing the Peacekeepers

United Nations peacekeeping management benefits from the prestige and authority of the secretary-general and his office and—during the first generation of U.N. peacekeeping—from the executive talent and prestige of Under Secretary–General Urquhart and his associates. The secretary-general, inevitably diverted to other concerns, cannot be expected to give sustained attention and direction to UNIFIL, UNFICYP, and UNDOF. He is brought into the picture only at times of critical decisions. The reverse is true of the MFO. The director-general must create his own authority and earn his prestige, which cannot be a reflection of the international institution he heads. At the same time he is never absent or diverted. Directing the force and serving as its chief diplomat and manager are his sole assignments. And he accumulates authority with performance. The vulnerability lies in the fact that without historical-institutional legitimacy, the director-general's effectiveness flows from his personal talents, and the success of the operation depends on the men who run it rather than on the institution. Fortunately, the MFO has had the right persons in the right places at the right time. By the same token, the prestige and authority they earn are not fully transferable to successors. In effect, the MFO government depends on the chance of having attracted good men.

Meeting the Costs

Financing peacekeeping—finding the money, collecting arrears, determining fair-shares among contributors—has been a critical problem in almost all cases of international peacekeeping. Uncertainty and delay in reimbursement, and in meeting bills, making payments, and withholding assessments have plagued U.N. peacekeeping since Congo days. About two-thirds of the U.N. short-term deficit of $300 million as of 1982 was due to shortfall in contributions to peacekeeping operations. UNIFIL's accumulated deficit totaled $130 million, UNDOF's (including bills left over from UNEF II) was about $26 million, and that of UNFICYP, financed through voluntary contributions, amounted to $107 million. Most participants may grumble but are willing to wait for their money from the United Nations. Indeed, nations such as Canada and Sweden may offer troops and services without requiring full reimbursement. Still, delay in reimbursement is a major impediment to effective management. Fiji, for example, indicated it might withdraw its contingent from UNIFIL at the end of the then-current term (October 1983) if reimbursement owed it was not paid up. (In the end, arrangements were made for partial reimbursement, which induced the Fiji battalion to remain.)

The supreme advantage of the MFO is that the parties share in direct funding, that is, they contribute cash according to MFO budget-estimates to meet operating and maintenance costs. The financial participation of Egypt and Israel has produced a sense of identification with the organization. In addition, the United States pays one-third of the cost and, in effect, assumed the obligation of financier of last resort. Assured financing makes it easier to recruit among nations like Fiji, which must budget on the economic edge and are concerned about full and prompt reimbursement.

At the same time, the MFO managers have been subjected to pressures from Egypt, Israel, and the United States to keep down expenses, while the participants demand that the MFO not skimp on the quality of life for their troops in the Sinai or on maintenance and support services. Money has been a problem from the outset. Israelis projected that the annual cost would run at $30–50 million a year; it mounted to almost three times that. Egypt and the U.S. have periodically expressed concern about increasing costs. Given that the parties are also the paymasters, the MFO must be unusually alert to both cost-effectiveness and accountability. Of course, the MFO management must be responsible for ensuring objectivity and independence; it must not become the client of the parties. It tries to be responsive without opening its books or giving the parties an auditor's access to the accounts.

The differences between U.N. and MFO procedures should not be exaggerated. Costing procedures in the MFO are patterned, by and large, on those of the United Nations which treats "extra and extraordinary costs" of maintaining men and equipment in the field, as well as transporting them, as an obligation of the organization. The basic MFO formula is that a participant-state bears the ordinary costs of domestic troop maintenance, while the institution meets "extraordinary" costs associated with Sinai duty. This formula is modified to accomodate troop-contributors less able to manage financially—there is thus greater flexibility than is customary with U.N. operations.

While more or less following the U.N. rule about reimbursement, the MFO's advantage again is flexibility: It can calibrate reimbursement to the particular circumstances of each participant and negotiate with each on particular terms. The MFO leadership started with the idea of finding a formula that would hold down expenses while adequately reimbursing participating countries. A rigorous definition of differences in costs between keeping troops at home and in the Sinai was applied, and for the developing countries, economic circumstances were taken into account. Differentials could thus be separately negotiated for each participant.

The formula for the developed countries was to negotiate on the nation's own scale with respect to overseas allowances and benefits. The participants pay the salaries and home allowances of the soldiers, while the MFO transports, houses, and feeds them, provides life-support in the desert (including medical service) in addition to transport and communications in the field. As a result, the cost for this group has varied from an annual $1,800 per soldier for Americans to as high as $7,200 for certain European contingents. (The reason for the differential is that while American military salaries tend to be higher, compensation for overseas duty tends to be proportionately lower.) For the developing-country participants, the MFO has paid the U.N. scale of $950 per man per month plus a small ammunition and uniform allowance; specialists get a supplement of 10 percent. So, the cost for the LDC soldier has averaged about $1,000 a month. But, the supreme advantage for all the contingents has been not so much the scale of reimbursement as its certainty and promptness.

In the MFO, also, capital equipment—aircraft from Australia, New Zealand, France, and the United States; patrol vessels from Italy; motor vehicles used by the U.S. battalions—has constituted an additional contribution from certain participating governments. This is not unlike some U.N. peacekeeping operations, like that in Cyprus, where certain battalions provide their own equipment without cost to the United Nations. The MFO has paid, however, for operating and maintenance costs.

On balance, the MFO system makes for greater financial stability and assures participants that authorized reimbursement will be forthcoming fully and without delay. Acquisition of spare parts and expeditious repair and maintenance have assured units of high operational readiness. (In contrast, a major problem in recruiting for the MNF was that each participant was expected to pay its own way and make its own equipment and logistical arrangements. Certain countries declined to participate because reimbursement could not be promised even for extraordinary costs.)

Still, costs could become a problem in sustaining the MFO over time. It took $200 million to establish the force, half of that just for construction; the United States paid two-thirds of the start-up costs. The first year's operating costs amounted to $103 million, with Egypt, Israel, and the United States sharing equally (that is, $34.5 million apiece); expenses were expected to rise during the second year. The procedure has been that each party provides the MFO a line of credit on which equal amounts are drawn as needed. And the parties (and Congress) have been sensitive to the need for minimizing costs. At the same time, the MFO has had a good record of rigorous budgeting and accountability and has made a solid case that high operational standards and the need to sustain troop morale justify the costs.

Looked at in raw comparison—without taking account of the costs occasioned by geography, climate, distances, availability of communication and local supplies, the effect of desert conditions on the life of equipment, and, above all, different operational assignments—on paper the MFO operation shows up as the most costly of any peacekeeping operation ever. With a complement of some 3,000 men (counting contract personnel), operating and maintenance costs have come to about $34,000 per person, per year. This compares with $30,000 for UNIFIL, $26,500 for UNDOF, and a low $12,000 for UNFICYP (where some battalions absorb costs).

Nonetheless, the advantage lies with the non-U.N. alternative because of the financial certainty and the widespread perception of a well-managed and rigorously accountable operation. In addition, the MFO has shown the superiority of a formula whereby the organization takes full responsibility not only for housing, feeding, and providing life-support in the desert, but does not ask the contingents to bring their own medical units, vehicles, or communications gear. These are provided in place and their maintenance is the MFO's responsibility. This system surmounts a major shortcoming in U.N. operations—logistical weakness.

In the U.N. system, financing can become a make-or-break factor, a determining consideration on whether to keep the operation going. The decision to terminate the Congo operation in June 1964 was due not inconsiderably to financial troubles. The MFO's advantages far outweigh the disadvantages of higher costs and inordinate dependence on the United States. Reliability and certainty that troops and equipment maintenance costs will be reimbursed expeditiously, the absence of an overhanging deficit, and financial participation of the parties, which makes for sensitivity to cost-effectiveness and accountability—all these add to assurances that administrative and operational decision making will not be unduly constrained by budgetary considerations.

8.
THIRD-PARTY PEACEKEEPERS FOR THE GOLAN AND THE WEST BANK?

IF THERE IS ONE LESSON that stands out from the contrasting experiences of the MFO in the Sinai and the MNF in Beirut, it is this: that propitious political circumstance, not institutional auspices or even a commitment of U.S. power, largely determines the utility of a peacekeeping operation in the region. Peacekeeping works best when only two parties are involved and both are politically stable. The major constraint on peacekeeping in Lebanon has been that, unlike the Sinai, the protagonists are many and are not necessarily peace-committed, responsible nations. The peacekeeping mission there has been complicated partly by the "third state"—namely Syria—whose security interests had to be factored in,[56] but mainly by the many indigenous players whose political interests had to be satisfied if peacekeeping were to be workable.

The complexity of this process was underestimated by the architects of the multinational force. The nature of the Lebanese situation, with myriad factions each ridden with intrigues and leadership struggles, militated against enlisting third-party peacekeepers as stabilizers except in the sense of fortifying local authority—presumably for just a short period. The social conflict meant that unless they were to become involved in the thankless and ultimately futile job of internal policing, third-party peacekeepers could not hope to be effective before factional fighting were brought under control and a modicum of "national reconciliation" achieved.

Another lesson has been that peacekeeping has the maximum prospect for success when it rests on a precedent agreement—whether peace treaty or disengagement accord—rather than a mandate imposed by the Security Council or other outside powers. At bottom, the reason for the MFO's success is that it bolsters the mutually agreed upon security arrangements in the peace treaty, which both states view as compatible with their security needs. Not the least of the favorable circumstances in which the MFO operates is that it is accepted neither as interposition force nor guarantor but, as one of the negotiators of the protocol observed, as an instrument to build confidence and help the parties work out their problems. In such circumstances, a peacekeeping presence can most effectively provide the stabilizing element.

Nowhere on other Arab-Israeli fronts are political circumstance and geography such as to replicate the favorable conditions of the Sinai: a sense of confidence on the part of the political leadership of both sides, and favorable circumstances on the ground—sparsely populated desert terrain offering natural barriers and a natural alert-system that require minimal monitoring and make verification duties uncomplicated. Some also contend that the unique circumstances leading to the peace—the Camp David process—is what induced Congress to approve an all-embracing commitment for the Sinai, and that these special circumstances are unlikely to be repeated. (Congressional hesitation to repeat the Sinai commitment has been reinforced by the traumatic experiences of the U.S. Marines in Lebanon in the fall of 1983.) Moreover, given that such mutual confidence and stability are unlikely on other fronts, recruitment of troop-contributors for non-U.N. peacekeeping enterprises will be even more difficult than was the case with the Sinai.

The important conclusion derived from my interviews in the spring of 1983 with officials, diplomats, and academicians in the area was that the possibility of adapting the MFO pattern elsewhere in the region is problematic. Still, none would completely rule out that situations may evolve on other fronts—notably Syria—that might open peacekeeping possibilities for which the Sinai experience could be relevant.

The Golan Front

The applicability of the MFO model to the Golan front is somewhat of a question mark. All those interviewed in the spring of 1983 stressed the complexity of the situation on the Golan and pointed to the differences with the Sinai, but none dismissed out of hand the utility of a third force there, and some saw possibilities in adapting the MFO experience.

Of course, these possibilities hinge on political change on both sides which might open the way to serious negotiation of either a final or interim settlement for the Golan. Despite differences in terrain and a history of extreme animosity (and the problem of the Israeli settlements), a case could then be made for negotiating the next step in the Golan similar to what transpired in the Sinai, that is, moving the disengagement line forward and adapting the policing machinery emplaced in 1974. In the 1974 troop-disengagement accord with Israel, Syria subscribed to the notion that the agreement was a "step toward a just and durable peace." The bolstering presence of UNDOF on the Golan has been more or less faithfully observed on both sides—despite flareups of friction and vituperative exchanges. In fact, as one authority pointed out, next to the Sinai, the Syrian front has been the most tranquil.

The current regimes are not likely to engage in serious peace negotiations. But should they be replaced by regimes willing to talk, the question of a third-party peacekeeping mechanism could arise. There the U.N. versus non-U.N. problem comes into play. The postulate is that Syria would prefer a U.N. to an autonomous multinational force dominated by the United States. Syria's preference would be reinforced by an international consensus favoring the adaptation and extension of UNDOF. On the other hand, it is reasonable to expect that Israel would prefer an MFO-type force that would put a U.S. presence in the area to buttress a peace settlement.

Given the complexities, it is safe to assume that even if the Syrians were willing to talk, a repeat of the Egypt-Israel course of negotiation is unlikely. One cannot foresee that a Syrian government would be willing to go so far as Sadat, or that Israel would be prepared to give up its hold on the strategic heights or to dismantle the settlements at this stage of Israel-Syrian relations. For this reason, Professor Itamar Rabinovich, director of the Shiloah Center at Tel Aviv University, among others, speculates that a "glorified interim settlement" is a more realistic possibility. In effect, this would be something similar to the interim 1975 agreement between Egypt and Israel: less than total withdrawal for less than total peace. The pattern might be: Israel to relinquish Mount Hermon plus a part of the adjoining territory via an arrangement similar to that of the 1975 interim agreement in the Sinai. The vacated territory would be demilitarized and the flanking zones made subject to restrictions on men and arms—the system would be monitored and verified by watchstations and a third-party peacekeeping mechanism. Some suggest this could be best monitored by adapting the present system of UNDOF.

Others say that Israel would not accept this arrangement without an American presence either on the pattern of 1975 (watchstations with early-warning systems manned by the parties themselves and monitored by an American presence), or the more elaborate 1979 system whereby the observer-inspectors verified the demilitarized and limited-forces zones.

On balance, it would appear that an adapted observer force on the pattern of UNDOF to monitor such an interim arrangement would be easier to negotiate. Syria should find this politically acceptable because it would represent a military, not political, arrangement, involve just an incremental change in the present system, and remain under U.N. auspices. For Israel, although an MFO-type would clearly be preferred for bolstering security arrangements in a *peace treaty*, other considerations come into play with respect to third-party peacekeepers to police an interim agreement. Short of a full peace and normalized relations with Damascus, Israel would view the Golan as a high-threat front where, like Lebanon, security concerns might compel the IDF to move despite the international peacekeeping presence. As argued earlier, Israel may very well be concerned that a multinational force (with an anchoring American presence) could risk IDF confrontation with U.S. soldiers. To avoid this ominous prospect, a U.N. mechanism might therefore be preferred. In any event, Israel would continue to rely on national-security means—the third force would play only a marginal role.

Although an interim arrangement appears to be the most realistic option, one finds two dissenting schools of thought at opposite poles. The pessimists believe even an interim agreement is not in the cards so long as the strategic understanding between Syria and the Soviet Union remains the basis of Syrian strategy; the only reason Syria agreed to disengage on the Golan in 1975 was because Egypt withdrew from the war, leaving Syria no choice. Certain American and Israeli experts argue that no parallel exists with the Egyptian front. From every perspective—political, strategic, historical—Israeli and Syrian interests are seen as incompatible. Differences in terrain, in the history of animosity, and in the strategic sensitivity of the Golan militate against a stable settlement that could be policed by U.N. or MFO peacekeepers. Syria regards the Golan as Syrian territory; it lies just forty kilometers from Damascus. And Israelis recall Syrian shelling from the Golan Heights on the Hula Valley and that Syrian forces reached Lake Tiberias during the Yom Kippur War. Apart from differences in terrain between the Sinai and the

Golan and in the history of animosities, many question the likelihood of Syria accepting a U.S. presence and guarantee (without which Israel might not be willing to relinquish the Golan). Given the greater risk of hostilities breaking even after the settlement, these skeptics also doubt that Congress would accept a MFO commitment on this front.

On the other hand, a surprisingly wide segment of those interviewed in the spring of 1983—embracing Americans, Israelis, and Egyptians—speculated that despite these weighty considerations, the constraints of politics and terrain were not intractable, as had been depicted. That is, the MFO model might be adapted once a basic political decision were reached on Israeli relinquishment of the Golan in exchange for peace (in effect, the Sinai formula). Although the Golan differs in terms of expanse, terrain, strategic sensitivity, and population, Syrian and Israeli security concerns could, with some adjustment, be met. Some believed an accommodation could even be reached on maintaining Israeli settlements on the Golan under Syrian sovereignty. Indeed, one expert, comparing the Golan's sparse population with that of the Sinai's Zone C thought the Golan settlements might actually be easier to accommodate because the inhabitants are primarily Israeli and Druse. The security arrangement would involve a demilitarized buffer, comparable to Zone C in the Sinai, with flanking, limited-forces zones on both Israeli and Syrian sides, to be monitored by the peacekeepers.

Given the sensitivities on both sides, the option of an MFO-type third force to monitor permanent security arrangements does not appear to be in the cards. The best prospect appears to be for an interim agreement along lines described earlier: Israel's relinquishment of Mount Hermon and adjoining territory, with much of the Golan to serve as a demilitarized buffer and to be monitored by an expanded UNDOF-type force equipped with a more authoritative mandate and authorized for longer than the current six-month pattern. Also, Israel would need to be assured that the U.S. aerial monitoring which now reinforces the UNDOF arrangements would be put on a more regular and frequent basis.

The West Bank

Israel's acute security concerns about control of Judea and Samaria inhibit any third-party role as a serious factor in a settlement. Despite deep differences among the political parties on defense policy during the

1967–73 period, a broad consensus emerged in Israel on the need for secure borders, particularly the need to secure the eastern front against surprise attack.[57] Although the Labor party has been much more flexible about territorial compromise or shared rule on the West Bank—given political and demographic realities—its leadership has been unified on the proposition that there must be sufficient Israeli military presence on the West Bank to guarantee Israel's security. Any external guarantee, even verified by third-party peacekeepers, is viewed, at best, as a supplement, not a substitute, for the IDF presence.

The consensus among officials and academics interviewed in Israel in the spring of 1983 was that it was idle to speculate about an MFO-type peacekeeping mechanism there since Israeli security concerns could not accommodate this kind of arrangement. The accepted doctrine was set forth by Brig. Gen. (ret.) Aryeh Shalev in *The West Bank: Line of Defense*.[58] An Israeli military presence at strategic points both in the Jordan Valley and along the ridges and western slopes of the mountain ranges of Judea and Samaria was judged so crucial for Israeli security that no Israeli government could afford to abandon them.

Essentially, the Shalev position reflects mainstream Labor party strategic doctrine: that although West Bank civilian administration or even formal sovereignty might in time be safely handed over to Arab rule as part of a territorial compromise, Israel must retain its hold on the strategic sites in the Jordan Valley and on the Judea-Samaria ridges. No demilitarization system or third-party guarantor could be relied on to prevent the massing of armor for a sweep into Israel which could cut Israel at the narrow waist before reserves were mobilized. Moreover, the emplacement of artillery and missiles could threaten Israel's airfields. Even the more dovish wing of Labor, which advocates handing over sovereignty to an Arab political entity, would insist on Israel's holding the strategic positions under a lease arrangement (comparable to that held at Guantanamo Bay in Cuba by the United States)[59] until full reconciliation and a durable peace had been firmly established. Apart from an Israeli military presence, the mainstream view remains that the West Bank would have to be demilitarized except for local police; but no need is seen for third-party peacekeepers to verify demilitarization since the IDF itself would do this through arrangements with local authorities.

With few dissenters, Israeli strategists challenged American (and European) military analysts like Drew Middleton who argue that security is not to be found in West Bank settlements and military positions since

THE GOLAN HEIGHTS AND THE WEST BANK

they are vulnerable to Arab surface-to-surface missiles and long-range (twenty-km) self-propelled artillery from the other side of the Jordan. A more flexible Arab strategy—using helicopters as gunships and troop transports—could effectively bypass Israeli strongpoints, says Middleton. Shalev argues that Israel has no alternative but to deny the highly mechanized and powerful Arab armies the dominant topography of Judea and Samaria so as to avert a swift battle of movement aimed at Israel's heartland. In his reasoning, the crucial element is to give Israel time to mobilize and equip reservists and move them to the front within forty-eight hours.

Nor would Shalev—and like-minded Israeli strategists who now articulate the mainstream doctrine in that country—accept that Israeli concerns can be met by third-party guarantees and multinational monitoring of a demilitarized West Bank and an array of electronic early-warning devices. (In the period following the 1967 war, no Israeli government considered as realistic U.S. proposals for such third-party guarantees for the West Bank.)[60] The narrow and densely populated West Bank presents a stark contrast to the vast and sparsely populated Sinai Desert. On the Sinai frontier, Israel enjoyed ample time to mobilize reserves to block any advancing land armies, but the eastern front could not begin to offer equivalent advantages. Any comparison between the two fronts and any suggestion that the Sinai peacekeeping operation could be a model for the West Bank was shrugged off as totally unrealistic. Few in Israel would challenge the accepted doctrine that the country had no choice but to station significant numbers of regular forces in fortified positions on a permanent basis.[61]

In the case of the West Bank, then, both security considerations, as set forth by Shalev, and cultural-historical associations inhibit Israeli consideration of a third-party peacekeeping presence (like that in the Sinai or even on the Golan). At the same time, some experts do not exclude the possibility of enlisting a third-party mechanism as part of a process whereby the Israeli military presence would be diluted and wind down as civilian functions are transferred to an autonomous administration.

The MFO may be entertained as a model only on the Syrian front—and even then, there is just a theoretical prospect of success. More likely would be an extension of an UNDOF-patterned force to monitor an interim agreement. In Lebanon, if any peacekeeping force could prove feasible—which now appears problematic—it would need to be a mixed system in view of the factional struggle over reforming the political order and the security sensitivities of both Syria and Israel about control of areas adjacent to their borders. On the West Bank, Israeli opposition to any substantive third-party role in policing a settlement will not soon be overcome.

NOTES

1. International Institute for Strategic Studies, *Strategic Survey 1978* (London: IIIS, 1979), p. 19.

2. Harlan Cleveland, *The Obligations of Power* (New York: Harper and Row, 1966), p. 51.

3. On the U.S. Sinai Support Mission, see the semiannual reports from the president to the Congress, beginning April 13, 1976. For a scholarly analysis of the period, see Nissim Bar-Yaacov, "Keeping the Peace between Egypt and Israel, 1973–1980," *Israel Law Review* 15 (April 1980).

4. Annual Report of the Director-General, Multinational Force & Observers, Rome, April 25, 1983. This first annual report is an account of the formation, structure, and first year's operation. It also includes the texts of the peace treaty and protocol governing the mission of the MFO.

As of that date, the composition of the force was as follows: The three infantry battalions—each of which was assigned patrolling and observation assignments in two of the six sectors into which Zone C is divided—consisted of a 500-man Colombian battalion and a 500-man Fijian battalion, housed and headquartered at the north base (El Gorah), and the U.S. infantry battalion of the 81st and 101st airborne divisions in rotation, housed and headquartered at MFO's south base. The U.S. battalion conducted its own reconnaissance patrols and provided its own helicopter and motor transport. Australia (100 men and eight UH-1H helicopters) and New Zealand (35 men and two helicopters) formed the ANZAC rotary-wing aviation unit which provided primary transportation for the MFO observers on their verification missions; the unit also provided flight control and meteorological services to all MFO aviation elements. France (40-man crew, two DH-6 Twin Otters, and one C-160 Transall aircraft) provided the air link between the two main bases and between Cairo and Tel Aviv. Italy's three minesweepers, organized as the coastal patrol unit (90 naval officers and sailors) and headquartered at Sharm el-Sheikh, patrolled the Strait of Tiran at the southern entrance to the Gulf of Aqaba, working closely with U.S.-manned observation posts north of Sharm el-Sheikh and on the island of Tiran. The Netherlands contingent was divided into two units: an 81-man military signals unit, which maintained the communications system between El Gorah headquarters and the units deployed in the Sinai, and a 21-man military police unit. The United Kingdom provided a 35-man headquarters company at El Gorah and personnel for the force commander's staff.

5. Annual Report of the Director-General, MFO, p. 8.

6. The judgment not only at U.N. headquarters but among independent observers such as Alan James of the University of Keele was that UNIFIL's shortcomings derived mainly from the impossible task imposed on it. Within the physical and political constraints under which UNIFIL labored, James observes that "from a number of angles, [UNIFIL] was a fairly successful operation." "Painful Peacekeeping: The United Nations in Lebanon, 1978–1982," *International Journal* 38 (Autumn 1983): 613–34.

7. Among the key problems posed for assessment of the MFO experience were the following:

Compared to a U.N. peacekeeping operation, what special problems or advantages does a non-U.N. force face in maintaining a reputation for effectiveness and impartiality and in enlisting the confidence and cooperation of the parties?

Does a non-U.N. structure complicate or facilitate organization and management? What special obstacles must a non-U.N. "international organization" overcome given the lack of a permanent political-institutional structure (Security Council, permanent secretary-general and Secretariat, institutionalized procedures) and the consequent need to improvise?

What special problems confront a non-U.N. force in recruiting the right mix of units, inducing troop-contributors to stay, finding replacements for dropouts? In particular, does the constitutional-political structure of nations inhibit their joining a multinational force except under U.N. authority and auspices?

In a period of budgetary constraint, relative costs are a major concern. Financing peacekeeping—both finding the money and justifying the lion's share paid by the U.S.— has been a major inhibition on American support of peacekeeping in some cases. A non-U.N. alternative like the MFO may pose even greater complications, partly because the U.S. pays a somewhat larger share than has been customary since Congo days, but mainly because the U.S. assumes the central commitment for the success and solvency of ventures like the MFO and the multinational force.

How does a non-U.N. multinational force compare with its U.N. counterpart in coping with the vulnerabilities that plague any peacekeeping operation: erosion of the political consensus over time, incidents that call into question effectiveness or impartiality, weariness of troop-contributors, all of which lead to dropouts, problems with rules of engagement, financial troubles, etc.?

To what extent are peacekeeping choices affected by the overall bilateral relationship between the parties and their direct involvement in security arrangements?

What happens if the constitutional-political underpinnings of a peacekeeping presence (authorization and renewal of mandate in U.N. cases, treaty-protocol structure in the MFO case) should crumble and the U.S. must find an alternative or go it alone?

8. U.N. Under Secretary–General Brian E. Urquhart, a pioneer of U.N. peacekeeping, has stressed that in such circumstances peacekeeping can function successfully only if it is sustained by a broad political base in support of a well-defined mandate, a geographically diverse military force, and a unified command sensitive to political considerations. Cooperation of conflicting parties is, of course, a prerequisite for peacekeeping whether under U.N. or autonomous auspices. Urquhart's remarks were quoted in Michael J. Berlin, "U.N. Peace-Keeper Sees Failure in Lebanon," *Washington Post*, December 12, 1983, and appear in Urquhart's op-ed piece, "On U.N. Peacekeeping," *New York Times*, December 19, 1983. For a recent appraisal of U.N. and regional peacekeeping, see Henry Wiseman, ed., *Peacekeeping: Appraisals & Proposals*, International Peace Academy, (New York: Pergamon Press, 1983).

9. James, "Painful Peacekeeping," pp. 616–17.

10. James's account of General Siilasvuo's views appear on p. 618.

11. An illustrative log of operational entries compiled by Mr. Timur Goksel, UNIFIL press and information officer, on the fifth anniversary of UNIFIL (April 1978–June 1982) portrays the battalions as both active and evenhanded. Thus, in the first six months (April–September 1978), nine direct attacks and ambushes on UNIFIL personnel by "armed elements," mainly out of the Tyre pocket, led to fire-fights that resulted in three UNIFIL deaths and many wounded; in the same period the DFF fired into UNIFIL positions ten times. In the second half of 1979 there were 110 infiltration attempts involving 785 "armed elements" which were "prevented"; four fire-fights with these elements left four UNIFIL soldiers dead. One hundred twenty-three infiltration attempts by armed elements and eight "close firings" on UNIFIL positions occurred during the first

half of 1980; by this time UNIFIL's main trouble was with Haddad and his de facto forces, with 143 close-firing incidents and six clashes resulting in five UNIFIL deaths. In the first half of 1981, 62 infiltration attempts by the PLO were blocked, apart from 490 persons who were denied entry through UNIFIL checkpoints because they were armed or in military uniform or refused to allow their vehicles to be searched. On the DFF side there were two clashes involving UNIFIL troops and 236 cases of close firing. A similar pattern is recorded for the periods from June to December of that year and for the first half of 1982. All this was at the cost of 40 killed in action (out of a casualty toll of 89) and 119 wounded in action. The secretary-general's report on UNIFIL, dated July 12, 1983, records a similar toll: Since the establishment of UNIFIL in 1978, 93 members of the force died, 41 as a result of firing and mine explosions, while 120 were wounded in armed clashes, shelling, and mine explosions.

12. James, "Painful Peacekeeping," p. 621; also Maureen Boerma, "The United Nations Interim Force in Lebanon: Peacekeeping in a Domestic Conflict," *Millennium: Journal of International Studies* 8 (Spring 1979): 51–62.

13. Embassy of Israel, Washington, D.C., "UNIFIL in the Lebanese Cauldron," Information Background, March 1981. An unidentified Israeli general is quoted as saying that the IDF could "get rid" of the PLO guerrillas easily. "The reason we are not doing so is that UNIFIL is in the area. UNIFIL would suffer casualties, and we don't want one finger of one UNIFIL soldier to get hurt." *Washington Post*, March 16, 1981.

14. In an assessment a year after the invasion, Amnon Rubinstein wrote in *Haaretz*, May 13, 1983: "I do not doubt that many would prefer a return to the arrangements we had before the Peace for Galilee Operation. . . . In the final analysis, the security strip under the rule of Haddad's men and the basically positive role fulfilled by the men of UNIFIL prevented at the least substantial infiltration across the border."

15. Based on conversations with UNIFIL and OGL officers held in Naquora and elsewhere in southern Lebanon on April 6–7, 1983. Report of the Secretary-General on UNIFIL (for the period January 19–July 12, 1983) S/15863, July 12, 1983, para. 12. The report notes the link between fostering stability and restoring Lebanese authority. "Although the circumstances under which the Force was established have been radically altered as a result of the Israeli invasion, the task of assisting the Government of Lebanon in ensuring the return of its effective authority in southern Lebanon remains especially relevant in the present situation."

16. Thomas L. Friedman in *New York Times*, September 28, 1983, and October 28, 1983; and Drew Middleton, *New York Times*, November 8, 1983. Flora Lewis observed: "There is really no such thing as a Multinational Force in Beirut. There are American, French, Italian, and British troops operating separately, without an agreed mission. There is spectacular evidence that each decides whether, when, and where to retaliate." "More Mideast Muddling," *New York Times*, op-ed, November 28, 1983.

17. Michael Getler, "Lebanon Worries U.S. Military," *Washington Post*, December 18, 1983, and Joel Brinkley, "Beirut's Envoy Doubts Value of Marines," *New York Times*, December 31, 1983; see also remarks by Senator Sam Nunn (D-Ga.), NBC's "Meet the Press," October 23, 1983. The decision to deploy the marines rather than army troops was based largely on the fact that the former appear more temporary. Command and logistics could be based offshore and "within 24 hours they could be packed up and gone," as U.S. Ambassador to Lebanon Robert C. Dillon subsequently observed.

18. Provisional Verbatim Record of the 419th Security Council meeting, October 18, 1983. S/PV.2480.

19. *Washington Post*, January 25, 1983.

20. Draper's remarks were made on ABC's "This Week with David Brinkley," June 12, 1983. In mid-August, in anticipation of Israeli redeployment, Lebanon again pressed for an increase in the size of the MNF, although the question of augmenting the U.S. contingent reportedly was not raised. *Washington Post*, August 14, 1983. The year-end forecast in Michael Getler, "Lebanon Worries U.S. Military," *Washington Post*, December 18, 1983.

21. Michael J. Berlin, "U.N. Peace-Keeper Sees Failure in Lebanon," *Washington Post*, December 12, 1983. The transformation of the situation facing the peacekeepers in Lebanon during the last three months of 1983 is addressed in Michael Dobbs, "Beirut Bombs Shatter Allies' Resolve," *Washington Post*, December 28, 1983.

22. "The 'Peacekeeping' Fraud," *New Republic*, November 14, 1983. Commentaries on President Reagan's radio broadcast of December 10, 1983, appeared in Hedrick Smith, *New York Times*, December 11, 1983, and James Reston, *New York Times*, December 14, 1983.

23. Multinational Force in Lebanon Resolution, October 12, 1983. The text of this resolution appears in Appendix B.

24. Fred Hiatt, "Marines Unlikely to Quit Airport," *Washington Post*, December 9, 1983, Margaret Shapiro, "Lawmakers Not Soothed by Briefing," *Washington Post*, December 10, 1983, Steven V. Roberts, "Congress Critical of Mideast Policy," *New York Times*, December 10, 1983, and Hedrick Smith, "Lebanon Rekindles U.S. Foreign Policy Troubles," *New York Times*, December 11, 1983. In an op-ed piece in the *New York Times*, December 22, 1983, former defense secretary Harold Brown concluded that in using naval guns to defend Gemayel's army against Syrian-backed militias, the United States had taken on a mission with an unattainable goal that could risk war with Syria. He called for the withdrawal of the marines even at the cost of an arrangement with Syria that would involve a de facto partition of Lebanon.

25. On the Pentagon's report see *New York Times*, December 29, 1983. Key portions of the report appear in Appendix B of this book. The commission was directed to examine the rules of engagement and the security measures in place at the time of the attack, but Adm. Robert L. J. Long (ret.), the chairman, and his colleagues interpreted their charter in the broadest sense. On Mondale's statement see Cass Peterson and Martin Schram, "Mondale Urges Lebanon Withdrawal," *Washington Post*, January 1, 1984.

26. President Reagan's press conference in *New York Times*, December 15, 1983. *The New Republic* (December 26, 1983) was one of the few opinion journals to approve the administration's aims, which it interpreted as ensuring the survival of a pro-Western government in Beirut. But the editors charged that the administration had failed to pursue vigorously the needed twofold strategy of expanding the political base of the Lebanon government and bringing military pressure on Syria to settle for half-a-loaf (as Secretary of State Shultz had proposed), that is, dominance over half of Lebanon.

27. On the Geneva talks, see *New York Times*, October 31, 1983, and November 4, 1983.

28. Shamir's television interview was reported in *Haaretz*, November 3, 1983, and interviews with Deputy Foreign Minister Yehuda Ben-Meir, "Condition for Pullback," and with Labor party leader, Shimon Peres, "Peres Plan for Withdrawal," appeared in *Jerusalem Post*, int'l ed., November 20–26, 1983. Plans for a staged withdrawal are covered by Michael Garty, "It Is Possible to Get Out of Lebanon," *Haaretz*, December 1, 1983. It should be noted that as of the end of 1983, the Israeli cabinet had not endorsed

these plans and continued to insist on a reciprocal Syrian pullout as a condition of total IDF withdrawal. But sources close to the top leadership confirmed that Israel would be as flexible as possible in finding ways to remove Israel's troops, provided security arrangements would be worked out to protect its northern border. David K. Shipler, "Top Israelis Deny Policy Change on Withdrawal," Washington Post, January 12, 1984.

29. The text of the May 17 agreement appears in Appendix B.

30. Economist, July 16, 1983, and Washington Post, July 8, 1983.

31. Talcott W. Seelye, "Misunderstanding Syria," Washington Post, July 17, 1983; "Is There a Way Out of Beirut?", Economist, December 10, 1983; and Sol M. Linowitz, "Lebanon: An Exit Plan," Washington Post, Outlook, December 25, 1983.

32. Puls, "Lebanon at the Crossroads," Haaretz, November 4, 1983, and Drew Middleton, "Syria Said to Pass Egypt as a Power," New York Times, November 19, 1983. Other military analysts and Middleton himself later wondered just how formidable the Syrian forces were and suggested that Syrian anxiety about how effectively the army could absorb high-technology weapons might induce Assad to strike a political bargain over Lebanon. Drew Middleton, "Syrians' Armed Forces: Playing a Waiting Game?", New York Times, January 7, 1984. Israeli political sentiment regarding accommodation with Syria is assessed by Daniel Gavron, "Assad's Secret," Jerusalem Post, int'l ed., December 4-10, 1983. Gavron recalls Begin's remark that Assad "knows how to honor an agreement" and senses "reluctant admiration" for Assad among Israeli experts. Itamar Rabinovich, director of Tel Aviv University's Shiloah Center, notes that Assad "can deliver the goods" if an agreement is reached with Syria. Moshe Maoz, chairman of the Islamic studies department at the Hebrew University, observes that any Syrian regime will safeguard what it regards as its legitimate interests in Lebanon.

33. "Lebanon: And Now What?", Economist, October 8, 1983. Faced with a deteriorating political situation in Beirut and a lack of progress on national reconciliation, the Italian government in mid-December 1983 renounced the idea of participating in the corps of ceasefire observers. According to Italian officials, this decision followed a judgment that prospects for a genuine truce had dimmed and that the proposal for neutral observers had become moot. Sari Gilbert, "Italy Won't Take Part in Truce Observer Unit," Washington Post, December 10, 1983.

34. Remarks of the Dutch and French representatives on Security Council consideration of the renewal of UNIFIL's mandate appear in U.N. Security Council, Provisional Verbatim Record of the 2,480th meeting, October 18, 1983.

35. In Britain, the government quieted the storm and received general endorsement of its view that an immediate withdrawal would sabotage any hope for peace and national reconciliation in Lebanon. And, in a television interview on January 4, 1984, Prime Minister Margaret Thatcher said there could be no possibility of a pullout by the multinational force, including the British contingent, because it would "leave a vacuum." The Italian government decided not to pull out, which brought sighs of relief in Washington because Italy not only fielded the largest MNF contingent but fulfilled the important peacekeeping role of protecting the refugee camps in south Beirut. Allied concerns about the MNF are detailed in Thomas L. Friedman, "American Air Strikes Change the Game in the Middle East," New York Times, December 11, 1983; "Huffing and Puffing over Tory Foreign Policy," Economist, December 10, 1983; "British Tell Gemayel They Don't Plan to Pull Out," New York Times, December 15, 1983, Alan Cowell, "Heavy Fighting Erupts in Beirut as French Shift," New York Times, December 26, 1983; and Michael Dobbs, "Beirut Bombs Shatter Allies' Resolve," Washington Post, December 28, 1983. It should be noted that Italian anxiety about the entanglement of its

force in Lebanon antedated the events of autumn 1983—concerns had already been voiced in the spring, as reported by Enrico Jacchia, "Beirut Role Has Italians Worrying," *International Herald Tribune*, May 6, 1983.

36. Richard Halloran, "Tower Says Withdrawing Troops in Lebanon Would Be 'Disastrous,' " *New York Times*, January 11, 1984.

37. "Marine Chief Optimistic on Beirut Withdrawal," *New York Times*, December 9, 1983. Syrian concerns regarding U.S. troops in Lebanon reported by Ze'ev Schiff, "Are They Leaving or Not?", *Haaretz*, May 13, 1983.

38. The remark about France being the "indispensable Western power" was made by Minister of Defense Charles Hernu, who was quoted by John Vinocur, "French Official Backs Beirut Role," *New York Times*, December 23, 1983. French views at the end of 1983 are reported in Michael Dobbs, "Beirut Bombs Shatter Allies' Resolve," *Washington Post*, December 28, 1983. Congress endorsed the eventual replacement of the MNF by a U.N. peacekeeping force in the Multinational Force in Lebanon Resolution of October 12, 1983. The resolution called for a concerted diplomatic effort at the United Nations to bring this about not later than one year after the enactment of the resolution. The day of the October 23 truck-bombing of the marine barracks in Beirut, Senator Nunn (D-Ga.) advocated that the "United Nations forces . . . eventually replace the marines," on NBC's "Meet the Press," and Walter F. Mondale, a Democratic candidate for president, urged that "American troops be replaced with U.N. forces, other Third World forces, and certainly with Lebanese army forces." *New York Times*, December 26, 1983.

39. On growing advocacy for replacing the MNF with U.N. peacekeepers, see articles and opinion pieces by Bernard Gwertzman, *New York Times*, September 28–29, 1983; John M. Goshko, *Washington Post*, October 1, 1983; Stephen S. Rosenfeld, *Washington Post*, December 16, 1983; Brian E. Urquhart, *New York Times*, December 18, 1983; Drew Middleton, *New York Times*, December 18, 1983; and Sol M. Linowitz, *Washington Post*, Outlook, December 15, 1983.

40. Bernard Gwertzman, *New York Times*, September 28, 1983, and David Ottaway, *Washington Post*, October 11, 1983.

41. In the 1970s the exact location of this notional line was assumed to lie somewhere north of the Litani River. Rabin, then Israel's prime minister and generally reputed to be the author of the "red line" concept, declares in his memoirs that a line was actually "drawn on a map and extended from just south of Sidon on the west in a straight line to a depth some 25 km north of the Litani. Both the Syrians and the Americans knew the boundaries." *Pinkas Sheruth* (Tel Aviv: Maariv, 1979), p. 503.

42. Shamir's television interview was reported in *Haaretz*, November 10, 1983.

43. On Assad's disciplining the PLO in a manner that coincidentally served Israel's interests, see Flora Lewis, "A New Look at Lebanon," *New York Times*, January 16, 1983; Puls, "Key to Golan Peace Lies in Damascus," *Haaretz*, September 23, 1983.

44. Rabin's remarks to Philip Geyelin, "Shedding Illusions in Israel," *Washington Post*, November 22, 1983. Yariv's analysis in the *Jerusalem Post*, int'l ed., November 6–12, 1983. For an Israeli analysis along similar lines, see Michael Garty, "It is Possible to Get Out of Lebanon," *Haaretz*, December 1, 1983. An opposing Israeli view, holding that Syria is in no mood for compromise and prepares for the ultimate showdown, is contained in Oded Zarai, "Talk with Syria—About What?" *Haaretz*, November 20, 1983.

45. Hirsh Goodman, "Quagmire in Lebanon," *Jerusalem Post*, int'l ed., January 9–14, 1984. Israel's approach to the United States to explore Israel-Syria disengagement in

Lebanon reported in David K. Shipler, "Israelis Deny Policy Change," *New York Times*, January 12, 1984.

46. *Jerusalem Post*, int'l ed., November 6–12, 1983. On the background and peacekeeping mechanism created to monitor the 1974 disengagement agreement, see my article, "U.N. Peacekeeping and the 1973 Arab-Israeli Conflict," *Orbis* (Spring 1975). The text of the 1974 disengagement agreement appears in the appendix.

47. The official account of the formation and first year's operation is set forth in Annual Report of the Director-General, Multinational Force & Observers, Rome, April 25, 1983.

48. Creation of the Multinational Force & Observers (MFO) for the Sinai, Hearings and Markup before the Committee on Foreign Affairs, 97th Cong., 1st sess., on H.J. Res. 349, July 21, 28, and October 27, 1981.

49. Similarly, in connection with the president's decision in July to conduct military exercises in Honduras, senior military officers expressed concern that worldwide commitments had overextended the armed forces and strained their ability to carry out planned military exercises elsewhere. Richard Halloran, "U.S. Held Unready for Show of Force," *New York Times*, July 31, 1983.

50. Article V, section 2 reads: "The Parties consider the Strait of Tiran and the Gulf of Aqaba to be international waterways open to all nations for unimpeded and non-suspendable freedom of navigation and overflight. The Parties will respect each other's right to navigation and overflight for access to either country through the Strait of Tiran and the Gulf of Aqaba."

51. Letter to the author from Maj. Barry Sprouse, senior visits officer, MFO Force Headquarters, Sinai, dated May 21, 1983.

52. The full text of Article II, section 2 reads: "Each party undertakes to ensure that acts or threats of belligerency, hostility, or violence do not originate from and are not committed from within its territory, or by any forces subject to its control or by any forces stationed on its territory, against the population, citizens or property of the other Party. Each Party also undertakes to refrain from organizing, instigating, inciting, assisting or participating in acts of belligerency, hostility, subversion or violence against the other Party, anywhere, and undertakes to ensure that perpetrators of such acts are brought to justice."

53. *Washington Post*, June 14, 1983. The issue has been aggravated by a related problem, which came to a head in June 1983. For the first time Egypt made public a protest it made privately in April that Israel was maintaining a police or military presence at three of the fifteen disputed points along the border between the two countries which, Egypt contended, violated the terms of the treaty and protocol. Israel argued that maintaining police or soldiers at the three points was not in violation of the agreement because of Egypt's failure to agree to procedures for stationing soldiers from the MFO at the disputed border points to guard against their use by guerrillas attempting to infiltrate. One of the disputed points was at Taba just outside the Israeli city of Eilat. The other two—one involving just a few feet of land, the other more than a mile of disputed territory—are in central Sinai, where the Israelis said they had encountered instances of the laying of land mines within Israel by infiltrators through these points. *Washington Post*, June 14, 1983.

54. "Way Open for Europe to Join Sinai Force in Wake of U.S.-Israeli Statement," *Jerusalem Post*, int'l ed., December 6–12, 1981.

55. See my article, "U.N. Peacekeeping," *Orbis* (Spring 1975).

56. As noted earlier, one should not discount the difficulties of overcoming Syrian

concerns (whether or not Soviet-inspired) that any American-dominated multinational force would camouflage American strategic presence and mask a long-range policy of bringing Lebanon into Western orbit. This concern could only reinforce American reluctance to deploy a U.S. contingent even as temporary peacekeeper to fill the vacuum caused by Israel's redeployment. See, e.g., Secretary Shultz's remarks during his Middle East trip in July 1983, reported in the *Washington Post*, July 8, 1983.

57. Dan Horowitz, *Israel's Concept of Defensible Borders*, Jerusalem Papers on Peace Problems, no. 16 (Jerusalem: The Hebrew University, 1975). The mainstream Labor party position was codified in the Allon Plan (named after Yigal Allon, the party's foreign minister and deputy prime minister) which called for negotiating a settlement with Jordan under which the largely populated areas of the West Bank would be returned to Jordanian sovereignty while Israel keep its forces and strategic positions along the largely unpopulated border area. See Yigal Allon, "Israel: The Case of Defensible Borders," *Foreign Affairs* 55 (October 1976): 38–53.

58. Published in Hebrew as *Kav Haganah Be-Yehudah Ve-Shomron* (Tel Aviv: Hakibbutz Hameuchad Publishing House, 1982). An English version is forthcoming.

59. Guantanamo Bay was leased by Cuba to the United States in 1903 by treaty, and the arrangement was renewed in 1934. The consent of both governments is needed to revoke the agreement. Since 1960 the Castro regime has refused to accept the token annual stipend and has pressed for surrender of the base.

60. Zbigniew Brzezinski, *Power and Principle* (New York: Farrar, Straus, and Giroux, 1983), pp. 85–86, 118–19.

61. Zalman Shoval, "Why the West Bank is Vital," *Jerusalem Post*, int'l ed., March 20–26, 1983. He concludes that "demilitarisation of Judea and Samaria is not . . . a reasonable answer to the potential security threats to Israel," and that any solution must allow Israel to "deploy warning devices, air force radar stations and at least two armoured or mechanized divisions from the eastern mountain plateau to the Jordan." *Jerusalem Post*, int'l ed., February 27–March 5, 1983, p. 13.

APPENDIX A

Documents Relating to the Sinai Multinational Force & Observers (MFO)

Letter of March 26, 1979, from President Jimmy Carter to Egyptian President Anwar El-Sadat and to Israeli Prime Minister Menachem Begin.

March 26, 1979

Dear Mr. President [Mr. Prime Minister]:

I wish to confirm to you that subject to United States Constitutional processes:

In the event of an actual or threatened violation of the Treaty of Peace between Egypt and Israel, the United States will, on request of one or both of the Parties, consult with the Parties with respect thereto and will take such other action as it may deem appropriate and helpful to achieve compliance with the Treaty.

The United States will conduct aerial monitoring as requested by the Parties pursuant to Annex I of the Treaty.

The United States believes the Treaty provision for permanent stationing of United Nations personnel in the designated limited force zone can and should be implemented by the United Nations Security Council. The United States will exert its utmost efforts to obtain the requisite action by the Security Council. If the Security Council fails to establish and maintain the arrangements called for in the Treaty, the President will be prepared to take those steps necessary to ensure the establishment and maintenance of an acceptable alternative multinational force.

Sincerely,

JIMMY CARTER

On August 3, 1981, at a ceremony at the U.S. Department of State, Ephraim Evron, ambassador of Israel to the United States, and Ashraf A. Gorbal, ambassador of Egypt to the United States, signed the protocol which established the Sinai Multinational Force & Observers (MFO); Secretary Haig signed as witness for the United States.

Following are the texts of identical letters from Secretary Haig to Yitzhak Shamir, foreign minister of Israel, and Kamal Hasan Ali, deputy prime minister and foreign minister of Egypt. The protocol, annex, and appendix for the MFO are also reprinted below, in addition to a statement by Nicholas A. Veliotes, assistant secretary of state for Near Eastern and South Asian affairs, before the U.S. Senate Foreign Relations Committee on July 20, 1981.

109

Letter from Secretary Haig to Egyptian and Israeli Foreign Ministers, August 3, 1981

Dear Mr. Minister:

I wish to confirm the understandings concerning the United States' role reached in your negotiations on the establishment and maintenance of the Multinational Force and Observers:

1. The post of the Director-General will be held by U.S. nationals suggested by the United States.

2. Egypt and Israel will accept proposals made by the United States concerning the appointment of the Director-General, the appointment of the Commander, and the financial issues related to paragraphs 24–26 of the Annex to the Protocol, if no agreement is reached on any of these issues between the Parties. The United States will participate in deliberations concerning financial matters. In the event of differences of view between the Parties over the composition of the MFO, the two sides will invite the United States to join them in resolving any issues.

3. Subject to Congressional authorization and appropriations:

A. The United States will contribute an infantry battalion and a logistics support unit from its armed forces and will provide a group of civilian observers to the MFO.

B. The United States will contribute one-third of the annual operating expenses of the MFO. The United States will be reimbursed by the MFO for the costs incurred in the change of station of U.S. Armed Forces provided to the MFO and for the costs incurred in providing civilian observers to the MFO. For the initial period (July 17, 1981–September 30, 1982) during which there will be exceptional costs connected with the establishment of the MFO, the United States agrees to provide three-fifths of the costs, subject to the same understanding concerning reimbursement.

C. The United States will use its best efforts to find acceptable replacements for contingents that withdraw from the MFO.

D. The United States remains prepared to take those steps necessary to ensure the maintenance of an acceptable MFO.

I wish to inform you that I sent today to the Minister of Foreign Affairs of Israel [of Egypt] an identical letter, and I propose that my letters and the replies thereto constitute an agreement among the three States.

Sincerely,

ALEXANDER M. HAIG, JR.

PROTOCOL

In view of the fact that the Egyptian-Israeli Treaty of Peace dated March 26, 1979 (hereinafter, "the Treaty"), provides for the fulfillment of certain functions by the United Nations Forces and Observers and that the President of the Security Council indicated on 18 May 1981 that the Security Council was unable to reach the necessary agreement on the proposal to establish the UN Forces and Observers, Egypt and Israel, acting in full respect for the purposes and principles of the United Nations Charter, have reached the following agreement:

1. A Multinational Force and Observers (hereinafter, "MFO") is hereby established as an alternative to the United Nations Forces and Observers. The two parties may

consider the possibility of replacing the arrangements hereby established with alternative arrangements by mutual agreement.

2. The provisions of the Treaty which relate to the establishment and functions and responsibilities of the UN Forces and Observers shall apply mutatis mutandis to the establishment and functions and responsibilities of the MFO or as provided in this Protocol.

3. The provisions of Article IV of the Treaty and the Agreed Minute thereto shall apply to the MFO. In accordance with paragraph 2 of this Protocol, the words "through the procedures indicated in paragraph 4 of Article IV and the Agreed Minute thereto" shall be substituted for "by the Security Council of the United Nations with the affirmative vote of the five permanent members" in paragraph 2 of Article IV of the Treaty.

4. The Parties shall agree on the nations from which the MFO will be drawn.

5. The mission of the MFO shall be to undertake the functions and responsibilities stipulated in the Treaty for the United Nations Forces and Observers. Details relating to the international nature, size, structure and operation of the MFO are set out in the attached Annex.

6. The Parties shall appoint a Director-General who shall be responsible for the direction of the MFO. The Director-General shall, subject to the approval of the Parties, appoint a Commander, who shall be responsible for the daily command of the MFO. Details relating to the Director-General and the Commander are set out in the attached Annex.

7. The expenses of the MFO which are not covered by other sources shall be borne equally by the Parties.

8. Disputes arising from the interpretation and application of this Protocol shall be resolved according to Article VII of the Treaty.

9. This Protocol shall enter into force when each Party has notified the other that all its Constitutional requirements have been fulfilled. The attached Annex shall be regarded as an integral part hereof. This Protocol shall be communicated to the Secretary General of the United Nations for registration in accordance with the provisions of Article 102 of the Charter of the United Nations.

For the Government of the
Arab Republic of Egypt:

ASHRAF A. GORBAL

For the Government of
the State of Israel:

EPHRAIM EVRON

Witnessed by:

ALEXANDER M. HAIG, JR.
For the Government of the
United States of America

ANNEX

Director-General

1. The Parties shall appoint a Director-General of the MFO within one month of the signing of this Protocol. The Director-General shall serve a term of four years, which may be renewed. The Parties may replace the Director-General prior to the expiration of his term.

2. The Director-General shall be responsible for the direction of the MFO in the fulfillment of its functions and in this respect is authorized to act on behalf of the MFO. In accordance with local laws and regulations and the privileges and immunities of the MFO, the Director-General is authorized to engage an adequate staff, to institute legal proceedings, to contract, to acquire and dispose of property, and to take those other actions necessary and proper for the fulfillment of his responsibilities. The MFO shall not own immovable property in the territory of either Party without the agreement of the respective government. The Director-General shall determine the location of his office, subject to the consent of the country in which the office will be located.

3. Subject to the authorization of the Parties, the Director-General shall request those nations agreeable to the Parties to supply contingents to the MFO and to receive the agreement of contributing nations that the contingents will conduct themselves in accordance with the terms of this Protocol. The Director-General shall impress upon contributing nations the importance of continuity of service in units with the MFO so that the Commander may be in a position to plan his operations with knowledge of what units will be available. The Director-General shall obtain the agreement of contributing nations that the national contingents shall not be withdrawn without adequate prior notification to the Director-General.

4. The Director-General shall report to the Parties on developments relating to the functioning of the MFO. He may raise with either or both Parties, as appropriate, any matter concerning the functioning of the MFO. For this purpose, Egypt and Israel shall designate senior responsible officials as agreed points of contact for the Director-General. In the event that either Party or the Director-General requests a meeting, it will be convened in the location determined by the Director-General within 48 hours. Access across the international boundary shall only be permitted through entry checkpoints designated by each Party. Such access will be in accordance with the laws and regulations of each country. Adequate procedures will be established by each Party to facilitate such entries.

Military Command Structure

5. In accordance with paragraph 6 of the Protocol, the Director-General shall appoint a Commander of the MFO within one month of the appointment of the Director-General. The Commander will be an officer of general rank and shall serve a term of three years which may, with the approval of the Parties, be renewed or curtailed. He shall not be of the same nationality as the Director-General.

6. Subject to paragraph 2 of this Annex, the Commander shall have full command authority over the MFO, and shall promulgate its Standing Operating Procedures. In making the command arrangements stipulated in paragraph 9 of Article VI of Annex I of the Treaty (hereinafter "Annex I"), the Commander shall establish a chain of command for the MFO linked to the commanders of the national contingents made available by contributing nations. The members of the MFO, although remaining in their national service, are, during the period of their assignment to the MFO, under the

Director-General and subject to the authority of the Commander through the chain of command.

7. The Commander shall also have general responsibility for the good order of the MFO. Responsibility for disciplinary action in national contingents provided for the MFO rests with the commanders of the national contingents.

Functions and Responsibilities of the MFO

8. The mission of the MFO shall be to undertake the functions and responsibilities stipulated in the Treaty for the United Nations Forces and Observers.

9. The MFO shall supervise the implementation of Annex I and employ its best efforts to prevent any violation of its terms.

10. With respect to the MFO, as appropriate, the Parties agree to the following arrangements:

(a) Operation of checkpoints, reconnaissance patrols, and observation posts along the international boundary and Line B, and within Zone C.

(b) Periodic verification of the implementation of the provisions of Annex I will be carried out not less than twice a month unless otherwise agreed by the Parties.

(c) Additional verifications within 48 hours after the receipt of a request from either Party.

(d) Ensuring the freedom of navigation through the Strait of Tiran in accordance with Article V of the Treaty of Peace.

11. When a violation has been confirmed by the MFO, it shall be rectified by the respective Party within 48 hours. The Party shall notify the MFO of the rectification.

12. The operations of the MFO shall not be construed as substituting for the undertakings by the Parties described in paragraph 2 of Article III of the Treaty. MFO personnel will report such acts by individuals as described in that paragraph in the first instance to the police of the respective Party.

13. Pursuant to paragraph 2 of Article II of Annex I, and in accordance with paragraph 7 of Article VI of Annex I, at the checkpoints at the international boundary, normal border crossing functions, such as passport inspection and customs control, will be carried out by officials of the respective Party.

14. The MFO operating in the Zones will enjoy freedom of movement necessary for the performance of its tasks.

15. MFO support flights to Egypt or Israel will follow normal rules and procedures for international flights. Egypt and Israel will undertake to facilitate clearances for such flights.

16. Verification flights by MFO aircraft in the Zones will be cleared with the authorities of the respective Party, in accordance with procedures to ensure that the flights can be undertaken in a timely manner.

17. MFO aircraft will not cross the international boundary without prior notification and clearance by each of the Parties.

18. MFO reconnaissance aircraft operating in Zone C will provide notification to the civil air control center and, thereby, to the Egyptian liaison officer therein.

Size and Organization

19. The MFO shall consist of a headquarters, three infantry battalions totalling not more than 2,000 troops, a coastal patrol unit and an observer unit, an aviation element and logistics and signal units.

20. The MFO units will have standard armament and equipment appropriate to their peacekeeping mission as stipulated in this Annex.

21. The MFO headquarters will be organized to fulfill its duties in accordance with the Treaty and this Annex. It shall be manned by staff-trained officers of appropriate rank provided by the troop contributing nations as part of their national contingents. Its organization will be determined by the Commander, who will assign staff positions to each contributor on an equitable basis.

Reports

22. The Commander will report findings simultaneously to the Parties as soon as possible, but not later than 24 hours, after a verification or after a violation has been confirmed. The Commander will also provide the Parties simultaneously a monthly report summarizing the findings of the checkpoints, observation posts, and reconnaissance patrols.

23. Reporting formats will be worked out by the Commander with the Parties in the Joint Commission. Reports to the Parties will be transmitted to the liaison offices to be established in accordance with paragraph 31 below.

Financing, Administration, and Facilities

24. The budget for each financial year shall be prepared by the Director-General and shall be approved by the Parties. The financial year shall be from October 1 through September 30. Contributions shall be paid in U.S. dollars, unless the Director-General requests contributions in some other form. Contributions shall be committed the first day of the financial year and made available as the Director-General determines necessary to meet expenditures of the MFO.

25. For the period prior to October 1, 1981, the budget of the MFO shall consist of such sums as the Director-General shall receive. Any contributions during that period will be credited to the share of the budget of the contributing state in Financial Year 1982, and thereafter as necessary, so that the contribution is fully credited.

26. The Director-General shall prepare financial and administrative regulations consistent with this Protocol and submit them no later than December 1, 1981, for the approval of the Parties. These financial regulations shall include a budgetary process which takes into account the budgetary cycles of the contributing states.

27. The Commander shall request the approval of the respective Party for the use of facilities on its territory necessary for the proper functioning of the MFO. In this connection, the respective Party, after giving its approval for the use by the MFO of land or existing buildings and their fixtures, will not be reimbursed by the MFO for such use.

Responsibilities of the Joint Commission Prior to Its Dissolution

28. In accordance with Article IV of the Appendix to Annex I, the Joint Commission will supervise the implementation of the arrangements described in Annex I and its Appendix, as indicated in subparagraphs b, c, h, i, and j of paragraph 3 of Article IV.

29. The Joint Commission will implement the preparations required to enable the Liaison System to undertake its responsibilities in accordance with Article VII of Annex I.

30. The Joint Commission will determine the modalities and procedures for the implementation of Phase Two, as described in paragraph 3(b) of Article I of Annex I, based on the modalities and procedures that were implemented in Phase One.

Liaison System

31. The Liaison System will undertake the responsibilities indicated in paragraph 1 of Article VII of Annex I, and may discuss any other matters which the Parties by agreement may place before it. Meetings will be held at least once a month. In the event that either Party or the Commander requests a special meeting, it will be convened within 24 hours. The first meeting will be held in El-Arish not later than two weeks after the MFO assumes its functions. Meetings will alternate between El-Arish and Beer Sheba, unless the Parties otherwise agree. The Commander shall be invited to any meeting in which subjects concerning the MFO are discussed, or when either Party requests MFO presence. Decisions will be reached by agreement of Egypt and Israel.

32. The Commander and each chief liaison officer will have access to one another in their respective offices. Adequate procedures will be worked out between the Parties with a view to facilitating the entry for this purpose of the representatives of either Party to the territory of the other.

Privileges and Immunities

33. Each Party will accord to the MFO the privileges and immunities indicated in the attached Appendix.

Schedule

34. The MFO shall assume its functions at 1300 hours on April 25, 1982.
35. The MFO shall be in place by 1300 hours, on March 20, 1982.

APPENDIX

Definitions

1. The "Multinational Force and Observers" (hereinafter referred to as "the MFO") is that organization established by the Protocol.

2. For the purposes of this Appendix, the term "Member of the MFO" refers to the Director-General, the Commander and any person, other than a resident of the Receiving State, belonging to the military contingent of a Participating State or otherwise under the authority of the Director-General, and his spouse and minor children, as appropriate.

3. The "Receiving State" means the authorities of Egypt or Israel as appropriate, and the territories under their control. "Government authorities" includes all national and local, civil and military authorities called upon to perform functions relating to the MFO under the provisions of this Appendix, without prejudice to the ultimate responsibility of the Government of the Receiving State.

4. "Resident of the Receiving State" includes (a) a person with citizenship of the Receiving State, (b) a person resident therein, or (c) a person present in the territory of the Receiving State other than a member of the MFO.

5. "Participating State" means a State that contributes personnel to the MFO.

Duties of members of the MFO in the Receiving State:

6. (a) Members of the MFO shall respect the laws and regulations of the Receiving State and shall refrain from any activity of a political character in the Receiving State and from any action incompatible with the international nature of their duties or inconsistent with the spirit of the present arrangements. The Director-General shall take all appropriate measures to ensure the observance of these obligations.

(b) In the performance of their duties for the MFO, members of the MFO shall receive their instructions only from the Director-General and the chain of command designated by him.

(c) Members of the MFO shall exercise the utmost discretion in regard to all matters relating to their duties and functions. They shall not communicate to any person any information known to them by reason of their position with the MFO which has not been made public, except in the course of their duties or by authorization of the Director-General. These obligations do not cease upon the termination of their assignment with the MFO.

(d) The Director-General will ensure that in the Standing Operating Procedures of the MFO, there will be arrangements to avoid accidental or inadvertent threats to the safety of MFO members.

Entry and exit: Identification

7. Individual or collective passports shall be issued by the Participating States for members of the MFO. The Director-General shall notify the Receiving State of the names and scheduled time of arrival of MFO members, and other necessary information. The Receiving State shall issue an individual or collective multiple entry visa as appropriate prior to that travel. No other documents shall be required for a member of the MFO to enter or leave the Receiving State. Members of the MFO shall be exempt from immigration inspection and restrictions on entering or departing from the territory of the Receiving State. They shall also be exempt from any regulations governing the residence of aliens in the Receiving State, including registration, but shall not be considered as acquiring any right to permanent residence or domicile in the Receiving State. The Receiving State shall also provide each member of the Force with a personal identity card prior to or upon his arrival.

8. Members of the MFO will at all times carry their personal identity cards issued by the Receiving State. Members of the MFO may be required to present, but not to surrender, their passport or identity cards upon demand of an appropriate authority of the Receiving State. Except as provided in paragraph 7 of this Appendix, the passport or identity card will be the only document required for a member of the MFO.

9. If a member of the MFO leaves the services of the Participating State to which he belongs and is not repatriated, the Director-General shall immediately inform the authorities of the Receiving State, giving such particulars as may be required. The Director-General shall similarly inform the authorities of the Receiving State of any member of the MFO who has absented himself for more than twenty-one days. If an expulsion order against the ex-member of the MFO has been made, the Director-General

shall be responsible for ensuring that the person concerned shall be received within the territory of the Participating State concerned.

Jurisdiction

10. The following arrangements respecting criminal and civil jurisdiction are made having regard to the special functions of the MFO and not for the personal benefit of the members of the MFO. The Director-General shall cooperate at all times with the appropriate authorities of the Receiving State to facilitate the proper administration of justice, secure the observance of laws and regulations, and prevent the occurrence of any abuse in connection with the privileges, immunities, and facilities mentioned in this Appendix.

Criminal jurisdiction

11. (a) Military members of the MFO and members of the civilian observer group of the MFO shall be subject to the exclusive jurisdiction of their respective national states in respect of any criminal offenses which may be committed by them in the Receiving State. Any such person who is charged with the commission of a crime will be brought to trial by the respective Participating State, in accordance with its laws.

(b) Subject to paragraph 25, other members of the MFO shall be immune from the criminal jurisdiction of the Receiving State in respect of words spoken or written and all acts performed by them in their official capacity.

(c) The Director-General shall obtain the assurances of each Participating State that it will be prepared to take the necessary measures to assure proper discipline of its personnel and to exercise jurisdiction with respect to any crime or offense which might be committed by its personnel. The Director-General shall comply with requests of the Receiving State for the withdrawal from its territory of any member of the MFO who violates its laws, regulations, customs, or traditions. The Director-General, with the consent of the Participating State, may waive the immunity of a member of the MFO.

(d) Without prejudice to the foregoing, a Participating State may enter into a supplementary arrangement with the Receiving State to limit or waive the immunities of its members of the MFO who are on periods of leave while in the Receiving State.

Civil jurisdiction

12. (a) Members of the MFO shall not be subject to the civil jurisdiction of the courts of the Receiving State or to other legal process in any matter relating to their official duties. In a case arising from a matter relating to official duties and which involves a member of the MFO and a resident of the Receiving State, and in other disputes as agreed, the procedure provided in paragraph 38(b) of this Appendix shall apply to the settlement.

(b) If the Director-General certifies that a member of the MFO is unable because of official duties or authorized absence to protect his interests in a civil proceeding in which he is a participant, the court or authority shall at his request suspend the proceeding until the elimination of the disability, but for not more than ninety days. Property of a member of the MFO which is certified by the Director-General to be needed by him for the fulfillment of his official duties shall be free from seizure for the satisfaction of a judgment, decision, or order, together with other property not subject thereto under the law of the Receiving State. The personal liberty of a member of the MFO shall not be restricted by a court or other authority of the Receiving State in a civil proceeding, whether to enforce a judgment, decision, or order, to compel an oath of disclosure, or for any other reason.

(c) In the cases provided for in subparagraph (b) above, the claimant may elect to have his claim dealt with in accordance with the procedure set out in paragraph 38(b) of this Appendix. Where a claim adjudicated or an award made in favor of the claimant by a court of the Receiving State or the Claims Commission under paragraph 38(b) of this Appendix has not been satisfied, the authorities of the Receiving State may, without prejudice to the claimant's rights, seek the good offices of the Director-General to obtain satisfaction.

Notification: certification

13. If any civil proceeding is instituted against a member of the MFO, before any court of the Receiving State having jurisdiction, notification shall be given to the Director-General. The Director-General shall certify to the court whether or not the proceeding is related to the official duties of such member.

Military police: arrest: transfer of custody and mutual assistance

14. The Director-General shall take all appropriate measures to ensure maintenance of discipline and good order among members of the MFO. To this end military police designated by the Director-General shall police the premises referred to in paragraph 19 of this Appendix, and such areas where the MFO is functioning.

15. The military police of the MFO shall immediately transfer to the civilian police of the Receiving State any individual, who is not a member of the MFO, of whom it takes temporary custody.

16. The police of the Receiving State shall immediately transfer to the MFO any member of the MFO, of whom it takes temporary custody, pending a determination concerning jurisdiction.

17. The Director-General and the authorities of the Receiving State shall assist each other concerning all offenses in respect of which either or both have an interest, including the production of witnesses, and in the collection and production of evidence, including the seizure and, in proper cases, the handing over, of things connected with an offense. The handing over of any such things may be made subject to their return within the time specified by the authority delivering them. Each shall notify the other of the disposition of any case in the outcome of which the other may have an interest or in which there has been a transfer of custody under the provisions of paragraphs 15 and 16 of this Appendix.

18. The government of the Receiving State will ensure the prosecution of persons subject to its criminal jurisdiction who are accused of acts in relation to the MFO or its members which, if committed in relation to the forces of the Receiving State or their members, would have rendered them liable to prosecution. The Director-General will take the measures within his power with respect to crimes or offenses committed against citizens of the Receiving State by members of the MFO.

Premises of the MFO

19. Without prejudice to the fact that all the premises of the MFO remain the territory of the Receiving State, they shall be inviolable and subject to the exclusive control and

authority of the Director-General, who alone may consent to the entry of officials to perform duties on such premises.

MFO flag

20. The Receiving States permit the MFO to display a special flag or insignia, of design agreed upon by them, on its headquarters, camps, posts, or other premises, vehicles, boats, and otherwise as decided by the Director-General. Other flags or pennants may be displayed only in exceptional cases and in accordance with conditions prescribed by the Director-General. Sympathetic consideration will be given to observations or requests of the authorities of the Receiving State concerning this last-mentioned matter. If the MFO flag or other flag is flown, the flag of the Receiving State shall be flown alongside it.

Uniform: Vehicle, boats and aircraft markings and registration: Operating permits

21. Military members of the MFO shall normally wear their national uniform with such identifying MFO insignia as the Director-General may prescribe. The conditions on which the wearing of civilian dress is authorized shall be notified by the Director-General to the authorities of the Receiving State and sympathetic consideration will be given to observations or requests of the authorities of the Receiving State concerning this matter. Members of the MFO shall wear civilian dress while outside the areas where they are functioning. Service vehicles, boats, and aircraft shall not carry the marks or license plates of any Participating State, but shall carry the distinctive MFO identification mark and license which shall be notified by the Director-General to the authorities of the Receiving State. Such vehicles, boats, and aircraft shall not be subject to registration and licensing under the laws and regulations of the Receiving State. Authorities of the Receiving State shall accept as valid, without a test or fee, a permit, or license for the operation of service vehicles, boats, and aircraft issued by the Director-General. MFO drivers shall be given permits by the Receiving State to enable them to drive outside the areas where they are functioning, if these permits are required by the Receiving State.

Arms

22. Members of the MFO who are off-duty shall not carry arms while outside the areas where they are functioning.

Privileges and immunities of the MFO

23. The MFO shall enjoy the status, privileges, and immunities accorded in Article II of the Convention on the Privileges and Immunities of the United Nations (hereinafter, "the Convention"). The provisions of Article II of the Convention shall also apply to the property, funds, and assets of Participating States used in the Receiving State in connection with the activities of the MFO. Such Participating States may not acquire immovable property in the Receiving State without agreement of the government of the Receiving State. The government of the Receiving State recognizes that the right of the MFO to import free of duty equipment for the MFO and provisions, supplies, and other goods for the exclusive use of members of the MFO, includes the right of the MFO to establish, maintain, and operate at headquarters, camps, and posts, service institutes providing amenities for the members of the MFO. The amenities that may be provided by service institutes shall be goods of a consumable nature (tobacco and tobacco products,

beer, etc.), and other customary articles of small value. To the end that duty-free importation for the MFO may be effected with the least possible delay, having regard to the interests of the government of the Receiving State, a mutually satisfactory procedure, including documentation, shall be arranged between the Director-General and the customs authorities of the Receiving State. The Director-General shall take all necessary measures to prevent any abuse of the exemption and to prevent the sale or resale of such goods to persons other than the members of the MFO. Sympathetic consideration shall be given by the Director-General to observations or requests of the authorities of the Receiving State concerning the operation of service institutes.

Privileges and immunities and delegation of authority of Director-General

24. The Director-General of the MFO may delegate his powers to other members of the MFO.

25. The Director-General, his deputy, the Commander, and his deputy, shall be accorded in respect of themselves, their spouses, and minor children, the privileges and immunities, exemptions, and facilities accorded to diplomatic envoys in accordance with international law.

Members of the MFO: Taxation, customs, and fiscal regulations

26. Members of the MFO shall be exempt from taxation by the Receiving State on the pay and emoluments received from their national governments or from the MFO. They shall also be exempt from all other direct taxes, fees, and charges, except for those levied for services rendered.

27. Members of the MFO shall have the right to import free of duty their personal effects in connection with their first taking up their post in the Receiving State. They shall be subject to the laws and regulations of the Receiving State governing customs and foreign exchange with respect to personal property not required by them by reason of their presence in the Receiving State with the MFO. Special facilities for entry or exit shall be granted by the immigration, customs, and fiscal authorities of the Receiving State to regularly constituted units of the MFO provided that the authorities concerned have been duly notified sufficiently in advance. Members of the MFO on departure from the area may, notwithstanding the foreign exchange regulations, take with them such funds as the Director-General certifies were received in pay and emoluments from their respective national governments or from the MFO and are a reasonable residue thereof. Special arrangements between the Director-General and the authorities of the Receiving State shall be made for the implementation of the foregoing provisions in the interests of the government of the Receiving State and members of the MFO.

28. The Director-General will cooperate with the customs and fiscal authorities of the Receiving State and will render all assistance within his power in ensuring the observance of the customs and fiscal laws and regulations of the Receiving State by the members of the MFO in accordance with this Appendix or any relevant supplemental arrangements.

Communications and postal services

29. The MFO shall enjoy the facilities in respect to communications provided for in Article III of the Convention. The Director-General shall have authority to install and operate communications systems as are necessary to perform its functions subject to the

provisions of Article 35 of the International Telecommunications Convention of April 11, 1973, relating to harmful interference. The frequencies on which any such station may be operated will be duly communicated by the MFO to the appropriate authorities of the Receiving State. Appropriate consultations will be held between the MFO and the authorities of the Receiving State to avoid harmful interference. The right of the Director-General is likewise recognized to enjoy the priorities of government telegrams and telephone calls as provided for the United Nations in Article 39 and Annex 3 of the latter Convention and in Article 5, No. 10 of the telegraph regulations annexed thereto.

30. The MFO shall also enjoy, within the areas where it is functioning, the right of unrestricted communication by radio, telephone, telegraph, or any other means, and of establishing the necessary facilities for maintaining such communications within and between premises of the MFO, including the laying of cables and land lines and the establishment of fixed and mobile radio sending and receiving stations. It is understood that the telegraph and telephone cables and lines herein referred to will be situated within or directly between the premises of the MFO and the areas where it is functioning, and that connection with the system of telegraphs and telephones of the Receiving State will be made in accordance with arrangements with the appropriate authorities of the Receiving State.

31. The Government of the Receiving State recognizes the right of the MFO to make arrangements through its own facilities for the processing and transport of private mail addressed to or emanating from members of the MFO. The government of the Receiving State will be informed of the nature of such arrangements. No interference shall take place with, and no censorship shall be applied to, the mail of the MFO by the government of the Receiving State. In the event that postal arrangements applying to private mail of members of the MFO are extended to operations involving transfer of currency, or transport of packages or parcels from the Receiving State, the conditions under which such operations shall be conducted in the Receiving State will be agreed upon between the government of the Receiving State and the Director-General.

Motor vehicle insurance

32. The MFO will take necessary arrangements to ensure that all MFO motor vehicles shall be covered by third party liability insurance in accordance with the laws and regulations of the Receiving State.

Use of roads, waterways, port facilities, airfields, and railways

33. When the MFO uses roads, bridges, port facilities, and airfields it shall not be subject to payment of dues, tolls, or charges either by way of registration or otherwise, in the areas where it is functioning and the normal points of access, except for charges that are related directly to services rendered. The authorities of the Receiving State, subject to special arrangements, will give the most favorable consideration to requests for the grant to members of the MFO of traveling facilities on its railways and of concessions with regard to fares.

Water, electricity, and other public utilities

34. The MFO shall have the right to the use of water, electricity, and other public utilities at rates not less favorable to the MFO than those to comparable consumers. The authorities of the Receiving State will, upon the request of the Director-General, assist

the MFO in obtaining water, electricity, and other utilities required, and in the case of interruption or threatened interruption of service, will give the same priority to the needs of the MFO as to essential government services. The MFO shall have the right where necessary to generate, within the premises of the MFO either on land or water, electricity for the use of the MFO and to transmit and distribute such electricity as required by the MFO.

Currency of the Receiving State

35. The Government of the Receiving State will, if requested by the Director-General, make available to the MFO, against reimbursement in U.S. dollars or other currency mutually acceptable, currency of the Receiving State required for the use of the MFO, including the pay of the members of the national contingents, at the rate of exchange most favorable to the MFO that is officially recognized by the government of the Receiving State.

Provisions, supplies, and services

36. The authorities of the Receiving State will, upon the request of the Director-General, assist the MFO in obtaining equipment, provisions, supplies, and other goods and services required from local sources for its subsistence and operation. Sympathetic consideration will be given by the Director-General in purchases on the local market to requests or observations of the authorities of the Receiving State in order to avoid any adverse effect on the local economy. Members of the MFO may purchase locally goods necessary for their own consumption, and such services as they need, under conditions prevailing in the open market.

If members of the MFO should require medical or dental facilities beyond those available within the MFO, arrangements shall be made with the appropriate authorities of the Receiving State under which such facilities may be made available. The Director-General and the appropriate local authorities will cooperate with respect to sanitary services. The Director-General and the authorities of the Receiving State shall extend to each other the fullest cooperation in matters concerning health, particularly with respect to the control of communicable diseases in accordance with international conventions; such cooperation shall extend to the exchange of relevant information and statistics.

Locally recruited personnel

37. The MFO may recruit locally such personnel as required. The authorities of the Receiving State will, upon the request of the Director-General, assist the MFO in the recruitment of such personnel. Sympathetic consideration will be given by the Director-General in the recruitment of local personnel to requests or observations of authorities of the Receiving State in order to avoid any adverse effect on the local economy. The terms and conditions of employment for locally recruited personnel shall be prescribed by the Director-General and shall generally, to the extent practicable, be no less favorable than the practice prevailing in the Receiving State.

Settlement of disputes or claims

38. Disputes or claims of a private law character shall be settled in accordance with the following provisions:

(a) The MFO shall make provisions for the appropriate modes of settlement of disputes or claims arising out of contract or other disputes or claims of a private law character to which the MFO is a party other than those covered in subparagraph (b) and paragraph 39 following. When no such provisions have been made with the contracting party, such claims shall be settled according to subparagraph (b) below.

(b) Any claim made by:

(i) a resident of the Receiving State against the MFO or a member thereof, in respect of any damages alleged to result from an act or omission of such member of the MFO relating to his official duties;

(ii) the Government of the Receiving State against a member of the MFO;

(iii) the MFO or the Government of the Receiving State against one another, that is not covered by paragraph 40 of this Appendix;

shall be settled by a Claims Commission established for that purpose. One member of the Commission shall be appointed by the Director-General, one member by the Government of the Receiving State, and a Chairman jointly by the two. If the Director-General and the Government of the Receiving State fail to agree on the appointment of a chairman, the two members selected by them shall select a chairman from the list of the Permanent Court of Arbitration. An award made by the Claims Commission against the MFO or a member or other employee thereof or against the Government of the Receiving State shall be notified to the Director-General or the authorities of the Receiving State as the case may be, to make satisfaction thereof.

39. Disputes concerning the terms of employment and conditions of service of locally recruited personnel shall be settled by administrative procedure to be established by the Director-General.

40. All disputes between the MFO and the Government of the Receiving State concerning the interpretation or application of this Appendix which are not settled by negotiation or other agreed mode of settlement shall be referred for final settlement to a tribunal of three arbitrators, one to be named by the Director-General, one by the Government of the Receiving State, and an umpire to be chosen jointly who shall preside over the proceedings of this tribunal.

41. If the two parties fail to agree on the appointment of the umpire within one month of the proposal of arbitration by one of the parties, the two members selected by them shall select a chairman from the list of the Permanent Court of Arbitration. Should a vacancy occur for any reason, the vacancy shall be filled within thirty days by the methods laid down in this paragraph for the original appointment. The tribunal shall come into existence upon the appointment of the chairman and at least one of the other members of the tribunal. Two members of the tribunal shall constitute a quorum for the performance of its functions, and for all deliberations and decisions of the tribunal a favorable vote of two members shall be sufficient.

Deceased members: disposition of personal property

42. The Director-General shall have the right to take charge of and dispose of the body of a member of the MFO who dies in the territory of the Receiving State and may dispose of his property after the debts of the deceased person incurred in the territory of the Receiving State and owing to residents of the Receiving State have been settled.

Supplemental arrangements

43. Supplemental details for the carrying out of this Appendix shall be made as required between the Director-General and appropriate authorities designated by the Government of the Receiving State.

Effective date and duration

44. This Appendix shall take effect from the date of the entry into force of the Protocol and shall remain in force for the duration of the Protocol. The provisions of paragraphs 38, 39, 40, and 41 of this Appendix, relating to the settlement of disputes, however, shall remain in force until all claims arising prior to the date of termination of this Appendix and submitted prior to or within three months following the date of termination, have been settled.

ASSISTANT SECRETARY VELIOTES, JULY 20, 1981

My purpose today is to begin the process of seeking congressional authorization for U.S. participation in and financial support for the multinational force and observers (MFO), which is being established in connection with the withdrawal of Israeli forces to the international border with Egypt, in keeping with the Treaty of Peace between them. On July 17 in London, representatives of Egypt and Israel, together with Ambassador Michael Sterner [Deputy Assistant Secretary for Near Eastern and South Asian Affairs] representing the United States, initialed the protocol and related documents which constitute the international agreement which establishes the MFO and determines its functions. The texts of the protocol and all related documents have been furnished to this committee. We have benefited, greatly, from your wise counsel during these months of negotiation.

It is important to U.S. interests in the Middle East that the MFO be established in as smooth a manner as possible and that it be enabled to carry out its functions as efficiently and effectively as possible. The establishment of this force represents the final step in the implementation of the Egyptian-Israeli treaty which, in turn, is the first step toward comprehensive peace in the Middle East. It is fair to say, therefore, that the documents we are discussing today represent the end of the beginning in our search for a just and lasting peace in that troubled region.

At the outset, the Treaty of Peace Between Egypt and Israel calls for the presence of a peacekeeping force and observers to monitor the parties' compliance with the terms of the treaty and to perform specified functions designed to enhance the mutual confidence of the parties. The treaty specifically mandates that the force should be under the direction of the U.N. Security Council.

In response to a formal request from the Permanent Representative of Egypt, however, the President of the Security Council on May 18 reported that the members of the Council were unable to reach the agreement necessary for the United Nations to provide a force and observers as envisioned in the treaty. This possibility had been foreseen and provided for during the treaty negotiations. In connection with the signing of the treaty, President Carter provided each party with a letter in which he assured them that, in the event the United Nations failed to provide a force, "the President will be prepared to take those steps necessary to ensure the establishment and maintenance of an acceptable alternative multinational force."

Pursuant to that assurance, a U.S. delegation led by Ambassador Sterner has participated over the past several months in negotiations with Egyptian and Israeli

APPENDIX A   125

delegations which have resulted in the agreement package which has been provided to the committee.

Financial Commitments

We have undertaken certain financial commitments, subject to congressional approval. Beginning in FY 1983, Egypt, Israel, and the United States will each provide one-third of the annual operating costs of the MFO, which we tentatively estimate will be approximately $35 million for each country. During the period prior to September 30, 1982, there will be unusual startup costs associated largely with necessary construction activities. We have undertaken, again subject to congressional authorization, to provide 60% of those costs, with Egypt and Israel dividing the remainder equally. Accordingly, the legislation we are submitting today, in addition to providing for the participation of U.S. personnel in the MFO, authorizes the appropriation of $125 million for our FY 1982 contribution.

We also intend to reprogram $10 million in FY 1981 from economic support fund assistance to the peacekeeping operations account to assist with the funding of initial activities necessary to prepare for the establishment of the MFO. Egypt and Israel are each making $20 million available immediately from their own resources for the same purpose.

We have agreed to contribute to the force an infantry battalion, a logistics support unit, and a group of civilian observers. The number of American personnel will be slightly more than 1,000, or a bit less than one-half of the total complement of the MFO, which may approach 2,500 persons.

The Administration intends to comply voluntarily with the reporting requirements of the war powers resolution concerning the introduction of U.S. Armed Forces equipped for combat into foreign countries.

The committee should also be aware that the United States has undertaken to propose to the parties a U.S. national to serve as Director-General of the MFO. In this connection, Egypt and Israel, on Friday, presented to Ambassador Sterner letters in which they appoint Mr. Leamon R. Hunt, a retired Foreign Service officer, to serve as interim Director-General.

Additional Actions

The United States has assured the parties that it will take certain additional actions as required and, as appropriate, subject to congressional authorization.

- In the event the parties are unable to agree on the appointment of the Director-General, the appointment of the force commander, or MFO financial matters, the United States will make proposals which the parties will accept.
- The United States will use its best efforts to find acceptable replacements for contingents that withdraw from the MFO.
- The United States will take steps necessary to insure the maintenance of an acceptable MFO.

Finally, let me say a word about troop contributions from other countries. Egypt and Israel have asked the United States to assume the primary role in approaching potential contributors. In this we have had encouraging success. It appears thus far that we will be able to count on one battalion from Latin America and another from Asia. However, our approaches constitute ongoing diplomatic discussions which, within the countries concerned, are considered politically sensitive. I, therefore, believe that that subject would best be addressed in closed session.

Conclusion

We will be consulting with Egypt and Israel concerning a mutually agreeable time for the protocol to be signed, an event at which the United States will act as witness as was the case with the Treaty of Peace. The agreement will then come into force when each party has notified the other that all its constitutional requirements have been fulfilled. In the meantime Mr. Hunt, as interim Director-General, is empowered by the parties to undertake construction activity in the Sinai and other activities necessary to assure that the MFO can be in place by March 20, 1982, as agreed.

The conclusion of this agreement represents a victory for creative diplomacy. It also reflects the determination of both Egypt and Israel to proceed with the strengthening of peace between them despite severe obstacles. Our own undertakings are nothing more than what should be expected of a nation that has been, and is pledged to remain, a full partner in their historic endeavor. It is in this light that I request this committee to lend its support to what is truly an essential cornerstone in the emerging structure of peace in the Middle East.

I would like to emphasize the urgency of the task before us. Much remains to be done before the MFO can be in place. All available FY 1981 funds will be obligated by September, and legislation is essential if the necessary preparations are to continue without interruption in October and be completed by next March. I know that you will carefully examine the joint resolution we have proposed. My colleagues and I are prepared to respond to your questions and to be of all possible assistance in your consideration of this important legislation. I hope that you will be able to conclude your deliberations as soon as possible and report the resolution favorably with a view to its early passage.

Public Law 97-132, Ninety-seventh Congress, authorizing U.S. participation in MFO, December 29, 1981

PUBLIC LAW 97–132—DECEMBER 29, 1981

Joint Resolution

To authorize the participation of the United States in a multinational force and observers to implement the Treaty of Peace between Egypt and Israel.

Whereas the Treaty of Peace between Egypt and Israel signed on March 26, 1979, calls for the supervision of security arrangements to be undertaken by United Nations Forces and Observers; and

Whereas the United Nations has been unable to assume those responsibilities at this time; and

Whereas a Protocol signed on August 3, 1981, by the Government of the Arab Republic of Egypt and the Government of the State of Israel provides for the creation of an alternative Multinational Force and Observers to implement the Treaty of Peace; and

Whereas the Government of the Arab Republic of Egypt and the Government of the State of Israel have requested that the United States participate in the Multinational Force and Observers: Now, therefore, be it

Resolved by the Senate and House of Representatives of the United States of America in Congress assembled,

SHORT TITLE

SECTION 1. This joint resolution may be cited as the "Multinational Force and Observers Participation Resolution".

STATEMENT OF POLICY

SEC. 2. The Congress considers the establishment of the Multinational Force and Observers to be an essential stage in the development of a comprehensive settlement in the Middle East. The Congress enacts this resolution with the hope and expectation that establishment of the Multinational Force and Observers will assist Egypt and Israel in fulfilling the Camp David accords and bringing about the establishment of a self-governing authority in order to provide full autonomy in the West Bank and Gaza.

PARTICIPATION OF UNITED STATES PERSONNEL IN THE MULTINATIONAL FORCE AND OBSERVERS

SEC. 3. (a)(1) Subject to the limitations contained in this resolution, the President is authorized to assign, under such terms and conditions as he may determine, members of the United States Armed Forces to participate in the Multinational Force and Observers.

(2) The Congress declares that the participation of the military personnel of other countries in the Multinational Force and Observers is essential to maintain the international character of the peacekeeping function in the Sinai. Accordingly—

(A) before the President assigns or details members of the United States Armed Forces to the Multinational Force and Observers, he shall notify the Congress of the names of the other countries that have agreed to provide military personnel for the Multinational Force and Observers, the number of military personnel to be provided by each country, and the functions to be performed by such personnel; and

(B) if a country withdraws from the Multinational Force and Observers with the result that the military personnel of less than four foreign countries remain, every possible effort must be made by the United States to find promptly a country to replace that country.

(3) Members of the United States Armed Forces, and United States civilian personnel, who are assigned, detailed, or otherwise provided to the Multinational Force and Observers may perform only those functions or responsibilities which are specified for United Nations Forces and Observers in the Treaty of Peace and in accordance with the Protocol.

(4) The number of members of the United States Armed Forces who are assigned or detailed by the United States Government to the Multinational Force and Observers may not exceed one thousand two hundred at any one time.

(b) Subject to the limitations contained in this resolution, the President is authorized to provide, under such terms and conditions as he may determine, United States civilian personnel to participate as observers in the Multinational Force and Observers.

(c) The status of United States Government personnel assigned to the Multinational Force and Observers under subsection (a)(1) or (b) of this section shall be as provided in section 629 of the Foreign Assistance Act of 1961.

UNITED STATES CONTRIBUTIONS TO COSTS

SEC. 4. (a) In accordance with the agreement set forth in the exchanges of letters between the United States and Egypt and between the United States and Israel which were signed on August 3, 1981, the United States share of the costs of the Multinational Force and Observers—

(1) shall not exceed 60 per centum of the budget for the expenses connected with the establishment and initial operation of the Multinational Force and Observers during the period ending September 30, 1982; and

(2) shall not exceed 33^1/$_3$ per centum of the budget for the annual operating expenses of the Multinational Force and Observers for each financial year beginning after that date.

(b)(1) There are authorized to be appropriated to the President to carry out chapter 6 of part II of the Foreign Assistance Act of 1961, in addition to amounts otherwise available to carry out that chapter, $125,000,000 for the fiscal year 1982 for use in paying the United States contribution to the budget of the Multinational Force and Observers. Amounts appropriated under this subsection are authorized to remain available until expended.

(2) Expenditures made pursuant to section 138 of the joint resolution entitled "Joint resolution making continuing appropriations for the fiscal year 1982, and for other purposes", approved October 1, 1981 (Public Law 97–51), or pursuant to any subsequent corresponding provision applicable to the fiscal year 1982, shall be charged to the appropriation authorized by this subsection.

(c) Unless required by law, reimbursements to the United States by the Multinational Force and Observers shall be on the basis of identifiable costs actually incurred as a result of requirements imposed by the Multinational Force and Observers, and shall not include administrative surcharges.

NONREIMBURSED COSTS

SEC. 5. (a) Any agency of the United States Government is authorized to provide administrative and technical support and services to the Multinational Force and Observers, without reimbursement and upon such terms and conditions as the President may direct, when the provision of such support or services would not result in significant incremental costs to the United States.

(b) The provision by the United States to the Multinational Force and Observers under the authority of this resolution or any other law of any property, support, or services, including the provision of military and civilian personnel under section 3 of this resolution, on other than a reimbursable basis shall be kept to a minimum.

(c) The President may provide military training to members of the armed forces of other countries participating in the Multinational Force and Observers.

REPORTS TO THE CONGRESS

SEC. 6. (a) Not later than April 30, 1982, the President shall transmit to the speaker of the House of Representatives, and to the chairman of the Committee on Foreign Relations of the Senate, a detailed written report with respect to the period ending two weeks prior to that date which contains the information specified in subsection (b).

(b) Not later than January 15 of each year (beginning in 1983), the President shall transmit to the Speaker of the House of Representatives, and to the chairman of the Committee on Foreign Relations of the Senate, a written report which describes—

(1) the activities performed by the Multinational Force and Observers during the preceding year;

(2) the composition of the Multinational Force and Observers, including a description of the responsibilities and deployment of the military personnel of each participating country;

(3) All costs incurred by the United States Government (including both normal and incremental costs), set forth by category, which are associated with the United States relationship with the Multinational Force and Observers and which were incurred during the preceding fiscal year (whether or not the United States was reimbursed for those costs), specifically including but not limited to—

   (A) the costs associated with the United States units and personnel participating in the Multinational Force and Observers (including salaries, allowances, retirement and other benefits, transportation, housing, and operating and maintenance costs), and

   (B) the identifiable costs relating to property, support, and services provided by the United States to the Multinational Force and Observers;

(4) the costs which the United States Government would have incurred in maintaining in the United States those United States units and personnel participating in the Multinational Force and Observers;

(5) amounts received by the United States Government from the Multinational Force and Observers as reimbursement;

(6) the types of property, support, or services provided to the Multinational Force and Observers by the United States Government, including identification of the types of property, support, or services provided on a nonreimbursable basis; and

(7) the results of any discussions with Egypt and Israel regarding the future of the Multinational Force and Observers and its possible reduction or elimination.

(c)(1) The reports required by this section shall be as detailed as possible.

(2) The information pursuant to subsection (b)(3) shall, in the case of costs which are not identifiable, be set forth with reasonable accuracy.

(3) The information with respect to any administrative and technical support and services provided on a nonreimbursed basis under section 5(a) of this resolution shall include a description of the types of support and services which have been provided and an estimate of both the total costs of such support and services and the incremental costs incurred by the United States with respect to such support and services.

STATEMENTS OF CONGRESSIONAL INTENT

SEC. 7. (a) Nothing in this resolution is intended to signify approval by the Congress of any agreement, understanding, or commitment made by the executive branch other than the agreement to participate in the Multinational Force and Observers as set forth in the exchanges of letters between the United States and Egypt and between the United States and Israel which were signed on August 3, 1981.

(b) The limitations contained in this resolution with respect to United States participation in the Multinational Force and Observers apply to the exercise of the authorities provided by this resolution or provided by any other provision of law. No funds appropriated by the Congress may be obligated or expended for any activity which is contrary to the limitations contained in this resolution.

(c) Nothing in this resolution shall affect the responsibilities of the President or the Congress under the War Powers Resolution (Public Law 93–148).

DEFINITIONS

SEC. 8. As used in this resolution—
(1) the term "Multinational Force and Observers" means the Multinational Force and Observers established in accordance with the Protocol between Egypt and Israel signed on August 3, 1981, relating to the implementation of the security arrangements of the Treaty of Peace; and
(2) the term "Treaty of Peace" means the Treaty of Peace between the Arab Republic of Egypt and the State of Israel signed on March 26, 1979, including the Annexes thereto.

Approved December 29, 1981.

The Deployment and Mission of U.S. Forces in the MFO: President Reagan's Letter to Congress, March 19, 1982

THE WHITE HOUSE,
Washington, March 19, 1982.

Hon. THOMAS P. O'NEILL , Jr.,
Speaker of the House of Representatives,
Washington, D.C.

DEAR MR. SPEAKER : On December 29, 1981, I signed into law Public Law 97–132, a Joint Resolution authorizing the participation of the United States in the Multinational Force and Observers (MFO) which will assist in the implementation of the 1979 Treaty of Peace between Egypt and Israel. The U.S. military personnel and equipment which the United States will contribute to the MFO are now in the process of deployment to the Sinai. In accordance with my desire that the Congress be fully informed on this matter, and consistent with Section 4(a)(2) of the War Powers Resolution, I am hereby providing a report on the deployment and mission of these members of the U.S. Armed Forces.

As you know, the 1979 Treaty of Peace between Egypt and Israel terminated the existing state of war between those countries, provided for the complete withdrawal from the Sinai of Israeli armed forces and civilians within three years after the date of the Treaty's entry into force (that is, by April 25, 1982), and provided for the establishment of normal friendly relations. To assist in assuring compliance with the terms of Annex I to the Treaty, so as to enhance the mutual confidence of the parties in the security of the Sinai border area, the Treaty calls for the establishment of a peacekeeping force and observers to be deployed prior to the final Israeli withdrawal. Although the Treaty called on the parties to request the United Nations to provide the peacekeeping force and observers, it was also recognized during the negotiations that it might not be possible to reach agreement in the United Nations for this purpose. For this reason, President Carter assured Israel and Egypt in separate letters that "if the Security Council fails to establish and maintain the arrangements called for in the Treaty, the President will be prepared to take those steps necessary to ensure the establishment and maintenance of an acceptable alternative multinational force."

In fact, it proved impossible to secure U.N. action. As a result, Egypt and Israel, with the participation of the United States, entered into negotiations for the creation of an alternative multinational force and observers. These negotiations resulted in the signing on August 3, 1981, by Egypt and Israel of a Protocol for that purpose. The Protocol established the MFO and provided in effect that the MFO would have the same functions and responsibilities as those provided in the 1979 Treaty for the planned U.N. force.

Included are: the operation of checkpoints, reconnaissance patrols, and observation posts; verification of the implementation of Annex I of the Peace Treaty; and ensuring freedom of navigation through the Strait of Tiran in accordance with Article V of the Peace Treaty. By means of an exchange of letters with Egypt and Israel dated August 3, 1981, the United States agreed, subject to Congressional authorization and appropriations, to contribute an infantry battalion, a logistics support unit and civilian observers to the MFO, as well as a specified portion of the annual costs of the MFO. The U.S. military personnel to be contributed comprise less than half of the anticipated total MFO military complement of approximately 2,500 personnel.

In Public Law 97–132, the Multinational Force and Observers Participation Resolution, Congress affirmed that it considered the establishment of the MFO to be an essential stage in the development of a comprehensive settlement in the Middle East. The President was authorized to assign, under such terms and conditions as he might determine, members of the United States Armed Forces to participate in the MFO, provided that these personnel perform only the functions and responsibilities specified in the 1979 Treaty and the 1981 Protocol, and that their number not exceed 1,200 at any one time.

In accordance with the 1981 Egypt-Israel Protocol, the MFO must be in place by 1300 hours on March 20, 1982, and will assume its functions at 1300 hours on April 25, 1982. Accordingly, the movement of U.S. personnel and equipment for deployment to the Sinai is currently underway. On February 26 five unarmed UH-1H helicopters (which will provide air transportation in the Sinai for MFO personnel), together with their crews and support personnel, arrived at Tel Aviv; on March 2 approximately 88 logistics personnel arrived at Tel Aviv; on March 17, the first infantry troops of the First Battalion, 505th Infantry, 82nd Airborne Division arrived in the Southern Sinai; and by March 18 a total of 808 infantry troops, together with their equipment, will have arrived. These troops will be equipped with standard light infantry weapons, including M-16 automatic rifles, M-60 machine guns, M203 grenade launchers and Dragon anti-tank missiles.

The duration of this involvement of U.S. forces in the Sinai will depend, of course, on the strengthening of mutual confidence between Egypt and Israel. The U.S. contribution to the MFO is not limited to any specific period; however, each country which contributes military forces to the MFO retains a right of withdrawal upon adequate prior notification to the MFO Director-General. U.S. participation in future years will, of course, be subject to the Congressional authorization and appropriations process.

I want to emphasize that there is no intention or expectation that these members of the U.S. Armed Forces will become involved in hostilities. Egypt and Israel are at peace, and we expect them to remain at peace. No hostilities are occurring in the area and we have no expectation of hostilities. MFO forces will carry combat equipment appropriate for their peacekeeping missions, to meet the expectations of the parties as reflected in the 1981 Protocol and related documents, and as a prudent precaution for the safety of MFO personnel.

The deployment of U.S. forces to the Sinai for this purpose is being undertaken pursuant to Public Law 97–132 of December 29, 1981, and pursuant to the President's constitutional authority with respect to the conduct of foreign relations and as Commander-in-Chief of U.S. Armed Forces.

Sincerely,

RONALD REAGAN.

Text of the European Community (EC) Communiqué on MFO Participation, London, November 23, 1981.

Statement by the Ten on the participation of member states in the Sinai peacekeeping force.

The Ten consider that the decision of France, Italy, the Netherlands and the United Kingdom to participate in the multinational Force in the Sinai meets the wish frequently expressed by the Members of the Community to facilitate any progress in the direction of a comprehensive peace settlement in the Middle East on the basis of the mutual acceptance of the right to existence and security of all the States in the area and the need for the Palestinian people to exercise fully its right to self-determination.

Israeli-American MFO Agreement [on European participation], December 3, 1981

The United States and Israel note the decision of the United Kingdom, France, Italy and the Netherlands to contribute to the Multinational Force and Observers [MFO], to be established in accordance with the treaty of peace between Egypt and Israel.

The United States and Israel reviewed the participation of these four countries in light of the following clarifications which they have provided to the United States on November 26, 1981:

— That they recognize that the function of the MFO is as defined in the relevant Egyptian-Israeli agreements, and includes that of insuring freedom of navigation through the Strait of Tiran in accordance with Article V of the treaty of peace, and

— That they have attached no political conditions, linked to Venice or otherwise, to their participation.

The United States and Israel understand that the participation of the four and any other participating state is based upon the following:

— The basis for participation in the MFO is the treaty of peace between Egypt and Israel originated in the Camp David accords and the protocol signed between Egypt and Israel and witnessed by the United States on August 3, 1981 based upon the letter from President Carter to President as-Sadat and Prime Minister Begin on March 26, 1979.

— All of the functions and responsibilities of the MFO and of its constituent elements, including any contingents that may be formed through European participation, are defined in the treaty of peace and the protocol, and there can be no derogation or reservation from any of them.

As provided in the protocol, all participants in the MFO undertake to conduct themselves in accordance with the terms of the protocol under the direction of the director general appointed by Egypt and Israel. The MFO shall employ its best efforts to prevent any violation of the terms of the treaty of peace. The functions of the MFO will specifically include the following in accordance with the treaty of peace and the protocol:

(A) Operation of checkpoints, reconnaissance patrols, and observation posts along the international boundary and Line B, within Zone C.

(B) Periodic verification of the implementation of the provisions of Annex 1 will be carried out not less than twice a month unless otherwise agreed by the parties.

(C) Additional verifications within 48 hours after the receipt of a request from either party.

(D) Insuring the freedom of navigation through the Strait of Tiran in accordance with Article V of the treaty of peace.

The United States understands and appreciates the concerns expressed by the government of Israel regarding the statements made by the four European contributors in explaining their decision to participate in the MFO to their own legislatures and publics. The United States recognizes that some positions set forth in the statement are at variance with its own positions with respect to the future of the peace process as well as with positions held by Israel as a party to the treaty of peace. The United States and Israel recognize that the positions held on any other aspects of the problems in the area by any state which agrees to participate in the MFO do not affect the obligation of that state to comply fully with the terms of the protocol which was negotiated in accordance with the letter from President Carter to President as-Sadat and Prime Minister Begin of March 26, 1979, and which is designed to help implement the treaty of peace, which was concluded pursuant to the Camp David accords.

The treaty of peace, in accordance with which the MFO is established, represents the first step in a process agreed on at Camp David whose ultimate goal is a just, comprehensive, and durable settlement of the Middle East conflict through the conclusion of peace treaties based on Security Council Resolutions 242 and 338. The United States and Israel reiterate their commitment to the Camp David accords as the only viable and ongoing negotiating process. They renew their determination to make early meaningful progress in the autonomy talks.

Egypt-Israel: Agreement on the Sinai and Suez Canal, Done at Geneva, September 4, 1975

AGREEMENT BETWEEN EGYPT AND ISRAEL

The Government of the Arab Republic of Egypt and the Government of Israel have agreed that:

Article I

The conflict between them and in the Middle East shall not be resolved by military force but by peaceful means.

The Agreement concluded by the parties 18 January 1974, within the framework of the Geneva Peace Conference, constituted a first step towards a just and durable peace according to the provisions of Security Council Resolution 338 of 22 October 1973.

They are determined to reach a final and just peace settlement by means of negotiations called for by Security Council Resolution 338, this Agreement being a significant step towards that end.

Article II

The parties hereby undertake not to resort to the threat or use of force or military blockage against each other.

Article III

The parties shall continue scrupulously to observe the cease-fire on land, sea and air and to refrain from all military or para-military actions against each other. The parties also confirm that the obligations contained in the annex and, when concluded, the Protocol shall be an integral part of this Agreement.

Article IV

A. The military forces of the parties shall be deployed in accordance with the following principles:

(1) All Israeli forces shall be deployed east of the lines designated as lines J and M on the attached map [not attached].

(2) All Egyptian forces shall be deployed west of the line designated as line E on the attached map.

(3) The area between the lines designated on the attached map as lines E and F and the area between the lines designated on the attached map as lines J and K shall be limited in armament and forces.

(4) The limitations on armament and forces in the areas described by paragraph (3) above shall be agreed as described in the attached annex.

(5) The zone between the lines designated on the attached map as lines E and J will be a buffer zone. In this zone the United Nations Emergency Force will continue to perform its functions as under the Egyptian-Israeli Agreement of 18 January 1974.

(6) In the area south from line E and west from line M, as defined on the attached map, there will be no military forces, as specified in the attached annex.

B. The details concerning the new lines, the redeployment of the forces and its timing, the limitation on armaments and forces, aerial reconnaissance, the operation of the early warning and surveillance installations and the use of the roads, the United Nations functions and other arrangements will all be in accordance with the provisions of the annex and map which are an integral part of this Agreement and of the protocol which is to result from negotiations pursuant to the annex and which, when concluded, shall become an integral part of this Agreement.

Article V

The United Nations Emergency Force is essential and shall continue its functions and its mandate shall be extended annually.

Article VI

The parties hereby establish a joint commission for the duration of this Agreement. It will function under the aegis of the chief co-ordinator of the United Nations peacekeeping missions in the Middle East in order to consider any problem arising from this Agreement and to assist the United Nations Emergency Force in the execution of its mandate. The joint commission shall function in accordance with procedures established in the Protocol.

Article VII

Non-military cargoes destined for or coming from Israel shall be permitted through the Suez Canal.

Article VIII

This Agreement is regarded by the parties as a significant step toward a just and lasting peace. It is not a final peace agreement.

The parties shall continue their efforts to negotiate a final peace agreement within the framework of the Geneva peace conference in accordance with Security Council Resolution 338.

Article IX

This Agreement shall enter into force upon signature of the Protocol and remain in force until superseded by a new agreement.

ANNEX TO THE EGYPT-ISRAEL AGREEMENT

Within five days after the signature of the Egypt-Israel Agreement, representatives of the two parties shall meet in the military working group of the Middle East peace conference at Geneva to begin preparation of a detailed Protocol for the implementation of the Agreement. The working group will complete the Protocol within two weeks. In order to facilitate preparation of the Protocol and implementation of the agreement, and to assist in maintaining the scrupulous observance of the cease-fire and other elements of the Agreement, the two parties have agreed on the following principles, which are an integral part of the Agreement, as guidelines for the working group.

1. Definitions of Lines and Areas

The deployment lines, areas of limited forces and armaments, buffer zones, the area south from line E and west from line M, other designated areas, road sections for common use and other features referred to in Article IV of the Agreement shall be as indicated on the attached map.

2. Buffer Zones

(A) Access to the buffer zones will be controlled by the United Nations Emergency Force, according to procedures to be worked out by the working group and the United Nations Emergency Force.

(B) Aircraft of either party will be permitted to fly freely up to the forward line of that party. Reconnaissance aircraft of either party may fly up to the middle line of the buffer zone between E and J on an agreed schedule.

(C) In the buffer zone, between lines E and J, there will be established under article IV of the Agreement an early warning system entrusted to United States civilian personnel as detailed in a separate proposal, which is a part of this Agreement.

(D) Authorized personnel shall have access to the buffer zone for transit to and from the early warning system; the manner in which this is carried out shall be worked out by the working group and the United Nations Emergency Force.

3. Area South of Line E and West of Line M

(A) In this area, the United Nations Emergency Force will assure that there are no military or para-military forces of any kind, military fortifications and military installations; it will establish checkpoints and have the freedom of movement necessary to perform this function.

(B) Egyptian civilians and third-country civilian oil field personnel shall have the right to enter, exit from, work and live in the above indicated area, except for buffer zones 2A, 2B and the United Nations posts. Egyptian civilian police shall be allowed in the area to perform normal civil police functions among the civilian population in such number and with such weapons and equipment as shall be provided for in the Protocol.

(C) Entry to and exit from the area, by land, by air or by sea, shall be only through United Nations Emergency Force checkpoints. The United Nations Emergency Force shall also establish checkpoints along the road, the dividing line and at either points, with the precise locations and number to be included in the Protocol.

(D) Access to the airspace and the coastal area shall be limited to unarmed Egyptian civilian vessels and unarmed civilian helicopters and transport planes involved in the civilian activities of the area as agreed by the working group.

(E) Israel undertakes to leave intact all currently existing civilian installations and infrastructures.

(F) Procedures for use of the common sections of the coastal road along the Gulf of Suez shall be determined by the working group and detailed in the Protocol.

4. Aerial Surveillance

There shall be a continuation of aerial reconnaissance missions by the United States over the areas covered by the Agreement (the area between lines F and K), following the same procedures already in practice. The missions will ordinarily be carried out at a frequency of one mission every 7–10 days, with either party or the United Nations Emergency Force empowered to request an earlier mission. The United States Government will make the mission results available expeditiously to Israel, Egypt and the chief co-ordinator of the United Nations peace-keeping missions in the Middle East.

5. Limitation of Forces and Armaments

(A) Within the areas of limited forces and armaments (the areas between lines J and K and lines E and F) the major limitations shall be as follows:

(1) Eight (8) standard infantry battalions.

(2) Seventy-five (75) tanks.

(3) Seventy-two (72) artillery pieces, including heavy mortars (i.e. with caliber larger than 120 mm), whose range shall not exceed twelve (12) km.

(4) The total number of personnel shall not exceed eight thousand (8,000).

(5) Both parties agree not to station or locate in the area weapons which can reach the line of the other side.

(6) Both parties agree that in the areas between line A (of the disengagement agreement of 18 January 1974) and line E they will construct no new fortifications or installations for forces of a size greater than that agreed herein.

(B) The major limitations beyond the areas of limited forces and armament will be:

(1) Neither side will station nor locate any weapon in areas from which they can reach the other line.

APPENDIX A   137

(2) The parties will not place anti-aircraft missiles within an area of ten (10) kilometres east of line K and west of line F, respectively.

(C) The United Nations Emergency Force will conduct inspections in order to ensure the maintenance of the agreed limitations within these areas.

6. Process of Implementation

The detailed implementation and timing of the redeployment of forces, turnover of oil fields, and other arrangements called for by the Agreement, Annex and Protocol shall be determined by the working group, which will agree on the stages of this process, including the phased movement of Egyptian troops to line E and Israeli troops to line J. The first phase will be the transfer of the oil fields and installations to Egypt. This process will begin within two weeks from the signature of the Protocol with the introduction of the necessary technicians, and it will be completed no later than eight weeks after it begins. The details of the phasing will be worked out in the military working group.

Implementation of the redeployment shall be completed within five months after signature of the Protocol.

Proposal

In connexion with the early warning system referred to in Article IV of the Agreement between Egypt and Israel concluded on this date and as an integral part of that Agreement (hereafter referred to as the basic Agreement), the United States proposes the following:

1. The early warning system to be established in accordance with Article IV in the area shown on the map attached to the basic Agreement will be entrusted to the United States. It shall have the following elements:

A. There shall be two surveillance stations to provide strategic early warning, one operated by Egyptian and one operated by Israeli personnel. Their locations are shown on the map attached to the basic Agreement. Each station shall be manned by not more than 250 technical and administrative personnel. They shall perform the functions of visual and electronic surveillance only within their stations.

B. In support of these stations, to provide tactical early warning and to verify access to them, three watch stations shall be established by the United States in the Mitla and Giddi Passes as will be shown on the map attached to the basic Agreement. These stations shall be operated by United States civilian personnel. In support of these stations, there shall be established three unmanned electronic sensor fields at both ends of each Pass and in the general vicinity of each station and the roads leading to and from those stations.

2. The United States civilian personnel shall perform the following duties in connexion with the operation and maintenance of these stations.

A. At the two surveillance stations described in paragraph 1 A. above, United States civilian personnel will verify the nature of the operations of the stations and all movement into and out of each station and will immediately report any detected divergency from its authorized role of visual and electronic surveillance to the parties to the basic Agreement and to the United Nations Emergency Force.

B. At each watch station described in paragraph 1 B. above, the United States civilian personnel will immediately report to the parties to the basic Agreement and to the United Nations Emergency Force any movement of armed forces, other than the

United Nations Emergency Force, into either Pass and any observed preparations for such movement.

C. The total number of United States civilian personnel assigned to functions under this proposal shall not exceed 200. Only civilian personnel shall be assigned to functions under this proposal.

3. No arms shall be maintained at the stations and other facilities covered by this proposal, except for small arms required for their protection.

4. The United States personnel serving the early warning system shall be allowed to move freely within the area of the system.

5. The United States and its personnel shall be entitled to have such support facilities as are reasonably necessary to perform their functions.

6. The United States personnel shall be immune from local criminal, civil, tax and customs jurisdiction and may be accorded any other specific privileges and immunities provided for in the United Nations Emergency Force Agreement of 13 February 1957.

7. The United States affirms that it will continue to perform the functions described above for the duration of the basic Agreement.

8. Notwithstanding any other provision of this proposal, the United States may withdraw its personnel only if it concludes that their safety is jeopardized or that continuation of their role is no longer necessary. In the latter case the parties to the basic Agreement will be informed in advance in order to give them the opportunity to make alternative arrangements. If both parties to the basic Agreement request the United States to conclude its role under this proposal, the United States will consider such requests conclusive.

9. Technical problems including the location of the watch stations will be worked out through consultation with the United States.

HENRY A. KISSINGER
Secretary of State

APPENDIX B

Documents Relating to Peacekeeping in Lebanon

The following is the text of the letter from Fouad Boutros, deputy prime minister and minister of foreign affairs of Lebanon, to U.S. Ambassador Robert Dillon, whose reply also appears below.

Deputy Prime Minister Boutros' Letter

September 25, 1982

Your Excellency:

I have the honor to refer to the urgent discussions between representatives of our two Governments concerning the recent tragic events which have occurred in the Beirut area, and to consultations between my Government and the Secretary General of the United Nations pursuant to United Nations Security Council Resolution 521. On behalf of the Republic of Lebanon, I wish to inform your Excellency's Government of the determination of the Government of Lebanon to restore its sovereignty and authority over the Beirut area and thereby to assure the safety of persons in the area and bring an end to violence that has recurred. To this end, Israeli forces will withdraw from the Beirut area.

In its consultations with the Secretary General, the Government of Lebanon has noted that the urgency of the situation requires immediate action, and the Government of Lebanon, therefore, is, in conformity with the objectives in U.N. Security Council Resolution 521, proposing to several nations that they contribute forces to serve as a temporary Multinational Force (MNF) in the Beirut area. The mandate of the MNF will be to provide an interposition force at agreed locations and thereby provide the multinational presence requested by the Lebanese Government to assist it and the Lebanese Armed Forces (LAF) in the Beirut area. This presence will facilitate the restoration of Lebanese Government sovereignty and authority over the Beirut area, and thereby further efforts of my Government to assure the safety of persons in the area and bring to an end the violence which has tragically recurred. The MNF may undertake other functions only by mutual agreement.

In the foregoing context, I have the honor to propose that the United States of America deploy a force of approximately 1200 personnel to Beirut, subject to the following terms and conditions:

- The American military force shall carry out appropriate activities consistent with the mandate of the MNF.
- Command authority over the American force will be exercised exclusively by the United States Government through existing American military channels.
- The LAF and MNF will form a Liaison and Coordination Committee, composed of representatives of the MNF participating governments and chaired by the representatives of my Government. The Liaison and Coordination Committee will have two essential components: (A) Supervisory liaison; and (B) Military and technical liaison and coordination.
- The American force will operate in close coordination with the LAF. To assure effective coordination with the LAF, the American force will assign liaison officers to the LAF and the Government of Lebanon will assign liaison officers to the American force. The LAF liaison officers to the American force will, inter alia, perform liaison with the civilian population and with the U.N. observers and manifest the authority of the Lebanese Government in all appropriate situations. The American force will provide security for LAF personnel operating with the U.S. contingent.
- In carrying out its mission, the American force will not engage in combat. It may, however, exercise the right of self-defense.
- It is understood that the presence of the American force will be needed only for a limited period to meet the urgent requirements posed by the current situation. The MNF contributors and the Government of Lebanon will consult fully concerning the duration of the MNF presence. Arrangement for the departure of the MNF will be the subject of special consultations between the Government of Lebanon and the MNF participating governments. The American force will depart Lebanon upon any request of the Government of Lebanon or upon the decision of the President of the United States.
- The Government of Lebanon and the LAF will take all measures necessary to ensure the protection of the American force's personnel, to include securing assurances from all armed elements not now under the authority of the Lebanese Government that they will refrain from hostilities and not interfere with any activities of the MNF.
- The American force will enjoy both the degree of freedom of movement and the right to undertake those activities deemed necessary for the performance of its mission for the support of its personnel. Accordingly, it shall enjoy the privileges and immunities accorded the administrative and technical staff of the American Embassy in Beirut, and shall be exempt from immigration and customs requirements, and restrictions on entering or departing Lebanon. Personnel, property and equipment of the American force introduced into Lebanon shall be exempt from any form of tax, duty, charge or levy.

I have the further honor to propose, if the foregoing is acceptable to your Excellency's government, that your Excellency's reply to that effect, together with this note, shall constitute an agreement between our two Governments.

Please accept, Your Excellency, the assurances of my highest consideration.

[Fouad Boutros]
Deputy Prime Minister/
Minister of Foreign Affairs

APPENDIX B   141

Ambassador Dillon's Letter

September 25, 1982

Your Excellency:

I have the honor to refer to your Excellency's note of 25 September 1982 requesting the deployment of an American Force to the Beirut area. I am pleased to inform you on behalf of my Government that the United States is prepared to deploy temporarily a force of approximately 1200 personnel as part of a Multinational Force (MNF) to establish an environment which will permit the Lebanese armed forces (LAF) to carry out their responsibilities in the Beirut area. It is understood that the presence of such an American force will facilitate the restoration of Lebanese Government sovereignty and authority over the Beirut area, an objective which is fully shared by my Government, and thereby further efforts of the Government of Lebanon to assure the safety of persons in the area and bring to an end the violence which has tragically recurred.

I have the further honor to inform you that my Government accepts the terms and conditions concerning the presence of the American force in the Beirut area as set forth in your note, and that Your Excellency's note and this reply accordingly constitute an agreement between our two Governments.

[Robert Dillon]
United States Ambassador

War Powers Resolution and U.S. Troops in Lebanon

MESSAGE TO THE CONGRESS, September 29, 1982

On September 20, 1982, the Government of Lebanon requested the Governments of France, Italy, and the United States to contribute forces to serve as a temporary Multinational Force, the presence of which will facilitate the restoration of Lebanese Government sovereignty and authority, and thereby further the efforts of the Government of Lebanon to assure the safety of persons in the area and bring to an end the violence which has tragically recurred.

In response to this request, I have authorized the Armed Forces of the United States to participate in this Multinational Force. In accordance with my desire that the Congress be fully informed on this matter, and consistent with the War Powers Resolution, I am hereby providing a report on the deployment and mission of these members of the United States armed forces.

On September 29, approximately 1200 Marines of a Marine Amphibious Unit began to arrive in Beirut. Their mission is to provide an interposition force at agreed locations and thereby provide the multinational presence requested by the Lebanese Government to assist it and the Lebanese Armed Forces. In carrying out this mission, the American force will not engage in combat. It may, however, exercise the right of self-defense and will be equipped accordingly. These forces will operate in close coordination with the Lebanese Armed Forces, as well as with comparably sized French and Italian military contingents in the Multinational Force. Although it is not possible at this time to predict the precise duration of the presence of U.S. forces in Beirut, our agreement with the Government of Lebanon makes clear that they will be needed only for a limited period to meet the urgent requirements posed by the current situation.

I want to emphasize that, as was the case of the deployment of U.S. forces to Lebanon in August as part of the earlier multinational force, there is no intention or expectation that U.S. Armed Forces will become involved in hostilities. They are in Lebanon at the formal request of the Government of Lebanon, and our agreement with the Government of Lebanon expressly rules out any combat responsibilities for the U.S. forces. All armed elements in the area have given assurances that they will refrain from hostilities and will not interfere with the activities of the Multinational Force. Although isolated acts of violence can never be ruled out, all appropriate precautions have been taken to ensure the safety of U.S. military personnel during their temporary deployment in Lebanon.

This deployment of the United States Armed Forces is being undertaken pursuant to the President's constitutional authority with respect to the conduct of foreign relations and as Commander-in-Chief of the United States Armed Forces.

I believe that this step will support the objective of helping to restore the territorial integrity, sovereignty, and political independence of Lebanon. It is part of the continuing efforts of the United States Government to bring lasting peace to the troubled country, which has too long endured the trials of civil strife and armed conflict.

Sincerely,

RONALD REAGAN

Israel-Lebanon: Agreement on Withdrawal of Troops from Lebanon, Done at Kiryat Shemona and Khaldeh, May 17, 1983

AGREEMENT BETWEEN
THE GOVERNMENT OF THE STATE OF ISRAEL AND
THE GOVERNMENT OF THE REPUBLIC OF LEBANON

The Government of the State of Israel and the Government of the Republic of Lebanon:

Bearing in mind the importance of maintaining and strengthening international peace based on freedom, equality, justice, and respect for fundamental human rights;

Reaffirming their faith in the aims and principles of the Charter of the United Nations and recognizing their right and obligation to live in peace with each other as well as with all states, within secure and recognized boundaries;

Having agreed to declare the termination of the state of war between them;

Desiring to ensure lasting security for both their States and to avoid threats and the use of force between them;

Desiring to establish their mutual relations in the manner provided for in this Agreement;

Having delegated their undersigned representative plenipotentiaries, provided with full powers, in order to sign, in the presence of the representative of the United States of America, this Agreement;

Have agreed to the following provisions:

Article 1

1. The Parties agree and undertake to respect the sovereignty, political independence and territorial integrity of each other. They consider the existing international boundary between Israel and Lebanon inviolable.
2. The Parties confirm that the state of war between Israel and Lebanon has been terminated and no longer exists.
3. Taking into account the provisions of paragraphs 1 and 2, Israel undertakes to withdraw all its armed forces from Lebanon in accordance with the Annex of the present Agreement.

Article 2

The Parties, being guided by the principles of the Charter of the United Nations and of international law, undertake to settle their disputes by peaceful means in such a manner as to promote international peace and security, and justice.

Article 3

In order to provide maximum security for Israel and Lebanon, the Parties agree to establish and implement security arrangements, including the creation of a Security Region, as provided for in the Annex of the present Agreement.

Article 4

1. The territory of each Party will not be used as a base for hostile or terrorist activity against the other Party, its territory, or its people.
2. Each Party will prevent the existence or organization of irregular forces, armed bands, organizations, bases, offices or infrastructure, the aims and purposes of which include incursions or any act of terrorism into the territory of the other Party, or any other activity aimed at threatening or endangering the security of the other Party and safety of its people. To this end all agreements and arrangements enabling the presence and functioning on the territory of either Party of elements hostile to the other Party are null and void.
3. Without prejudice to the inherent right of self-defense in accordance with international law, each Party will refrain:
   a. from organizing, instigating, assisting, or participating in threats or acts of belligerency, subversion, or incitement or any aggression directed against the other Party, its population or property, both within its territory and originating therefrom, or in the territory of the other Party.
   b. from using the territory of the other Party for conducting a military attack against the territory of a third state.
   c. from intervening in the internal or external affairs of the other Party.

4. Each Party undertakes to ensure that preventive action and due proceedings will be taken against persons or organizations perpetrating acts in violation of this Article.

Article 5

Consistent with the termination of the state of war and within the framework of their constitutional provisions, the Parties will abstain from any form of hostile propaganda against each other.

Article 6

Each Party will prevent entry into, deployment in, or passage through its territory, its air space and, subject to the right of innocent passage in accordance with international law, its territorial sea, by military forces, armament, or military equipment of any state hostile to the other Party.

Article 7

Except as provided in the present Agreement, nothing will preclude the deployment on Lebanese territory of international forces requested and accepted by the Government of Lebanon to assist in maintaining its authority. New contributors to such forces shall be selected from among states having diplomatic relations with both Parties to the present Agreement.

Article 8

1. a. Upon entry into force of the present Agreement, a Joint Liaison Committee will be established by the Parties, in which the United States of America will be a participant, and will commence its functions. This Committee will be entrusted with the supervision of the implementation of all areas covered by the present Agreement. In matters involving security arrangements, it will deal with unresolved problems referred to it by the Security Arrangements Committee established in subparagraph c. below. Decisions of this Committee will be taken unanimously.
   b. The Joint Liaison Committee will address itself on a continuing basis to the development of mutual relations between Israel and Lebanon, *inter alia* the regulation of the movement of goods, products and persons, communications, etc.
   c. Within the framework of the Joint Liaison Committee, there will be a Security Arrangements Committee whose composition and functions are defined in the Annex of the present Agreement.
   d. Subcommittees of the Joint Liaison Committee may be established as the need arises.
   e. The Joint Liaison Committee will meet in Israel and Lebanon, alternately.
   f. Each Party, if it so desires and unless there is an agreed change of status, may maintain a liaison office on the territory of the other Party in order to carry out the above-mentioned functions within the framework of the Joint Liaison Committee and to assist in the implementation of the present Agreement.

g. The members of the Joint Liaison Committee from each of the Parties will be headed by a senior government official.
h. All other matters relating to these liaison offices, their personnel, and the personnel of each Party present in the territory of the other Party in connection with the implementation of the present Agreement will be the subject of a protocol to be concluded between the Parties in the Joint Liaison Committee. Pending the conclusion of this protocol, the liaison offices and the above-mentioned personnel will be treated in accordance with the pertinent provisions of the Convention on Special Missions of December 8, 1969, including those provisions concerning privileges and immunities. The foregoing is without prejudice to the positions of the Parties concerning that Convention.
2. During the six-month period after the withdrawal of all Israeli armed forces from Lebanon in accordance with Article 1 of the present Agreement and the simultaneous restoration of Lebanese governmental authority along the international boundary between Israel and Lebanon, and in the light of the termination of the state of war, the Parties shall initiate, within the Joint Liaison Committee, *bona fide* negotiations in order to conclude agreements on the movement of goods, products and persons and their implementation on a non-discriminatory basis.

Article 9

1. Each of the two Parties will take, within a time limit of one year as of entry into force of the present Agreement, all measures necessary for the abrogation of treaties, laws and regulations deemed in conflict with the present Agreement, subject to and in conformity with its constitutional procedures.
2. The Parties undertake not to apply existing obligations, enter into any obligations, or adopt laws or regulations in conflict with the present Agreement.

Article 10

1. The present Agreement shall be ratified by both Parties in conformity with their respective constitutional procedures. It shall enter into force on the exchange of the instruments of ratification and shall supersede the previous agreements between Israel and Lebanon.
2. The Annex, the Appendix and the Map attached thereto, and the Agreed Minutes to the present Agreement shall be considered integral parts thereof.
3. The present Agreement may be modified, amended, or superseded by mutual agreement of the Parties.

Article 11

1. Disputes between the Parties arising out of the interpretation or application of the present Agreement will be settled by negotiation in the Joint Liaison Committee. Any dispute of this character not so resolved shall be submitted to conciliation and, if unresolved, thereafter to an agreed procedure for a definitive resolution.
2. Notwithstanding the provisions of paragraph 1, disputes arising out of the interpretation or application of the Annex shall be resolved in the framework of the

Security Arrangements Committee and, if unresolved, shall thereafter, at the request of either Party, be referred to the Joint Liaison Committee for resolution through negotiation.

Article 12

The present Agreement shall be communicated to the Secretariat of the United Nations for registration in conformity with the provisions of Article 102 of the Charter of the United Nations.

Done at Kiryat Shemona and Khaldeh this seventeenth day of May, 1983, in triplicate in four authentic texts in the Hebrew, Arabic, English and French languages. In case of any divergence of interpretation, the English and French texts will be equally authoritative.

ANNEX
SECURITY ARRANGEMENTS

1. *Security Region*
   a. A Security Region in which the Government of Lebanon undertakes to implement the security arrangements agreed upon in this Annex is hereby established.
   b. The Security Region is bounded, as delineated on the Map attached to this Annex [map not attached], in the north by a line constituting "Line A", and in the south and east by the Lebanese international boundary.
2. *Security Arrangements*
   The Lebanese authorities will enforce special security measures aimed at detecting and preventing hostile activities as well as the introduction into or movement through the Security Region of unauthorized armed men or military equipment. The following security arrangements will apply equally throughout the Security Region except as noted:
   a. The Lebanese Army, Lebanese Police, Lebanese Internal Security Forces, and the Lebanese auxiliary forces (Ansar), organized under the full authority of the Government of Lebanon, are the only organized armed forces and elements permitted in the Security Region except as designated elsewhere in this Annex. The Security Arrangements Committee may approve the stationing in the Security Region of other official Lebanese armed elements similar to Ansar.
   b. Lebanese Police, Lebanese Internal Security Forces, and Ansar may be stationed in the Security Region without restrictions as to their numbers. These forces and elements will be equipped only with personal and light automatic weapons and, for the Internal Security Forces, armored scout or commando cars as listed in the Appendix.
   c. Two Lebanese Army brigades may be stationed in the Security Region. One will be the Lebanese Army Territorial Brigade stationed in the area extending from the Israeli-Lebanese boundary to "Line B" delineated on the attached Map. The other will be a regular Lebanese Army brigade stationed in the area extending from "Line B" to "Line A". These brigades may carry their organic weapons and equipment listed in the Appendix. Additional units equipped in accordance with the Appendix may be deployed in the Security Region for training purposes, including the training of conscripts, or, in the case of operational emergency situations, following

coordination in accordance with procedures to be established by the Security Arrangements Committee.
   d. The existing local units will be integrated as such into the Lebanese Army, in conformity with Lebanese Army regulations. The existing local civil guard shall be integrated into Ansar and accorded a proper status under Lebanese law to enable it to continue guarding the villages in the Security Region. The process of extending Lebanese authority over these units and civil guard, under the supervision of the Security Arrangements Committee, shall start immediately after the entry into force of the present Agreement and shall terminate prior to the completion of the Israeli withdrawal from Lebanon.
   e. Within the Security Region, Lebanese army units may maintain their organic anti-aircraft weapons as specified in the Appendix. Outside the Security Region, Lebanon may deploy personal, low, and medium altitude air defense missiles. After a period of three years from the date of entry into force of the present Agreement, the provision concerning the area outside the Security Region may be reviewed by the Security Arrangements Committee at the request of either Party.
   f. Military electronic equipment in the Security Region will be as specified in the Appendix. Deployment of ground radars within ten kilometers of the Israeli-Lebanese boundary should be approved by the Security Arrangements Committee. Ground radars throughout the Security Region will be deployed so that their sector of search does not cross the Israeli-Lebanese boundary. This provision does not apply to civil aviation or air traffic control radars.
   g. The provision mentioned in paragraph e. applies also to anti-aircraft missiles on Lebanese Navy vessels. In the Security Region, Lebanon may deploy naval elements and establish and maintain naval bases or other shore installations required to accomplish the naval mission. The coastal installations in the Security Region will be as specified in the Appendix.
   h. In order to avoid accidents due to misidentification, the Lebanese military authorities will give advance notice of all flights of any kind over the Security Region according to procedures to be determined by the Security Arrangements Committee. Approval of these flights is not required.
   i. (1) The forces, weapons and military equipment which may be stationed, stocked, introduced into, or transported through the Security Region are only those mentioned in this Annex and its Appendix.
      (2) No infrastructure, auxiliary installations, or equipment capable of assisting the activation of weapons that are not permitted by this Annex or its Appendix shall be maintained or established in the Security Region.
      (3) These provisions also apply whenever a clause of this Annex relates to areas outside the Security Region.
3. *Security Arrangements Committee*
   a. Within the framework of the Joint Liaison Committee, a Security Arrangements Committee will be established.
   b. The Security Arrangements Committee will be composed of an equal number of Israeli and Lebanese representatives, headed by senior officers. A representative of the United States of America will participate in meetings of the Committee at the request of either Party. Decisions of the Security Arrangements Committee will be reached by agreement of the Parties.
   c. The Security Arrangements Committee shall supervise the implementation of the security arrangements in the present Agreement and this Annex and the timetable and modalities, as well as all other aspects relating to withdrawals described in the

present Agreement and this Annex. To this end, and by agreement of the Parties, it will:
   (1) Supervise the implementation of the undertakings of the Parties under the present Agreement and this Annex.
   (2) Establish and operate Joint Supervisory Teams as detailed below.
   (3) Address and seek to resolve any problems arising out of the implementation of the security arrangements in the present Agreement and this Annex and discuss any violation reported by the Joint Supervisory Teams or any complaint concerning a violation submitted by one of the Parties.
d. The Security Arrangements Committee shall deal with any complaint submitted to it not later than 24 hours after submission.
e. Meetings of the Security Arrangements Committee shall be held at least once every two weeks in Israel and in Lebanon, alternately. In the event that either Party requests a special meeting, it will be convened within 24 hours. The first meeting will be held within 48 hours after the date of entry into force of the present Agreement.
f. *Joint Supervisory Teams*
   (1) The Security Arrangements Committee will establish Joint Supervisory Teams (Israel-Lebanon) subordinate to it and composed of an equal number of representatives from each Party.
   (2) The teams will conduct regular verification of the implementation of the provisions of the security arrangements in the Agreement and this Annex. The teams shall report immediately any confirmed violations to the Security Arrangements Committee and ascertain that violations have been rectified.
   (3) The Security Arrangements Committee shall assign a Joint Supervisory Team, when requested, to check border security arrangements on the Israeli side of the international boundary in accord with Article 4 of the present Agreement.
   (4) The teams will enjoy freedom of movement in the air, sea, and land as necessary for the performance of their tasks within the Security Region.
   (5) The Security Arrangements Committee will determine all administrative and technical arrangements concerning the functioning of the teams including their working procedures, their number, their manning, their armament, and their equipment.
   (6) Upon submission of a report to the Security Arrangements Committee or upon confirmation of a complaint of either Party by the teams, the respective Party shall immediately, and in any case not later than 24 hours from the report or the confirmation, rectify the violation. The Party shall immediately notify the Security Arrangements Committee of the rectification. Upon receiving the notification, the teams will ascertain that the violation has been rectified.
   (7) The Joint Supervisory Teams shall be subject to termination upon 90 days notice by either Party given at any time after two years from the date of entry into force of the present Agreement. Alternative verification arrangements shall be established in advance of such termination through the Joint Liaison Committee. Notwithstanding the foregoing, the Joint Liaison Committee may determine at any time that there is no further need for such arrangements.
g. The Security Arrangements Committee will ensure that practical and rapid contacts between the two parties are established along the boundary to prevent incidents and facilitate coordination between the forces on the terrain.

APPENDIX B   149

4. It is understood that the Government of Lebanon may request appropriate action in the United Nations Security Council for one unit of the United Nations Interim Force in Lebanon (UNIFIL) to be stationed in the Sidon area. The presence of this unit will lend support to the Government of Lebanon and the Lebanese Armed Forces in asserting governmental authority and protection in the Palestinian refugee camp areas. For a period of 12 months, the unit in the Sidon area may send teams to the Palestinian refugee camp areas in the vicinity of Sidon and Tyre to surveil and observe, if requested by the Government of Lebanon, following notification to the Security Arrangements Committee. Police and security functions shall remain the sole responsibility of the Government of Lebanon, which shall ensure that the provisions of the present Agreement shall be fully implemented in these areas.
5. Three months after completion of the withdrawal of all Israeli forces from Lebanon, the Security Arrangements Committee will conduct a full-scale review of the adequacy of the security arrangements delineated in this Annex in order to improve them.
6. *Withdrawal of Israeli Forces*
    a. Within 8 to 12 weeks of the entry into force of the present Agreement, all Israeli forces will have been withdrawn from Lebanon. This is consistent with the objective of Lebanon that all external forces withdraw from Lebanon.
    b. The Israel Defense Forces and the Lebanese Armed Forces will maintain continuous liaison during the withdrawal and will exchange all necessary information through the Security Arrangements Committee. The Israel Defense Forces and the Lebanese Armed Forces will cooperate during the withdrawal in order to facilitate the reassertion of the authority of the Government of Lebanon as the Israeli armed forces withdraw.

APPENDIX

In accordance with the provisions of the Annex, the Lebanese Armed Forces may carry, introduce, station, stock, or transport through the Security Region all weapons and equipment organic to each standard Lebanese Armed Forces brigade. Individual and crew-served weapons, including light automatic weapons normally found in a mechanized infantry unit, are not prohibited by this Appendix.

1. Weapon systems listed below presently organic to each brigade in the Security Region are authorized in the numbers shown:

Tanks
—40 tanks
—4 medium tracked recovery vehicles
Armored Cars
—10 AML-90/Saladin/etc.
Armored Personnel Carriers
—127 M113A1/VCC-L, plus 44 M113 family vehicles
Artillery/Mortars
—18 155MM towed howitzers (also 105MM/122MM)
—12 120MM mortars
—27 81MM mortars (mounted on M-125 tracked mortar carriers)
Anti-tank Weapons
—112 RPG
—30 anti-tank weapons (106MM recoilless rifle/TOW/MILAN)

Air Defense Weapons
—12 40MM or less guns (not radar-guided)

2. Brigade Communications Equipment:
—482 AN/GRC-160
—74 AN/VRC-46
—16 AN/VRC-47
—9 AN/VRC-49
—43 GRA-39
—539 TA-312
—27 SB-22
—8 SB-993
—4 AN/GRC-106

3. Brigade Surveillance Equipment:
—Mortar locating radars
—Artillery locating radars
—Ground surveillance radars
—Night observation devices
—Unattended ground sensors

4. In accordance with the provisions of the Annex, armored vehicles for the Internal Security Forces will be as follows:
—24 armored wheeled vehicles with guns up to 40mm

5. In accordance with the provisions of the Annex, there will be no limitations on the coastal installations in the Security Region, except on the following four categories:

—Coastal sea surveillance radars:	5
—Coastal defense guns:	15 40mm or less
—Coastal air defense guns:	15 40mm or less (not radar-guided)
—Shore-to-sea missiles:	None

6. The Lebanese Army Infantry Brigade and Territorial Brigade in the Security Region are each organized as follows:

1 Brigade headquarters and headquarters company	Off.: 14	Enl.: 173
3 infantry battalions	Off.: 31 ea.	Enl.: 654 ea.
1 artillery battalion	Off.: 39	Enl.: 672
1 tank battalion	Off.: 37	Enl.: 579
3 tank companies		
1 reconnaissance company		
1 logistics battalion	Off.: 26	Enl.: 344
1 engineer company	Off.: 6	Enl.: 125
1 anti-tank company	Off.: 4	Enl.: 117

APPENDIX B 151

AGREED MINUTES

Art. 4.4	Lebanon affirms that Lebanese law includes all measures necessary to ensure implementation of this paragraph.
Art. 6	Without prejudice to the provisions of the Annex regarding the Security Region, it is agreed that non-combat military aircraft of a foreign state on non-military missions shall not be considered military equipment.
Art. 6	It is agreed that, in the event of disagreement as to whether a particular state is "hostile" for purposes of Article 6 of the Agreement, the prohibitions of Article 6 shall be applied to any state which does not maintain diplomatic relations with both Parties.
Art. 8.1.b	It is agreed that, at the request of either Party, the Joint Liaison Committee shall begin to examine the question of claims by citizens of either Party on properties in the territory of the other Party.
Art. 8.1.h	It is understood that each Party will certify to the other if one of its personnel was on official duty or performing official functions at any given time.
Art. 8.2	It is agreed that the negotiations will be concluded as soon as possible.
Art. 9	It is understood that this provision shall apply *mutatis mutandis* to agreements concluded by the Parties pursuant to Article 8, paragraph 2.
Art. 11	It is agreed that both parties will request the United States of America to promote the expeditious resolution of disputes arising out of the interpretation or application of the present Agreement.
Art. 11	It is agreed that the phrase "an agreed procedure for a definitive resolution" means an agreed third-party mechanism which will produce a resolution of the dispute which is binding on the Parties.
ANNEX PARA 1.b	It is agreed that, in that portion of Jabal Baruk shown on the map attachment to the Annex, only civilian telecommunications installations, such as television facilities and radars for air traffic control purposes, may be emplaced. The restrictions on weapons and military equipment that are detailed in the Appendix to the Annex will also apply in that area.
ANNEX PARA 2.d	The Government of Lebanon affirms its decision that the Territorial Brigade established on April 6, 1983, mentioned in subparagraph c, will encompass the existing local units which had been formed into a near brigade-sized unit, along with Lebanese Army personnel from among the inhabitants of the Security Region, in conformity with Lebanese Army regulations. This brigade will be in charge of security in the area extending from the Israeli-Lebanese boundary to "Line B" delineated on the Map attachment to the Annex. All the Lebanese Armed Forces and elements in this area, including the Lebanese Police, Lebanese Internal Security Forces and Ansar, will be subordinated to the brigade commander. The organization of the existing local units will be adapted, under the supervision of the Security Arrangements Committee, in

conformity with the Table of Organization for the Territorial Brigade as shown in the Appendix.

ANNEX
PARA 2.g

1. An area extending from:

   33 degrees 15 minutes N
   35 degrees 12.6 minutes E; to

   33 degrees 05.5 minutes N
   35 degrees 06.1 minutes E; to

1 Anti-Air Artillery Company	Off.: 4	Enl.: 146
TOTAL 4,341	Off.: 223	Enl.: 4,118

2. If the Joint Supervisory Teams uncover evidence of a violation or a potential violation, they will contact the proper Lebanese authorities through the Security Arrangements Supervision Centers created pursuant to the Agreed Minute to paragraph 3.f.(5) of the Annex, in order to assure that Lebanese authorities take appropriate neutralizing and preventive action in a timely way. They will ascertain that the action taken rectified the violation and will report the results to the Security Arrangements Committee.
3. The Joint Supervisory Teams will commence limited activities as early as possible following the coming into force of the Agreement for the purpose of monitoring the implementation of the Israel Defense Forces withdrawal arrangements. Their other supervisory and verification activities authorized in the Annex will commence with the final withdrawal of the Israeli armed forces.
4. Joint Supervisory Teams will conduct daily verifications if necessary during day and night. Verifications will be carried out on the ground, at sea, and in the air.
5. Each Joint Supervisory Team will be commanded by a Lebanese officer, who will recognize the joint nature of the teams when making decisions in unforeseen situations, during the conduct of the verification mission.
6. While on a mission, the Joint Supervisory Team leader at his discretion could react to any unforeseen situation which could require immediate action. The team leader will report any such situation and the action taken to the Security Arrangements Supervision Center.
7. The Joint Supervisory Teams will not use force except in self-defense.
8. The Security Arrangements Committee will decide *inter alia* on the pattern of activity of the Joint Supervisory Teams, their weaponry and equipment, their mode of transport, and the areas in which the teams will operate on the basis of the rule of reason and pragmatic considerations. The Security Arrangements Committee will determine the overall pattern of activity with a view to avoiding undue disruption to normal civilian life as well as with a view to preventing the teams from becoming targets of attack.

APPENDIX B 153

9. Up to a maximum of eight Joint Supervisory Teams will function simultaneously.

ANNEX PARA 3.f.5

1. Two Security Arrangements Supervision Centers will be set up by the Security Arrangements Committee in the Security Region. The exact locations of the Centers will be determined by the Security Arrangements Committee in accord with the principle that the Centers should be located in the vicinity of Hasbaya and Mayfadun and should not be situated in populated areas.
2. Under the overall direction of the Security Arrangements Committee, the purpose of each Center is to:
   a) Control, supervise, and direct Joint Supervisory Teams functioning in the sector of the Security Region assigned to it.
   b) Serve as a center of communications connected to the Joint Supervisory Teams and appropriate headquarters.
   c) Serve as a meeting place in Lebanon for the Security Arrangements Committee.
   d) Receive, analyze, and process all information necessary for the function of the Joint Supervisory Teams, on behalf of the Security Arrangements Committee.
3. Operational Arrangements:
   a) The Centers will be commanded by Lebanese Army Officers.
   b) The Centers will function 24 hours a day.
   c) The exact number of personnel in each Center will be decided by the Security Arrangements Committee.
   d) Israeli personnel will be stationed in Israel when not engaged in activities in the Centers.
   e) The Government of Lebanon will be responsible for providing security and logistical support for the Centers.
   f) The Joint Supervisory Teams will ordinarily commence their missions from the Centers after receiving proper briefing and will complete their missions at the Centers following debriefing.
   g) Each Center will contain a situation room, communications equipment, facilities for Security Arrangements Committee meetings, and a briefing and debriefing room.

ANNEX PARA 3.g

In order to prevent incidents and facilitate coordination between the forces on the terrain, "practical and rapid contacts" will include direct radio and telephone communications between the respective military commanders and their staffs in the immediate border region, as well as direct face-to-face consultations.

154 PEACEKEEPING ON ARAB-ISRAELI FRONTS

PUBLIC LAW 98-119—October 12, 1983

Public Law 98-119

Ninety-eighth Congress

Joint Resolution

Providing statutory authorization under the War Powers Resolution for continued United States participation in the multinational peacekeeping force in Lebanon in order to obtain withdrawal of all foreign forces from Lebanon.

Resolved by the Senate and House of Representatives of the United States of America in Congress assembled,

SHORT TITLE

SECTION 1. This joint resolution may be cited as the "Multinational Force in Lebanon Resolution".

FINDINGS AND PURPOSE

SEC. (a) The Congress finds that—

(1) The removal of all foreign forces from Lebanon is an essential United States foreign policy objective in the Middle East;

(2) in order to restore full control by the Government of Lebanon over its own territory, the United States is currently participating in the multinational peacekeeping force (hereafter in this resolution referred to as the "Multinational Force in Lebanon") which was established in accordance with the exchange of letters between the Governments of the United States and Lebanon dated September 25, 1982;

(3) the Multinational Force in Lebanon better enables the Government of Lebanon to establish its unity, independence, and territorial integrity;

(4) progress toward national political reconciliation in Lebanon is necessary; and

(5) United States Armed Forces participating in the Multinational Force in Lebanon are now in hostilities requiring authorization of their continued presence under the War Powers Resolution.

(b) The Congress determines that the requirements of section 4(a)(1) of the War Powers Resolution became operative on August 29, 1983. Consistent with section 5(b) of the War Powers Resolution, the purpose of this joint resolution is to authorize the continued participation of United States Armed Forces in the Multinational Force in Lebanon.

(c) The Congress intends this joint resolution to constitute the necessary specific statutory authorization under the War Powers Resolution for continued participation by United States Armed Forces in the Multinational Force in Lebanon.

AUTHORIZATION FOR CONTINUED PARTICIPATION OF UNITED STATES ARMED FORCES IN THE MULTINATIONAL FORCE IN LEBANON

SEC. 3. The President is authorized, for purposes of section 5(b) of the War Powers Resolution, to continue participation by United States Armed Forces in the Multinational Force in Lebanon, subject to the provisions of section 6 of this joint resolution. Such participation shall be limited to performance of the functions, and shall be subject to the limitations, specified in the agreement establishing the Multinational Force in Lebanon as set forth in the exchange of letters between the Governments of the United States and Lebanon dated September 25, 1982, except that this shall not preclude such protective measures as may be necessary to ensure the safety of the Multinational Force in Lebanon.

REPORTS TO THE CONGRESS

SEC. 4. As required by section 4(c) of the War Powers Resolution, the President shall report periodically to the Congress with respect to the situation in Lebanon, but in no event shall he report less often than once every three months. In addition to providing the information required by that section on the status, scope, and duration of hostilities involving United States Armed Forces, such reports shall describe in detail—

(1) the activities being performed by the Multinational Force in Lebanon;

(2) the present composition of the Multinational Force in Lebanon, including a description of the responsibilities and deployment of the armed forces of each participating country;

(3) the results of efforts to reduce and eventually eliminate the Multinational Force in Lebanon;

(4) how continued United States participation in the Multinational Force in Lebanon is advancing United States foreign policy interests in the Middle East; and

(5) what progress has occurred toward national political reconciliation among all Lebanese groups.

STATEMENTS OF POLICY

SEC. 5. (a) The Congress declares that the participation of the armed forces of other countries in the Multinational Force in Lebanon is essential to maintain the international character of the peacekeeping function in Lebanon.

(b) The Congress believes that it should continue to be the policy of the United States to promote continuing discussions with Israel, Syria, and Lebanon with the objective of bringing about the withdrawal of all foreign troops from Lebanon and establishing an environment which will permit the Lebanese Armed Forces to carry out their responsibilities in the Beirut area.

(c) It is the sense of the Congress that, not later than one year after the date of enactment of this joint resolution and at least once a year thereafter, the United States should discuss with the other members of the Security Council of the United Nations the establishment of a United Nations peacekeeping force to assume the responsibilities of the Multinational Force in Lebanon. An analysis of the implications of the response to such discussions for the continuation of the Multinational Force in Lebanon shall be included in the reports required under paragraph (3) of section 4 of this resolution.

DURATION OF AUTHORIZATION FOR UNITED STATES PARTICIPATION IN THE MULTINATIONAL FORCE IN LEBANON

SEC. 6. The participation of the United States Armed Forces in the Multinational Force in Lebanon shall be authorized for purposes of the War Powers Resolution until the end of the eighteen-month period beginning on the date of enactment of this resolution unless the Congress extends such authorization, except that such authorization shall terminate sooner upon the occurrence of any one of the following:

(1) the withdrawal of all foreign forces from Lebanon, unless the President determines and certifies to the Congress that continued United States Armed Forces participation in the Multinational Force in Lebanon is required after such withdrawal in order to accomplish the purposes specified in the September 25, 1982, exchange of letters providing for the establishment of the Multinational Force in Lebanon; or

(2) the assumption by the United Nations or the Government of Lebanon of the responsibilities of the Multinational Force in Lebanon; or

(3) the implementation of other effective security arrangements in the area; or

(4) the withdrawal of all other countries from participation in the Multinational Force in Lebanon.

INTERPRETATION OF THIS RESOLUTION

SEC. 7. (a) Nothing in this joint resolution shall preclude the President from withdrawing United States Armed Forces participation in the Multinational Force in Lebanon if circumstances warrant, and nothing in this joint resolution shall preclude the Congress by joint resolution from directing such a withdrawal.

(b) Nothing in this joint resolution modifies, limits, or supersedes any provision of the War Powers Resolution or the requirement of section 4(a) of the Lebanon Emergency Assistance Act of 1983, relating to congressional authorization for any substantial expansion in the number or role of United States Armed Forces in Lebanon.

CONGRESSIONAL PRIORITY PROCEDURES FOR AMENDMENTS

SEC. 8. (a) Any joint resolution or bill introduced to amend or repeal this Act shall be referred to the Committee on Foreign Affairs of the House of Representatives or the Committee on Foreign Relations of the Senate, as the case may be. Such joint resolution or bill shall be considered by such committee within fifteen calendar days and may be reported out, together with its recommendations, unless such House shall otherwise determine pursuant to its rules.

(b) Any joint resolution or bill so reported shall become the pending business of the House in question (in the case of the Senate the time for debate shall be equally divided between the proponents and the opponents) and shall be voted on within three calendar days thereafter, unless such House shall otherwise determine by the yeas and nays.

(c) Such a joint resolution or bill passed by one House shall be referred to the committee of the other House named in subsection (a) and shall be reported out by such committee together with its recommendations within fifteen calendar days and shall thereupon become the pending business of such House and shall be voted upon within three calendar days, unless such House shall otherwise determine by the yeas and nays.

(d) In the case of any disagreement between the two Houses of Congress with respect to a joint resolution or bill passed by both Houses, conferees shall be promptly appointed and the committee of conference shall make and file a report with respect to such joint resolution within six calendar days after the legislation is referred to the committee of conference. Notwithstanding any rule in either House concerning the printing of conference reports in the Record or concerning any delay in the consideration of such reports, such report shall be acted on by both Houses not later than six calendar days after

APPENDIX B   157

the conference report is filed. In the event the conferees are unable to agree within forty-eight hours, they shall report back to their respective Houses in disagreement.

Approved October 12, 1983.

Report of the Department of Defense (Long) Commission on Beirut International Airport Terrorist Act, October 23, 1983, issued on December 20, 1983.

The following text is excerpted from the Long Commission Report, specifically parts one and two, which describe the military mission and the rules of engagement established for the U.S. Marine contingent of the MNF in Beirut.

PART ONE—THE MILITARY MISSION

I. MISSION DEVELOPMENT

A. *Principal Findings.*

Following the Sabra and Shatila massacres, a Presidential decision was made that the United States would participate in a Multinational Force (MNF) to assist the Lebanese Armed Forces (LAF) in carrying out its responsibilities in the Beirut area. Ambassador Habib, the President's Special Envoy to the Middle East, was charged with pursuing the diplomatic arrangements necessary for the insertion of U.S. forces into Beirut. His efforts culminated in an Exchange of Diplomatic Notes on 25 September 1982 between the United States and the Government of Lebanon which formed the basis for U.S. participation in the MNF. The national decision having been made, the Secretary of Defense tasked the Joint Chiefs of Staff (JCS) to develop the mission statement and to issue the appropriate Alert Order to the Commander in Chief United States European Command (USCINCEUR). Commission discussions with the principals involved disclosed that the mission statement was carefully drafted in coordination with USCINCEUR to ensure that it remained within the limits of national political guidance.

The Joint Operational Planning System (JOPS) Volume IV (Crisis Action System) provides guidance for the conduct of joint planning and execution concerning the use of military forces during emergency or time-sensitive situations.

The mission statement provided to USCINCEUR by the JCS Alert Order of 23 September 1983 read as follows:

"To establish an environment which will permit the Lebanese Armed Forces to carry out their responsibilities in the Beirut area. When directed, USCINCEUR will introduce U.S. forces as part of a multinational force presence in the Beirut area to occupy and secure positions along a designated section of the line from south of the Beirut International Airport to a position in the vicinity of the Presidential Palace; be prepared to protect U.S. forces; and, on order, conduct retrograde operations as required."

The wording " . . . occupy and secure positions along . . . the line . . . " was incorporated into the mission statement by the JCS on the recommendation of USCINCEUR to avoid any inference that the USMNF would be responsible for the security of any given area. Additional mission-related guidance provided in the JCS Alert Order included the direction that:

—The USMNF would not be engaged in combat.

—Peacetime rules of engagement would apply (i.e. use of force is authorized only in self-defense or in defense of collocated LAF elements operating with the USMNF.)
—USCINCEUR would be prepared to extract U.S. forces in Lebanon if required by hostile action.

USCINCEUR repromulgated the mission statement, essentially unchanged, to Commander United States Naval Forces Europe (CINCUSNAVEUR) on 24 September 1982. That OPREP-1 message designated CTF 61 (Commander Amphibious Task Force) as Commander, U.S. forces Lebanon and provided the following concept of operations:

" . . . land U.S. Marine Landing Force in Port of Beirut and/or vicinity of Beirut Airport. U.S. forces will move to occupy positions along an assigned section of a line extending from south of Beirut Airport to vicinity of Presidential Palace. Provide security posts at intersections of assigned section of line and major avenues of approach into city of Beirut from south/southeast *to deny passage of hostile armed elements* in order to provide an environment which will permit LAF to carry out their responsibilities in city of Beirut. Commander U.S. Forces will establish and maintain continuous coordination with other MNF units, EUCOM liaison team and LAF. Commander U.S. Forces will provide air/naval gunfire support as required." (Emphasis added)

The USCINCEUR concept of operations also tasked CTF 61 to conduct combined defensive operations with other MNF contingents and the LAF and to be prepared to execute retrograde or withdrawal operations.

The USCINCEUR OPREP-1 tasked CINCUSNAVEUR, when directed, to:

—Employ Navy/Marine forces to land at Beirut.
—Provide required air and naval gunfire support to forces ashore as required.
—Be prepared to conduct withdrawal operations if hostile actions occur.
—Provide liaison teams to each member of the MNF and to the LAF.

That OPREP-1 also included tasking for other Component Commands and supporting CINC's.

On 25 September 1982, JCS modified USCINCEUR's concept of operations for CTF 61 to read " . . . assist LAF to deter passage of hostile armed elements . . . " (vice "deny passage of hostile armed elements . . . ").

The original mission statement was formally modified by directive on four occasions. Change One reduced the estimated number of Israeli Defense Force (IDF) troops in Beirut. Change Two, issued on 6 October 1982, defined the line along which the USMNF was to occupy and secure positions. The third change (undesignated) was issued on 2 November 1982, and expanded the mission to include patrols in the East Beirut area. The fourth change (designated Change Three), was issued on 7 May 1983 and further expanded the mission to allow the USMNF to provide external security for the U.S. Embassy in Beirut.

B. *Discussion.*

Although some operational details were added, the original mission statement was repromulgated unchanged down the chain of command through Alert/Execute Orders and OPREP-1's. CINCUSNAVEUR provided position locations for the USMNF forces ashore in Beirut. Commander Sixth Fleet (COMSIXTHFLT) designated CTF 61 as On-Scene Commander and CTF 62 as Commander U.S. Forces Ashore Lebanon and defined the chain of command. CTF 61 promulgated detailed operational procedures for amphibious shipping, boats and aircraft to facilitate ship-to-shore movement. CTF 62

APPENDIX B 159

provided the detailed ship-to-shore movement plan for the MAU [Marine Amphibious Unit] and the concept of operations for the initial three days ashore.

USCINCEUR engaged in some mission analysis (e.g., crafting the concept of operations and working operational constraint wording with JCS) and provided detailed tasking to subordinates and to supporting CINC's. However, the mission statement and the concept of operations were passed down the chain of command with little amplification. As a result, perceptual differences as to the precise meaning and importance of the "presence" role of the USMNF existed throughout the chain of command. Similarly, the exact responsibilities of the USMNF commander regarding the security of Beirut International Airport were not clearly delineated in his mission tasking.

Clarification of the mission tasks and concepts of operations would not only have assisted the USMNF commanders to better understand what was required, it would also have alerted higher headquarters to the differing interpretations of the mission at intermediate levels of command. The absence of specificity in mission definition below the USCINCEUR level concealed differences of interpretation of the mission and tasking assigned to the USMNF.

The commission's inquiry clearly established that perceptions of the basic mission varied at different levels of command. The MAU commanders, on the ground in Beirut, interpreted their "presence" mission to require the USMNF to be visible but not to appear to be threatening to the populace. This concern was a factor in most decisions made by the MAU Commanders in the employment and disposition of their forces. The MAU Commander regularly assessed the effect of contemplated security actions on the "presence" mission.

Another area in which perceptions varied was the importance of Beirut International Airport (BIA) to the USMNF mission and whether the USMNF had any responsibility to ensure the operation of the airport. While all echelons of the military chain of command understood that the security of BIA was not a part of the mission, perceptions of the USMNF's implicit responsibility for airport operations varied widely. The U.S. Ambassador to Lebanon, and others in the State Department, saw an operational airport as an important symbolic and practical demonstration of Lebanese sovereignty. On television on 27 October 1983, the President stated: "Our Marines are not just sitting in an airport. Part of their task is to guard that airport. Because of their presence the airport remained operational." The other MNF commanders asserted to the Commission that, while BIA is not specifically the responsibility of any one MNF contingent, an operational airport is important to the viability of the MNF concept. The MAU Commanders interviewed by the Commission all believed they had some responsibility for ensuring an open airport as an implicit part of their mission.

C. *Conclusion.*

The Commission concludes that the "presence" mission was not interpreted in the same manner by all levels of the chain of command and that perceptual differences regarding that mission, including the responsibility of the USMNF for the security of Beirut International Airport, should have been recognized and corrected by the chain of command.

II. THE CHANGING ENVIRONMENT

A. *Principal Findings.*

The mission of the USMNF was implicitly characterized as a peace-keeping operation, although "peace-keeping" was not explicit in the mission statement. In September 1982, the President's public statement, his letter to the United Nations' Secretary General and his report to the Congress, all conveyed a strong impression of the peace-keeping nature of the operation. The subject lines of the JCS Alert and Execute Orders read, "U.S. Force participation in Lebanon Multinational Force (MNF) *Peacekeeping* Operations." (Emphasis added) Alert and Execute Orders were carefully worded to emphasize that the USMNF would have a non-combatant role. Operational constraint sections included guidance to be prepared to withdraw if required by hostile action. This withdrawal guidance was repeated in CINCEUR's OPREP-1.

A condition precedent to the insertion of U.S. forces into Beirut was that the Government of Lebanon and the LAF would ensure the protection of the MNF, including the securing of assurances from armed factions to refrain from hostilities and not to interfere with MNF activities. Ambassador Habib received confirmation from the Government of Lebanon that these arrangements had been made. These assurances were included by the Government of Lebanon in its exchange of notes with the United States.

It was contemplated from the outset that the USMNF would operate in a relatively benign environment. Syrian forces were not considered a significant threat to the MNF. The major threats were thought to be unexploded ordnance and possible sniper and small unit attacks from PLO and Leftist militias. It was anticipated that the USMNF would be perceived by the various factions as evenhanded and neutral and that this perception would hold through the expected 60 day duration of the operation.

The environment into which the USMNF actually deployed in September 1982, while not necessarily benign was, for the most part, not hostile. The Marines were warmly welcomed and seemed genuinely to be appreciated by the majority of Lebanese.

By mid-March 1983, the friendly environment began to change as evidenced by a grenade thrown at a USMNF patrol in 16 March, wounding five Marines. Italian and French MNF contingents were the victims of similar attacks.

The destruction of the U.S. Embassy in Beirut on 18 April, was indicative of the extent of the deterioration of the political/military situation in Lebanon by the Spring of 1983. That tragic event also signaled the magnitude of the terrorist threat to the U.S. presence. A light truck detonated, killing over 60 people (including 17 Americans) and destroying a sizable portion of the building. An FBI investigation into the explosion later revealed that the bomb was a "gas enhanced" device capable of vastly more destructive force than a comparable conventional explosive. Although the technique of gas-enhanced bombs had been employed by Irish Republican Army terrorists in Northern Ireland and, on at least two occasions, in Lebanon, the magnitude of the explosive force of the device used in the Embassy bombing was, in the opinion of FBI explosive experts, unprecedented.

During August, rocket, artillery and mortar fire began impacting at BIA. On 28 August 1983, the Marines returned fire for the first time. Following the deaths of two Marines in a mortar attack the following day, the USMNF responded with artillery fire. On 31 August, Marine patrols were terminated in the face of the sniper, RPG and artillery threats.

Fighting between the LAF and the Druze increased sharply with the withdrawal of the IDF from the Alayh and Shuf Districts on 4 September 1983. Two more Marines were killed by mortar or artillery rounds at BIA on 6 September 1983. By 11 September, the battle for Suq-Al-Gharb was raging. The USMNF, under frequent attack, responded with counterbattery fire and F-14 tactical air reconnaissance pod (TARPS) missions were commenced over Lebanon.

On 16 September 1983, U.S. Naval gunfire support was employed in response to shelling of the U.S. Ambassador's residence and USMNF positions at BIA. On 19 September, following a National Command Authority (NCA) decision, Naval gunfire support was employed to support the LAF fighting at Suq-Al-Gharb. On 20 September, the F-14 TARPS aircraft were fired on by SA-7 missiles.

During the period 14–16 October 1983, two Marines were killed on the BIA perimeter in separate sniper incidents.

By the end of September 1983, the situation in Lebanon had changed to the extent that not one of the initial conditions upon which the mission statement was premised was still valid. The environment clearly was hostile. The assurances the Government of Lebanon had obtained from the various factions were obviously no longer operative as attacks on the USMNF came primarily from extralegal militias. Although USMNF actions could properly be classified as self-defense and not "engaging in combat," the environment could no longer be characterized as peaceful. The image of the USMNF, in the eyes of the factional militias, had become pro-Israel, pro-Phalange, and anti-Muslim. After the USMNF engaged in direct fire support of the LAF, a significant portion of the Lebanese populace no longer considered the USMNF a neutral force.

B. *Discussions.*

The inability of the Government of Lebanon to develop a political consensus, and the resultant outbreak of hostilities between the LAF and armed militias supported by Syria, effectively precluded the possibility of a successful peacekeeping mission. It is abundantly clear that by late summer 1983, the environment in Lebanon changed to the extent that the conditions upon which the USMNF mission was initially premised no longer existed. The Commission believes that appropriate guidance and modification of tasking should have been provided to the USMNF to enable it to cope effectively with the increasingly hostile environment. The Commission could find no evidence that such guidance was, in fact, provided.

III. THE EXPANDING MILITARY ROLE

A. *Principal Findings.*

The "presence" mission assigned to the USMNF contemplated that the contending factions in Lebanon would perceive the USMNF as a neutral force, evenhanded in its dealings with the confessional groups that comprise Lebanese society. The mission statement tasked the USMNF to "establish an environment which will permit the Lebanese Armed Forces to carry out their responsibilities in the Beirut area." When hostilities erupted between the LAF and Shiite and Druze militias, USMNF efforts to support the LAF were perceived to be both pro-Phalangist and anti-Muslim.

USMNF support to the LAF increased substantially following their arrival in September 1982. The first direct military support to the LAF was in the form of training which the USMNF began to provide in November 1982.

In August and September 1983, the U.S. resupplied the LAF with ammunition. The LAF were engaged in intense fighting against the Druze and various Syrian surrogates. The ammunition came from MAU, CONUS and USCINCEUR stocks and was delivered by Military Sealift Command, Mobile Logistic Support Force (CTF 63), and CTF 61 ships.

On 19 September 1983, naval gunfire was employed in direct support of the LAF at Suq-Al-Gharb.

Following the U.S. action in providing Naval gunfire support for the LAF at Suq-Al-Gharb, hostile acts against the USMNF increased and the Marines began taking significantly more casualties. A direct cause and effect linkage between Suq-Al-Gharb and the terrorist bombing on 23 October 1983, cannot be determined. The views of the senior civilian and military officials interviewed by the Commission varied widely on this issue. Some believe that it was not a consequence of our relationship with any faction; that regardless of its actions, the USMNF would still have been targeted by terrorists. Others believe that certain factions wanted to force the MNF out of Lebanon and that the bombing of the BLT [Battalion Landing Team] Headquarters building was the tactic of choice to produce that end. The prevalent view within the USCINCEUR chain of command, however, is that there was some linkage between the two events. Whether or not there was a direct connection between Suq-Al-Gharb and the increase in terrorist attacks on the USMNF, the public statements of factional leaders confirmed that a portion of the Lebanese populace no longer considered the USMNF neutral.

B. *Discussion.*

The Commission believes that from the very beginning of the USMNF mission on 29 September 1982, the security of the USMNF was dependent upon the continuing validity of four basic conditions.

(1)   That the force would operate in a relatively benign environment;
(2)   That the Lebanese Armed Forces would provide for the security of the areas in which the force was to operate;
(3)   That the mission would be of limited duration; and
(4)   That the force would be evacuated in the event of attack.

As the political/military situation evolved, three factors were impacting adversely upon those conditions. First, although the mission required that the USMNF be perceived as neutral by the confessional factions, the tasks assigned to the USMNF gradually evolved to include active support of the LAF. A second factor was the deep-seated hostility of Iran and Syria toward the United States combined with the capability to further their own political interests by sponsoring attacks on the USMNF. And finally, the progress of diplomatic efforts to secure the withdrawal of all foreign forces from Lebanon faltered. The combination of these three factors served to invalidate the first two conditions and to complicate the third.

U.S. policy makers recognized that the conditions upon which the mission of the USMNF was premised were tenuous and that the decision to deploy the USMNF into Beirut involved considerable risk. The military mission was directed in concert with extensive diplomatic initiatives designed to shore up the Government of Lebanon and establish a climate for political reconciliation. At the same time that the political/military conditions in Lebanon deteriorated, the U.S. military role expanded in the form of increased USMNF training and logistic support for the LAF and in the form of changes to the rules of engagement of the USMNF to permit active support of LAF units engaged in combat with factional forces. That expanded role was directed in an effort to adjust to the changing situation and to continue to move toward realization of U.S. policy objectives in Lebanon. On the diplomatic front, achieving the withdrawal of foreign troops proved to be more difficult than had been anticipated. The overall result was the continued erosion of the security of the USMNF.

C. *Conclusion.*

The Commission concludes that U.S. decisions regarding Lebanon taken over the past fifteen months have been to a large degree characterized by an emphasis on military options and the expansion of the U.S. military role, notwithstanding the fact that the conditions upon which the security of the USMNF were based continued to deteriorate as progress toward a diplomatic solution slowed. The Commission further concludes that these decisions may have been taken without clear recognition that these initial conditions had dramatically changed and that the expansion of our military involvement in Lebanon greatly increased the risk to, and adversely impacted upon the security of, the USMNF. The Commission therefore concludes that there is an urgent need for reassessment of alternative means to achieve U.S. objectives in Lebanon and at the same time reduce the risk to the USMNF.

D. *Recommendation.*

The Commission recommends that the Secretary of Defense continue to urge that the National Security Council undertake a reexamination of alternative means of achieving U.S. objectives in Lebanon, to include a comprehensive assessment of the military security options being developed by the chain of command and a more vigorous and demanding approach to pursuing diplomatic alternatives.

PART TWO—RULES OF ENGAGEMENT

"Rules of Engagement: Directives issued by competent authority which delineate the circumstances and limitations under which United States forces will initiate and/or continue combat engagement with other forces encountered."

—JCS Pub 1

I. RULES OF ENGAGEMENT DEVELOPMENT

A. *Principal Findings.*

The basic Rules of Engagement (ROE) for USMNF forces in Beirut have been in effect since the second USMNF insertion on 29 September 1982. The ROE were promulgated on 24 September 1982 by USCINCEUR, the responsible authority for contingency operations in the Eastern Mediterranean. They are consistent with the guidance provided in the JCS Alert Order of 23 September 1983. The ROE developed by USCINCEUR are derived from U.S. European Command Directive 55-47A, "Peacetime Rules of Engagement." They were tailored to the Lebanon situation by the adaptation of ROE developed through the summer of 1982 for use in the evacuation of PLO elements in Beirut from 24 August to 10 September 1982. There had been extensive dialogue on ROE up and down the European Theater chain of command during July and August 1982.

JCS guidance to USCINCEUR was that USMNF forces were not to engage in combat and would use normal USEUCOM peacetime ROE. Force was to be used only when required for self-defense against a hostile threat, in response to a hostile act, or in defense of LAF elements operating with the USMNF. USCINCEUR incorporated the JCS guidance and elaborated thereon. Reprisals or punitive measures were forbidden. USMNF elements were enjoined to seek guidance from higher authority prior to using armed force for self-defense unless an emergency existed. The ROE defined "hostile act" and "hostile force," and designated the Combined Amphibious Task Force Commander (CTF 61) as the authority to declare a force hostile. "Hostile threat" was not defined. If non-LAF forces infiltrated or violated USMNF assigned areas or lines, they were to be informed they were in an unauthorized area and could not proceed. If they failed to depart, the USMNF Commander (CTF 62) was to be informed and would determine the action to be taken. The LAF had responsibility for apprehension and detention of any intruders. The USMNF was authorized to use force only if the intruder committed a hostile act. Finally, commanders were to be prepared to extract forces if necessary.

By message to subordinate commands on 28 September 1982, CINCUSNAVEUR elaborated on the ROE provided by USCINCEUR and directed that further ROE development for U.S. forces ashore be for self-defense only. Detailed ROE, consistent with command guidance, were issued by CTF 62 on 27 October 1982, and again on 12 November 1982.

Following the terrorist bombing of the U.S. Embassy in Beirut on 18 April 1983, a USMNF unit was formed to provide external security for U.S. Embassy functions relocated at the Duraffourd Building, the British Embassy, and the U.S. Ambassador's Residence at Yarze. On 1 May 1983, CTF 62 requested specific ROE to counter the vehicular and pedestrian terrorist threat to those buildings. On 7 May 1983, USCINCEUR promulgated ROE specifically for that security force which expanded the definition of a hostile act to encompass attempts by personnel or vehicles to breach barriers or roadblocks established on approaches to the Duraffourd Building, the British Embassy or the U.S. Ambassador's Residence.

Following the 4 September 1983 IDF pull-back to the Awwali River, fighting intensified in the mountainous Shuf region southeast of Beirut. Phalange and Druze militias fought for control of the territory vacated by the IDF. LAF units also moved to gain control of the strategically important Shuf high ground, and were engaged by Druze forces in heavy fighting at Suq-Al-Gharb. When defeat of the LAF appeared imminent, the National Command Authorities (NCA) authorized the use of naval gunfire and tactical air strikes in support of the LAF at Suq-Al-Gharb. Occupation of the dominant terrain in the vicinity of Suq-Al-Gharb by hostile forces would pose a danger of USMNF positions at BIA. Direct support of the LAF in those circumstances was to be considered as an act of self-defense authorized by the existing ROE. Early on 12 September 1983, the acting CJCS notified USCINCEUR of that decision. Later that day, USCINCEUR directed CINCUSNAVEUR to inform his subordinate commands to provide fire support to the LAF when the U.S. ground commander (CTF 62) determined that Suq-Al-Gharb was in danger of falling to an attack by non-Lebanese forces. USCINCEUR directed in the same message, "Nothing in this message shall be construed as changing the mission or ROE for USMNF."

In the aftermath of the 23 October 1983 terrorist attack at the BLT Headquarters, review of the basic USMNF ROE was conducted at virtually every level of command. ROE were promulgated to govern the use of electronic warfare, and reviews of specific ROE for F-14/Tactical Aerial Reconnaissance Pods (TARPS) flights, for air defense, and for defensive activities of afloat elements of the U.S. presence (i.e. CTF 60 and CTF 61) were conducted. Late on 23 October, CTF 61 submitted a ROE change request to COMSIXTHFLT requesting that USMNF personnel at BIA be authorized to take under fire any civilian vehicle which approached USMNF positions at a high rate of speed and failed to acknowledge signals to stop. COMSIXTHFLT forwarded the request up the chain of command. On 25 October 1983, USCINCEUR responded that the authority requested was already covered under the self-protection rules of the ROE in effect. The USCINCEUR response noted that the promulgation in early May 1983 of additional ROE for the U.S. Embassy security tasking was considered necessary because the USMNF had been assigned an additional mission which went beyond its self-defense. On 26 October 1983, CINCUSNAVEUR approved the ROE modification requested by CTF 61. On 26 November 1983, COMSIXTHFLT proposed to CINCUSNAVEUR that the ROE be further changed to authorize the taking of prompt, forceful action against any unauthorized attempt to gain entry into an area occupied by the USMNF. CINCUSNAVEUR and USCINCEUR responded on 27 November 1983 that such

APPENDIX B   165

action was already authorized by existing ROE. USCINCEUR, however, agreed to provide specific rules in a forthcoming revision of the original ROE.

B. *Discussion.*

The ROE were developed in accordance with established JCS guidance, and promulgated by the appropriate command authority, USCINCEUR. Although the rapid deterioration of the situation in Beirut which led to reinsertion of the USMNF caused understandable compression in the process, each command echelon participated in the development of the ROE provided to the USMNF.

The environment into which the USMNF was inserted on 29 September 1982 was clearly permissive. The judgement that the USMNF was perceived as a neutral, stabilizing presence by most, if not all, factions in the Beirut area can be drawn from the general absence of hostile reactions in the initial months of their presence. The ROE were appropriate for such a permissive environment. But the environment proved to be dynamic, and became increasingly hostile to the USMNF component as the U.S. presence stretched beyond the brief stay envisioned by the original Exchange of Notes.

The Commission believes that for any ROE to be effective, they should incorporate definitions of hostile intent and hostile action which correspond to the realities of the environment in which they are to be implemented. To be adequate, they must also provide the commander explicit authority to respond quickly to acts defined as hostile. Only when these two criteria are satisfied do ROE provide the on-scene commander with the guidance and the flexibility he requires to defend his force. By these measures, the ROE in force at BIA subsequent to the U.S. Embassy bombing in April were neither effective nor adequate. That event clearly signaled a change in the environment: the employment of terrorist tactics by hostile elements.

The emergence of the terrorist threat brought the guidance and flexibility afforded by the ROE into question. The modified ROE promulgated for the security force assigned to U.S. Embassy facilities were necessary. For the first time, threatening actions such as attempts to breach barriers or checkpoints were specifically defined as hostile acts justifying the use of military force. USMNF personnel providing security for the Embassy were authorized to take adequate defensive action in those circumstances. But the commander of the USMNF perceived that the new ROE from USCINCEUR were for use only by the Embassy security element. The presumption at HQ USEUCOM, subsequently apparent in both messages and discussions with principals, was that the USMNF Commander had already been given sufficient guidance and authority to respond to vehicular terrorist attacks against his forces at BIA in the original ROE promulgated on 24 September 1982. In the view of the Commission, the ROE provided in May for the Embassy security contingent should have been explicitly extended to the entire USMNF.

The Commission believes that ROE developed for the insertion of the USMNF into Lebanon in late September 1982, were appropriate to the relatively benign environment that existed at that time. That environment, however, was dynamic and became increasingly anti-USMNF. The Commission also believes that development by the chain of command of ROE guidance for the USMNF at BIA did not keep pace with the changing threat.

II. RULES OF ENGAGEMENT IMPLEMENTATION

A. *Principal Findings.*

The ROE contained in the 24 September 1982 USCINCEUR OPREP-1 were implemented by Commander Amphibious Task Force/Commander U.S. Forces Lebanon (CTF 61), and Commander 32d Marine Amphibious Unit/Commander U.S. Forces Ashore Lebanon (CTF 62), upon insertion of the USMNF into Beirut on 29 September 1982. CTF 62 implemented the ROE for the USMNF through the issuance of specific instructions to his personnel on 27 October and 12 November 1982. (COMSIXTHFLT and CTF 61 were information addressees on that traffic.) The central guidance for implementation of the ROE was that USMNF elements would only engage in defensive actions.

Briefly summarized, the following points constitute the ROE guidance utilized by the individual members of the USMNF from 29 September 1982 until 7 May 1983.

— Action taken by U.S. forces ashore in Lebanon would be for self-defense only.
— Reprisal or punitive measures would not be initiated.
— Commanders were to seek guidance from higher headquarters prior to using armed force, if time and situation allowed.
— If time or the situation did not allow the opportunity to request guidance from higher headquarters, commanders were authorized to use that degree of armed force necessary to protect their forces.
— Hostile ground forces which had infiltrated and violated USMNF lines by land, sea, or air would be warned that they could not proceed and were in a restricted area. If the intruder force failed to leave, the violation would be reported and guidance requested.
— Riot control agents would not be used unless authorized by the Secretary of Defense.
— Hostile forces would not be pursued.
— A "hostile act" was defined as an attack or use of force against the USMNF, or against MNF or LAF units operating with the USMNF, that consisted of releasing, launching, or firing of missiles, bombs, individual weapons, rockets or any other weapon.

Following the 18 April 1983 destruction of the U.S. Embassy, USCINCEUR promulgated an expanded set of ROE for use by USMNF personnel assigned to provide security for the British Embassy and the Duraffourd Building where U.S. Embassy functions had been relocated. Those expanded ROE were implemented by CTF 62 through the issuance to each Marine assigned to Embassy security duty of an ROE card, the so-called "Blue Card". Since the USCINCEUR expanded ROE were promulgated for specific use of those members of the USMNF assigned to provide security for the Embassy, USMNF elements at BIA continued to operate under the ROE previously provided. In order to ensure that each Marine of the USMNF understood what set of ROE were applicable to him at any given time, CTF 62 issued a "White Card" delineating the ROE for those not assigned to Embassy duty, as follows:

"The mission of the Multi-national Force (MNF) is to keep the peace. The following rules of engagement will be read and fully understood by all members of the U.S. contingent of the MNF:

— When on post, mobile or foot patrol, keep a loaded magazine in the weapon, weapons will be on safe, with no rounds in the chamber.
— Do not chamber a round unless instructed to do so by a commissioned officer unless you must act in immediate self-defense where deadly force is authorized.

APPENDIX B   167

—Keep ammunition for crew-served weapons readily available but not loaded in the weapon. Weapons will be on safe at all times.
—Call local forces to assist in all self-defense efforts. Notify next senior command immediately.
—Use only the minimum degree of force necessary to accomplish the mission.
—Stop the use of force when it is no longer required.
—If effective fire is received, direct return fire at a distinct target only. If possible, use friendly sniper fire.
—Respect civilian property; do not attack it unless absolutely necessary to protect friendly forces.
—Protect innocent civilians from harm.
—Respect and protect recognized medical agencies such as Red Cross, Red Crescent, etc.

These rules of engagement will be followed by all members of the U.S. MNF unless otherwise directed."

All USMNF personnel were required to carry the appropriate card and know its content at all times while on duty. The practical result was that USMNF elements operated under two sets of ROE from early May 1983 until after the 23 October 1983 bombing of the BLT Headquarters building.

The Blue Card/White Card ROE guidance continued in effect until 24 October 1983 (the day following the BLT Headquarters bombing) when CTF 62 sought a ROE change from USCINCEUR, via the chain of command, to allow USMNF personnel to take under fire speeding vehicles approaching USMNF positions at BIA. On 26 November 1983, COMSIXTHFLT requested that USMNF personnel be authorized to fire, without warning if necessary, on vehicles attempting unauthorized access to an area of USMNF positions. As noted in Section I of this Part, on both of those occasions CINCUSNAVEUR and USCINCEUR held the view that the original ROE (24 September 1982) authorized CTF 62 to take such actions as he, the on-scene commander, considered necessary to defend his force against hostile action. Nonetheless, approval was provided to CTF 62.

B. *Discussion.*

CTF 62 determined that restraint in the use of force was key to accomplishing the presence mission he was assigned, and that strict adherence to the ROE was necessary if his forces were to maintain the "neutral" stance that the presence role entailed.

The Commission views with concern the fact that there were two different sets of ROE being used by USMNF elements in Beirut after the Embassy bombing on 18 April 1983. Those ROE used by the Embassy security detail were designed to counter the terrorist threat posed by both vehicles and personnel. Marines on similar duty at BIA, however, did not have the same ROE to provide them specific guidance and authority to respond to a vehicle or person moving through a perimeter. Their "White Card" ROE required them to call local forces to assist in all self-defense efforts.

Message transmissions up and down the USCINCEUR chain of command revealed that COMSIXTHFLT subordinate elements had different perceptions of the commander's latitude in implementing ROE than did CINCUSNAVEUR and USCINCEUR. The latter believed authority to forcibly halt vehicles attempting unauthorized entry into the area of USMNF positions was inherent in the original 24 September 1982 ROE. CTF 62 obviously did not share that view.

The Commission believes there were a number of factors which cumulatively affected the "mind-set" of the Marines at BIA. One factor was the mission, with its emphasis on highly visible presence and peace-keeping. Another was the ROE, which underscored the need to fire only if fired upon, to avoid harming innocent civilians, to respect civilian property, and to share security and self-defense efforts with the LAF. Promulgation of different ROE for those performing Embassy security duties contributed to a sense among the officers and men at BIA that the terrorist threat confronting them was somehow less dangerous than that which prevailed at the Embassy. The "White Card–Blue Card" dichotomy tended to formalize that view. Interviews of individual Marines who performed duty at the two locations confirm this mind-set. In short, the Commission believes the Marines at BIA were conditioned by their ROE to respond less aggressively to unusual vehicular or pedestrian activity at their perimeter than were those Marines posted at the Embassy locations.

C. *Conclusions.*

The Commission concludes that a single set of ROE providing specific guidance for countering the type of vehicular terrorist attacks that destroyed the U.S. Embassy on 18 April 1983 and the BLT Headquarters building on 23 October 1983 had not been provided to, nor implemented by, CTF 62.

The Commission further concludes that the mission statement, the original ROE, and the implementation in May 1983 of dual "Blue Card"–"White Card" ROE contributed to a mind-set that detracted from the readiness of the USMNF to respond to the terrorist threat which materialized on 23 October 1983.

APPENDIX C

Document Relating to the United Nations Disengagement Observer Force (UNDOF)

Israel-Syria: Agreement on Disengagement (Done at Geneva, June 5, 1974).

Report of the Secretary-General

1. I wish to transmit to the Council the text of the Agreement on Disengagement between Iraeli and Syrian forces, which is attached as Annex A to this report, and the Protocol to the Agreement between Israeli and Syrian forces concerning the United Nations Disengagement Observer Force, which is attached as Annex B.

2. The Security Council will note that this Agreement and the Protocol, which are to be signed in Geneva not later than 31 May 1974, calls for the creation of a United Nations Disengagement Observer Force. I shall take the necessary steps in accordance with the provisions of the Protocol, if the Security Council so decides.

3. It is my intention that the United Nations Disengagement Observer Force will be drawn, in the first instance at any rate, from United Nations military personnel already in the area.

4. I shall keep the Council fully informed of future developments in this regard.

ANNEX A
AGREEMENT ON DISENGAGEMENT BETWEEN ISRAELI AND SYRIAN FORCES

A. Israel and Syria will scrupulously observe the cease-fire on land, sea and air and will refrain from all military actions against each other, from the time of the signing of this document, in implementation of United Nations Security Council resolution 338 dated 22 October 1973.

B. The military forces of Israel and Syria will be separated in accordance with the following principles:

1. All Israeli military forces will be west of the line designated as Line A on the Map attached hereto, except in the Quneitra area, where they will be west of Line A-1 [map not attached].

2. All territory east of Line A will be under Syrian administration, and Syrian civilians will return to this territory.

3. The area between Line A and the line designated as Line B on the attached Map will be an area of separation. In this area will be stationed the United Nations Disengagement Observer Force established in accordance with the accompanying protocol.

4. All Syrian military forces will be east of the line designated as Line B on the attached Map.

5. There will be two equal areas of limitation in armament and forces, one west of Line A and one east of Line B as agreed upon.

6. Air forces of the two sides will be permitted to operate up to their respective lines without interference from the other side.

C. In the area between Line A and Line A-1 on the attached Map there shall be no military forces.

D. This Agreement and the attached Map will be signed by the military representatives of Israel and Syria in Geneva not later than 31 May 1974, in the Egyptian-Israeli Military Working Group of the Geneva Peace Conference under the aegis of the United Nations, after that group has been joined by a Syrian military representative, and with the participation of representatives of the United States and the Soviet Union. The precise delineation of a detailed Map and a plan for the implementation of the disengagement of forces will be worked out by military representatives of Israel and Syria in the Egyptian-Israeli Military Working Group who will agree on the stages of this process. The Military Working Group described above will start their work for this purpose in Geneva under the aegis of the United Nations within 24 hours after the signing of this Agreement. They will complete this task within five days. Disengagement will begin within 24 hours after the completion of the task of the Military Working Group. The process of disengagement will be completed not later than 20 days after it begins.

E. The provisions of paragraphs A, B and C shall be inspected by personnel of the United Nations comprising the United Nations Disengagement Observer Force under this Agreement.

F. Within 24 hours after the signing of this Agreement in Geneva all wounded prisoners of war which each side holds of the other as certified by the ICRC [International Committee of the Red Cross] will be repatriated. The morning after the completion of the task of the Military Working Group, all remaining prisoners of war will be repatriated.

G. The bodies of all dead soldiers held by either side will be returned for burial in their respective countries within 10 days after the signing of this Agreement.

H. This Agreement is not a Peace Agreement. It is a step towards a just and durable peace on the basis of Security Council Resolution 338 dated 22 October 1973.

ANNEX B
PROTOCOL TO AGREEMENT ON DISENGAGEMENT BETWEEN ISRAELI AND SYRIAN FORCES CONCERNING THE UNITED NATIONS DISENGAGEMENT OBSERVER FORCE

Israel and Syria agree that:

The function of the United Nations Disengagement Observer Force (UNDOF) under the agreement will be to use its best efforts to maintain the ceasefire and to see that it is scrupulously observed. It will supervise the agreement and protocol thereto with regard to the areas of separation and limitation. In carrying out its mission, it will comply with generally applicable Syrian laws and regulations and will not hamper the functioning of local civil administration. It will enjoy freedom of movement and communication and other facilities that are necessary for its mission. It will be mobile and provided with personal weapons of a defensive character and shall use such weapons only in self-defence. The number of the UNDOF shall be about 1,250, who will be selected by the Secretary-General of the United Nations in consultation with the parties from members of the United Nations who are not permanent members of the Security Council.

The UNDOF will be under the command of the United Nations, vested in the Secretary-General, under the authority of the Security Council.

The UNDOF shall carry out inspections under the agreement, and report thereon to the parties, on a regular basis, not less often than once every 15 days, and, in addition, when requested by either party. It shall mark on the ground the respective lines shown on the map attached to the agreement.

Israel and Syria will support a resolution of the United Nations Security Council which will provide for the UNDOF contemplated by the agreement. The initial authorization will be for six months subject to renewal by further resolution of the Security Council.

Report of the Secretary-General
Addendum

1. Pursuant to paragraph D of the Agreement on Disengagement betwen Israeli and Syrian Forces (S/11302(Add.1, annex A), the Egyptian-Israeli Military Working Group of the Geneva Peace Conference under the aegis of the United Nations held six meetings in Geneva from 31 May to 5 June 1974. Military representatives of Syria joined the Working Group, and representatives of the Co-chairmen of the conference also participated in the meetings.

2. At the meeting held on 31 May, the military representatives of Israel and Syria signed the Agreement on Disengagement and a map attached to it. Following a brief intermission, the Military Working Group began work, in accordance with the agreement, on the precise delineation of a detailed map and a plan for the implementation of the disengagement of forces.

3. In the subsequent meetings, the Working Group reached full agreement on the following:

   (a) A map showing different phases of disengagement;

   (b) A disengagement plan and areas and a timetable;

   (c) A statement read by Lt. General E. Siilasvuo, who presided over the meetings.

The map, to which the disengagement plan was attached was signed by the military representatives of Israel and Syria at the final meeting held on 5 June 1974. The agreed statement was also signed by General Siilasvuo at the same meeting, in conformity with an understanding between the parties.

4. The plan of separation of forces involves the redeployment of Israeli forces from the area east of the 1967 cease-fire line. It also provides for Israeli redeployment from Quneitra and Rafid and the demilitarization of an area west of Quneitra still held by Israel.

5. Prior to any Israeli redeployment, the United Nations Disengagement Observer Force (UNDOF) will occupy, between 6 and 8 June, a buffer zone between the parties. The plan is to be implemented in the area of separation as specified in the Agreement. Separation of forces should be completed by 26 June. There is also provision for the return of Syrian civilian administration to the UNDOF area of separation.

6. UNDOF will carry out an inspection of the redeployment of forces after the completion of each phase on dates fixed in the time-table attached to the plan of separation of forces and will report its findings forthwith to the parties. In order to determine that both parties have redeployed their forces in the limited forces areas, UNDOF will verify on 26 June 1974 that the limitation of forces agreed to by the parties

is observed by the parties, and it will thereafter effect regular bi-weekly inspections of the 10-kilometre restricted forces areas.

7. Agreement was also reached within the Working Group on the following points:

(a) Israel and Syria undertake to repatriate all prisoners-of-war still detained by them, not later than 6 June;

(b) Israel and Syria will co-operate with the International Committee of the Red Cross in carrying out its mandate, including the exchange of dead bodies, which is to be completed on 6 June 1974;

(c) Israel and Syria will make available all information and maps of minefields concerning their respective areas and the areas to be handed over by them.

APPENDIX D

Security Council Resolutions on the United Nations Interim Force in Lebanon (UNIFIL)

Resolution 425 (1978) of 19 March 1978

The Security Council,

Taking note of the letters from the Permanent Representative of Lebanon and from the Permanent Representative of Israel,

Having heard the statements of the Permanent Respresentatives of Lebanon and Israel,

Gravely concerned at the deterioration of the situation in the Middle East and its consequences to the maintenance of international peace,

Convinced that the present situation impedes the achievement of a just peace in the Middle East,

1. *Calls* for strict respect for the territorial integrity, sovereignty and political independence of Lebanon within its internationally recognized boundaries;

2. *Calls upon* Israel immediately to cease its military action against Lebanese territorial integrity and withdraw forthwith its forces from all Lebanese territory;

3. *Decides,* in the light of the request of the Government of Lebanon, to establish immediately under its authority a United Nations interim force for Southern Lebanon for the purpose of confirming the withdrawal of Israeli forces, restoring international peace and security and assisting the Government of Lebanon in ensuring the return of its effective authority in the area, the force to be composed of personnel drawn from Member States;

4. *Requests* the Secretary-General to report to the Council within twenty-four hours on the implementation of the present resolution.

> *Adopted at the 2074th meeting by 12 votes to none, with 2 abstentions (Czechoslovakia, Union of Soviet Socialist Republics).*

Resolution 509 (1982) of 6 June 1982

The Security Council,
Recalling its resolutions 425 (1978) and 508 (1982),

Gravely concerned at the situation as described by the Secretary-General in his report to the Council,

Reaffirming the need for strict respect for the territorial integrity, sovereignty and political independence of Lebanon within its internationally recognized boundaries,

1. *Demands* that Israel withdraw all its military forces forthwith and unconditionally to the internationally recognized boundaries of Lebanon;

2. *Demands* that all parties observe strictly the terms of paragraph 1 of resolution 508 (1982) which called on them to cease immediately and simultaneously all military activities within Lebanon and across the Lebanese-Israeli border;

3. *Calls* on all parties to communicate to the Secretary-General their acceptance of the present resolution within twenty-four hours;

4. *Decides* to remain seized of the question.

Adopted unanimously at the 2375th meeting.

Resolution 512 (1982) of 19 June 1982

The Security Council,

Deeply concerned at the sufferings of the Lebanese and Palestinian civilian populations,

Referring to the humanitarian principles of the Geneva Conventions of 1949 and to the obligations arising from the regulations annexed to the Hague Convention of 1907,

Reaffirming its resolutions 508 (1982) and 509 (1982),

1. *Calls upon* all the parties to the conflict to respect the rights of the civilian populations, to refrain from all acts of violence against those populations and to take all appropriate measures to alleviate the suffering caused by the conflict, in particular, by facilitating the dispatch and distribution of aid provided by United Nations agencies and by non-governmental organizations, in particular, the International Committee of the Red Cross (ICRC);

2. *Appeals* to Member States to continue to provide the most extensive humanitarian aid possible;

3. *Stresses* the particular humanitarian responsibilities of the United Nations and its agencies, including the United Nations Relief and Works Agency for Palestine Refugees in the Near East (UNRWA), towards civilian populations and calls upon all the parties to the conflict not to hamper the exercise of those responsibilities and to assist in humanitarian efforts;

4. *Takes note* of the measures taken by the Secretary-General to co-ordinate the activities of the interantional agencies in this field and requests him to make every effort to ensure the implementation of and compliance with this resolution and to report on these efforts to the Council as soon as possible.

Adopted by the Security Council at its 2380th meeting

Resolution 516 (1982) of 1 August 1982

The Security Council,

Reaffirming its resolutions 508 (1982), 509 (1982), 511 (1982), 512 (1982) and 513 (1982),

APPENDIX D 175

Recalling its resolution 515 (1982) of 29 July 1982,
Alarmed by the continuation and intensification of military activities in and around Beirut,
Taking note of the latest massive violations of the cease-fire in and around Beirut,
1. *Confirms* its previous resolutions and demands an immediate cease-fire, and a cessation of all military activities within Lebanon and across the Lebanese-Israeli border;
2. *Authorizes* the Secretary-General to deploy immediately on the request of the Government of Lebanon, United Nations observers to monitor the situation in and around Beirut;
3. *Requests* the Secretary-General to report back to the Council on compliance with this resolution as soon as possible and not later than four hours from now.

Adopted by the Security Council at its 2386th meeting

Resolution 517 (1982) of 4 August 1982

The Security Council,
Deeply shocked and alarmed by the deplorable consequences of the Israeli invasion of Beirut on 3 August 1982,
1. *Reconfirms* its resolutions 508 (1982), 509 (1982), 512 (1982), 513 (1982), 515 (1982) and 516 (1982);
2. *Confirms once again* its demand for an immediate cease-fire and withdrawal of Israeli forces from Lebanon;
3. *Censures* Israel for its failure to comply with the above resolutions;
4. *Calls* for the prompt return of Israeli troops which have moved forward subsequent to 1325 hours EDT on 1 August 1982;
5. *Takes note* of the decision of the Palestine Liberation Organization to move the Palestinian armed forces from Beirut;
6. *Expresses* its appreciation for the efforts and steps taken by the Secretary-General to implement the provisions of Security Council resolution 516 (1982), and authorizes him, as an immediate step, to increase the number of United Nations observers in and around Beirut;
7. *Requests* the Secretary-General to report to the Security Council on the implementation of the present resolution as soon as possible and not later than 1000 hours EDT on 5 August 1982;
8. *Decides* to meet at that time if necessary in order to consider the report of the Secretary-General and, in case of failure to comply by any of the parties to the conflict, to consider adopting effective ways and means in accordance with the provisions of the Charter of the United Nations.

Adopted by the Security Council at its 2389th meeting

Resolution 518 (1982) of 12 August 1982

The Security Council,
Recalling its resolutions 508 (1982), 509 (1982), 511 (1982), 512 (1982), 513 (1982), 515 (1981), 516 (1982), and 517 (1982),

Expressing its most serious concern about continued military activities in Lebanon and, particularly, in and around Beirut,

1. *Demands* that Israel and all parties to the conflict observe strictly the terms of Security Council resolutions relevant to the immediate cessation of all military activities within Lebanon and, particularly, in and around Beirut;

2. *Demands* the immediate lifting of all restrictions on the city of Beirut in order to permit the free entry of supplies to meet the urgent needs of the civilian population of Beirut;

3. *Requests* United Nations observers in and in the vicinity of Beirut to report on the situation;

4. *Demands* that Israel co-operate fully in the effort to secure the effective deployment of the United Nations observers, as requested by the Government of Lebanon, and in such a manner as to ensure their safety;

5. *Requests* the Secretary-General to report soonest to the Security Council on the implementation of the present resolution;

6. *Decides* to meet if necessary in order to consider the situation upon receipt of the report of the Secretary-General.

Adopted by the Security Council at its 2392nd meeting

Resolution 521 (1982) of 19 September 1982

The Security Council,

Appalled at the massacre of Palestinian civilians in Beirut,

Having heard the report of the Secretary-General (S/15400),

Noting that the Government of Lebanon has agreed to the dispatch of United Nations Observers to the sites of greatest human suffering and losses in and around that city,

1. *Condemns* the criminal massacre of Palestinian civilians in Beirut;

2. *Reaffirms* once again its resolutions 512 (1982) and 513 (1982) which call for respect for the rights of the civilian population without any discrimination and repudiates all acts of violence against that population;

3. *Authorizes* the Secretary-General as an immediate step to increase the number of United Nations observers in and around Beirut from 10 to 50 and insists that there shall be no interference with the deployment of the observers and that they shall have full freedom of movement;

4. *Requests* the Secretary-General, in consultation with the Government of Lebanon, to ensure the rapid deployment of those observers in order that they may contribute in every way possible within their mandate, to the effort to ensure full protection for the civilian population;

5. *Requests* the Secretary-General as a matter of urgency to initiate appropriate consultations and in particular consultations with the Government of Lebanon on additional steps which the Council might take, including the possible deployment of United Nations forces, to assist that Government in ensuring full protection for the civilian population in and around Beirut and requests him to report to the Council within forty-eight hours;

6. *Insists* that all concerned must permit United Nations observers and forces established by the Security Council in Lebanon to be deployed and to discharge their

mandates and in this connexion solemnly calls attention to the obligation of all Member States under Article 25 of the Charter to accept and carry out the decisions of the Council in accordance with the Charter;

7. *Requests* the Secretary-General to keep the Council informed on an urgent and continuing basis.

Adopted by the Security Council at its 2396th meeting

Resolution 523 (1982) of 18 October 1982

The Security Council,
Having heard the statement of the President of the Lebanese Republic,
Recalling its resolutions 425 (1978), 426 (1978) and 519 (1982),
Reaffirming its resolutions 508 (1982) and 509 (1982), as well as all subsequent resolutions on the situation in Lebanon,
Having studied the report of the Secretary-General (S/15455 and Corr.1), and taking note of its conclusions and recommendations,
Responding to the request of the Government of Lebanon,

1. *Decides* to extend the present mandate of UNIFIL for a further interim period of three months, that is, until 19 January 1983;
2. *Insists* that there shall be no interference under any pretext with the operations of UNIFIL and that the Force shall have full freedom of movement in the discharge of its mandate;
3. *Authorizes* the Force during that period to carry out, with the consent of the Government of Lebanon, interim tasks in the humanitarian and administrative fields, as indicated in resolutions 511 (1982) and 519 (1982), and to assist the Government of Lebanon in assuring the security of all the inhabitants of the area without any discrimination;
4. *Requests* the Secretary-General, within the three-month period, to consult with the Government of Lebanon and to report to the Council on ways and means of ensuring the full implementation of the UNIFIL mandate as defined in resolutions 425 (1978) and 426 (1978), and the relevant decisions of the Security Council;
5. *Requests* the Secretary-General to report to the Security Council on the progress of his consultations.

Adopted by the Security Council at its 2400th meeting

Resolution 529 (1983) of 18 January 1983

The Security Council,
Recalling its resolutions 425 (1978) and 426 (1978), and all subsequent resolutions on the United Nations Interim Force in Lebanon,
Recalling further its resolutions 508 (1982) and 509 (1982),
Having taken note of the letter of the Permanent Representative of Lebanon to the President of the Security Council and to the Secretary-General of 13 January 1983 (s/15557, annex), and of the statement he made at the meeting of the Council,

178   PEACEKEEPING ON ARAB-ISRAELI FRONTS

Having studied the report of the Secretary-General (S/15557) and taken note of his observations,
Responding to the request of the Government of Lebanon,
1. *Decides* to extend the present mandate of the United Nations Interim Force in Lebanon for a further interim period of six months, that is, until 19 July 1983;
2. *Calls upon* all parties concerned to co-operate with the United Nations Interim Force in Lebanon for the full implementation of this resolution;
3. *Requests* the Secretary-General to report to the Council on the progress made in this respect.

Adopted by the Security Council at its 2411th meeting

Resolution 538 (1983) of 18 October 1983

The Security Council,
Having heard the statement of the representative of Lebanon,
Recalling its resolutions 425 (1978) and 426 (1978) and all subsequent resolutions on the United Nations Interim Force in Lebanon,
Recalling further its resolutions 508 (1982), 509 (1982) and 520 (1982), as well as all its other resolutions on the situation in Lebanon,
Reiterating its strong support for the territorial integrity, sovereignty and political independence of Lebanon within its internationally recognized boundaries,
Having studied the report of the Secretary-General on the United Nations Interim Force in Lebanon (S/16036) and taking note of the conclusions and recommendations expressed therein,
Taking note of the letter of the Permanent Representative of Lebanon to the Secretary-General of the United Nations (S/16036, para. 20),
Responding to the request of the Government of Lebanon,
1. *Decides* to extend the present mandate of the United Nations Interim Force in Lebanon for a further interim period of six months, that is, until 19 April 1984;
2. *Calls upon* all parties concerned to fully co-operate with the United Nations Interim Force in Lebanon for the full implementation of its mandate (as defined in resolutions 425 (1978) and 426 (1978) and the relevant decisions of the Security Council);
3. *Requests* the Secretary-General to report to the Council on the progress made in this respect.

Adopted by the Security Council at its 2480th meeting

INDEX

Assad, al- Hafez, 45, 55, 63

Begin, Menachem, 28
Blum, Yehuda, 40n
Bull-Hansen, Frederik, 72, 86

Cairo Agreement, 21
Callaghan, William, 19
Camp David accords, 7, 85
Carter, Jimmy: and establishment of UNIFIL, 18; and origins of MFO, 81
Cheysson, Claude, 58n

Draper, Morris, 35

Eban, Abba, 65
Egypt: and the MFO, 17–18, 70–71, 74, 77–79, 88
Erskine, Emanuel, 13, 21, 27

France: role in MNF 10, 32–33, 54–55, 57

Gemayel, Amin 10, 34, 39, 40, 52; and the MNF, 34–35, 46
Golan: Israel-Syria disengagement agreement, 65–66, 95; peacekeeping options in, 94–97
Goodman, Hirsh, 65
Great Britain: role in the MNF, 53–55
Greece: and third-party peacekeeping in Lebanon, 62
Gromyko, Andrei, 58

Haddad, Saad: and UNIFIL, 18, 26n, 40n, 41
Hamdy, Mohsen, 17, 73
Hammarskjold, Dag, 5, 83–84
Hernu, Charles, 34
Hunt, Leamon (Ray), 72

Israel: and May 17 agreement, 40; and the MFO, 17–18, 70–71, 74, 76–79, 88; and peacekeeping options in the Bekaa, 63–67; and peacekeeping options on the West Bank, 97–100; relations with UNIFIL, 18–19, 22–28; and third-party peacekeeping, 26–30, 83
Israel Defense Forces (IDF), 12, 26, 27, 40, 64; and May 17 agreement, 41–42
Italy: role in MNF, 10, 53–55, 57; and third-party peacekeeping in Lebanon, 62

James, Alan, 20
Jebel Baruk, 63, 65, 66
Jumblatt, Walid, 59

Khaddam, Abdel Halim, 45

Lagorio, Lelio, 34
Lebanon: armed forces of, 43–44, 56; and May 17 agreement, 39–43; peacekeeping options in, 47–67 *passim*, 93
Linowitz, Sol, 45
Litani Operation, 18, 20, 23
Long Commission Report, 38, 157–68

May 17 agreement: conditions of, 40n, 40–42, 47–48; and Israel, 40
Middleton, Drew, 98–99
Mitterrand, François: on French role in MNF, 57
Multinational Force (MNF): creation of, 7, 10; mandate and mission of, 31, 36–37, 51–52; and May 17 agreement, 42–43; structure of, 32–33; and Syria, 45–46; and U.S. Congress, 37–38

179

Multinational Force and Observers (MFO): and charges of treaty violations, 75–78; composition of, 7, 101n.4; contrasted with U.N. peacekeeping forces, 81–90, 92, 101n.7; cost and financing of, 89–90, 92; and freedom of navigation, 74–75; mandate and mission, 8, 69–70, 81; as peacekeeping model, 94, 97–99; structure of, 87–88; success of, 14, 81, 94; vulnerabilities, 73–80

Observer Group Lebanon, 23; *see also*, UNTSO.

Palestine Liberation Organization (PLO) 19–24, 40n
Perez de Cuellar, Javier 58; on UNIFIL, 10
Pertini, Sandro, 53
Phalangists, 39

Rabin, Yitzhak, 30, 48, 65
Reagan, Ronald: on the MNF, 10, 35n, 34–38

Salem, Elie, 31
Seelye, Talcott, 44
Shalev, Aryeh, 98, 99
Shamir, Yitzhak, 29, 64
Shultz, George, 29, 44
Siilasvuo, Ensio, 18
Sinai Field Mission, 73, 78, 83
Sinai Support Mission: establishment and functions of, 7; *see also* Sinai Field Mission
Sion, Dov, 17, 73
Sterner, Michael, 72
Syria: and May 17 agreement, 39, 44–46; and the MNF, 45–46, 55; and peacekeeping options in the Bekaa, 63, 65–67; and peacekeeping options in Golan, 95–97; and U.N. peacekeeping in Lebanon, 59–60

Tiran, Strait of, 71, 74
Thatcher, Margaret, 105n.35
Tower, John: on U.S. role in MNF, 57

Union of Soviet Socialist Republics: and U.N. peacekeeping in Lebanon, 59
United Nations: and May 17 agreement, 42–43; and peacekeeping operations in the Bekaa, 67; and third-party peacekeeping, 5–7, 30, 58, 82–85, 88; and third-party peacekeeping in Lebanon, 60–61
U.N. Disengagement Observer Force (UNDOF), 47, 63, 66, 67, 95, 96; mandate and mission of, 66n
U.N. Emergency Force (UNEF), 5, 66, 67
U.N. Force in Cyprus (UNFICYP), 6, 7, 25, 50
U.N. Interim Force in Lebanon (UNIFIL): establishment of, 20; future of, 11; and Israeli invasion of Lebanon, 10; mandate and mission of, 20, 23–24, 34, 49–51; and May 17 agreement, 48–49; and the PLO, 19–24; as a peacekeeping model, 61; relations with Israel, 18–28; relations with Maj. Saad Haddad, 18
U.N. Security Council: on Israeli siege of Beirut, 12–13; on Litani Operation, 20; on protection of civilians and refugees in Lebanon, 49–50; and U.N. forces in Lebanon, 59, 61; and UNIFIL, 20, 49

U.N. Truce Supervisory Organization (UNTSO), 5, 23, 60
United States: and the MNF, 10–11, 32–39, 51–56; and the MFO, 7, 16, 69–72, 78–80, 83–84, 86; and peacekeeping role in southern Lebanon, 28–30; and U.N. peacekeeping, 6–7
United States Congress: and U.S. role in MNF, 37–38, 53; and the MFO, 71, 78, 80; and peacekeeping options in Golan, 97; and third-party peacekeeping, 84, 94
Urquhart, Brian, 19, 58, 61, 88; on the MNF, 36; on successful third-party peacekeeping, 102n.8

War Powers Resolution, 71
Weinberger, Caspar, 33, 35, 53
West Bank: peacekeeping options in, 97–100

Yariv, Aharon, 64